SAP® System Landscape Optimization

SAP PRESS

SAP PRESS is issued by
Bernhard Hochlehnert, SAP AG

SAP PRESS is a joint initiative of SAP and Galileo Press. The know-how offered by SAP specialists combined with the expertise of the publishing house Galileo Press offers the reader expert books in the field. SAP PRESS features first-hand information and expert advice, and provides useful skills for professional decision-making.

SAP PRESS offers a variety of books on technical and business related topics for the SAP user. For further information, please visit our website: *www.sap-press.com*.

Missbach, Sosnitzka, Stelzel, Wilhelm
SAP System Operations
2004, 355 pp., ISBN 1-59229-025-8

Thomas Schneider
SAP Performance Optimization Guide
Analyzing and Tuning SAP Systems
2003, 494 pp. ISBN 1-59229-022-1

Sigrid Hagemann, Liane Will
SAP R/3 System Administration
2003, approx. 450 pp., ISBN 1-59229-014-4

Helmut Stefani
Archiving Your SAP Data
A comprehensive guide to plan and execute archiving projects
2003, 360 pp., ISBN 1-59229-008-6

Gerhard Oswald (Ed.)
SAP Service and Support
An A-to-Z guide to optimizing ROI and TCO
2003, 208 pp. ISBN 1-59229-015-9

Andreas Schneider-Neureither (Ed.)

SAP® System Landscape Optimization

SAP PRESS

Translation Lemoine International, Inc., Salt Lake City, UT
Copy Editor Nancy Etscovitz, UCG, Inc., Boston, MA
Cover Design department, Cologne, Germany

ISBN 1-59229-026-4

Contents

Foreword

In the late 1990s, considerable financial investment advanced the development of information technology in enterprises. The "Best-of-Breed" approach was frequently used as a basis for IT investment decisions. This method often produces a heterogeneous, complex system landscape that is costly to implement and maintain, and has a lot of potential for optimization, which should not be underestimated.

In this book, we present various different options for optimizing an SAP system infrastructure. We do so by addressing different approaches—from business process optimization to performance analysis.

Therefore, this book is primarily intended for IT managers, system or solution architects, and senior consultants.

I would now like to express my gratitude to my co-authors Daniel Baumann, Dr. Björn Gelhausen, Johannes Hurst, Gerhard Krauss, and Achim Westermann, who, despite their grueling daily workload, found the time and energy to make valuable contributions that greatly helped with the creation of this book.

Finally, I would like to thank Galileo Press for their pleasant and constructive collaboration and, in particular, Florian Zimniak for his painstaking assistance.

I hope that you enjoy reading this book and that you find many useful suggestions for optimizing your SAP system landscape.

Heidelberg, May 2004
Andreas Schneider-Neureither

Introduction

"There is a time in the life of every problem when it is big enough to see, yet small enough to solve."
(Mike Levitt)

There can be no doubt that SAP applications have a very strong influence on how enterprises structure their work processes and do business today.

Even with a successful SAP implementation, however, if it is to run efficiently in the long term, there is still always a need to customize an ERP solution so it meets the demands of the market, business requirements, and the enterprise.

Many enterprises currently use SAP products to control production planning, purchasing and logistics, warehouse management and inventory management, production, vendor management, customer service, finance, personnel management, and other basic business activities. In addition, numerous enterprises also use other applications (best-of-breed) to meet the requirements of other areas. All of these different applications must be integrated and work collectively with the central SAP system.

SAP Systems Change Business Processes

During the last decade, the use of SAP systems and supporting applications has led to important cost savings and productivity gains in various different areas of business. SAP has provided the necessary integration and the standardized data models to help link and coordinate separate functional units in the organization. SAP implementations usually involve a high level of training due to the definition and implementation of strict procedure instructions and new business processes for adjusting the enterprise process flows to the SAP system. Many enterprises find the cultural aspects of an implementation and the constraint of adjusting to SAP processes more challenging than the actual technical tasks.

SAP has built a lot of flexibility into its solutions. If, however, the requirements and process flows of an organization don't map to the range of possible customizing settings, the results of an implementation can prove very frustrating. In trying to satisfy the requirements of a real-time enterprise, many companies today are faced with a no-win situation. They can either adjust internal process flows to reflect the processes of the SAP application, or they can invest in solutions to integrate SAP with other enterprise applications.

Modification of the Enterprise

In addition to economic challenges, many enterprises must deal with a further complication. As a result of mergers and takeovers, enterprises must move from a traditional, vertically integrated organization to an enterprise made up of many different organizational parts. Consequently, they often have to concentrate on several different business areas. This complexity is heightened with the inclusion of dependencies among partner, vendor, and customer relations.

In business relations between enterprises—whereby companies aim to increase efficiency through closely linked internal systems—business processes have a direct influence on the architecture and functions required of ERP systems. Accordingly, enterprises are also increasingly forced to base the planning of ERP solutions on integrative and external requirements and less on internal or even application-specific requirements.

"Next Generation ERP"

The IT industry has recognized this situation and SAP also offers what is known as a "Next-Generation-ERP" or "ERP II" solution in the form of SAP NetWeaver. The integration of different ERP solutions is made possible with appropriately flexible tools and adapters and is increasingly geared toward the requirements of enterprises and their business processes.

Despite existing solutions, it is still difficult to map business processes generally across enterprise boundaries and heterogeneous systems. Quite often, however, these integration solutions are based purely on the exchange of data, so that the enterprise once again has to reflect the technical process flows. The already complex technical environment is often further complicated by partly inflexible processes that don't always cover all business requirements or dovetail completely into the existing landscape. Consequently, because of this integrative approach, the total costs of ownership (TCO)—the necessary time and capital for implementing and maintaining ERP solutions—can grow exponentially.

Many enterprises have discovered that implemented ERP solutions implemented don't always yield the added value anticipated. Based on our own experience and subsequent publications, it is apparent that in 2003, almost all companies are trying to gain more value from investments made in technology and services. This, in turn, leads to individual initiatives or complete improvement projects whose goal is to use existing resources optimally, and continually check and improve processes. We will now describe the most important initiatives.

The absolute highest priority is to improve the quality of the systems used, that is, the processes, and above all, the data in the systems. Until recently, the central data basis was the most important priority. Today, the central priority is ensuring the quality of data right from the start. This alone is not sufficient. It must be supported by high quality and consistent master data, even beyond system boundaries. Data quality is important for all systems, but it is critical for the SAP key systems and the related CRM or SCM solutions.

System and Data Quality

New business processes typically require new systems, new modes of operation, new roles, new training concepts, and targeted implementation. Because complete implementations can take up a lot of time and therefore, eat up a lot of money, the current trend is to tap the full potential of existing systems. A change to an existing system often requires only a few months, whereas a complete implementation can easily take several years. Reusability is supported by SAP applications that already provide the bases for the functions and technologies needed to implement new processes.

Reusability of Solutions

Given that a quick time-to-market is always imperative for the success of enterprises, usually, the reusability of existing systems for developing new or adjusted processes is the logical option for saving time and therefore costs.

The operation of systems and the support of business processes is evermore complex and requires an increasingly high number of systems. Ensuring availability and the speed of process flows in accordance with enterprise requirements and guidelines is becoming increasingly difficult. In the past, this was only possible if both the user and the service personnel—who was responsible for the operation—monitored the processes and intervened if necessary. With processes that go beyond system and enterprise boundaries, however, this is no longer possible. The requirements of a real-time enterprise can be met only if processes are automatically monitored for duration, integrity, and outcome, and if there are predefined roles and responsibilities for handling any problems that arise. Useful data and knowledge are a by-product of this real-time business monitoring and can provide a basis for the continued improvement of business processes.

Real-Time Business Monitoring

The lead times for business processes should be as low as possible. To optimize this, the work packages of a process must be exchanged quickly and completely between systems, made readily available to the person responsible and, if necessary, forwarded to other people. The Internet

Quick Process Execution Times

represents only the transport layer of the process. For this, processes often require synchronous interfaces between individual components, but frequently, however, the current forms of Enterprise Application Integration (EAI) and Electronic Data Interchange (EDI) can execute them only asynchronously. Business Services Orchestration (BSO) is one possible alternative to shorten each individual process step and therefore, reduce the runtime of the entire process.

Integral Communication and Training

Changes or continual improvements to business processes require a fully developed training concept to keep all relevant employees up to date. This will be even more difficult to achieve with future systems and cross-enterprise processes because the employees of the virtual enterprise can be in different organizations, enterprises, continents, and time zones. New communication and training concepts will have to be developed to address these challenges.

Optimizing Service & Support

One prerequisite for optimized business processes is that any problems that occur must be identified automatically, addressed quickly, and then, resolved efficiently. Support processes outside system and enterprise boundaries with scattered users and, above all, support organizations, require completely new support concepts and processes to deal with these new requirements. Not only must the data that forms the basis for the support processes exist electronically; you must be able to forward this data between different support systems to the relevant support teams, without compromising its quality. The users and the support organizations must always be cognizant of what phase the solution process is currently at.

Solutions for the Virtual Enterprise

Today, the integration of systems and different organizations is frequently achieved by the use of EDI. However, with this process, only the data that corresponds to the paper documents of old is exchanged. It is often difficult to ensure that data is complete and synchronous beyond system borders. There is a need for intelligent solutions to develop optimal systems, to integrate systems and, in doing so, save interfaces or counteract incompatibilities with central master data systems or templates.

This book addresses the aspects listed in the three main areas of optimizing business processes, optimizing system landscapes, and the associated optimization of service and support concepts.

In **Chapter 1**, we provide you with an overview of the current range of SAP products. We present the functions and the technical components involved and show the first possibilities for optimization.

Chapter 2 introduces you to the different architectures of SAP systems. First, we deal with the conventional system architecture of SAP R/3 and show how a system landscape can be represented with SAP NetWeaver. The essential SAP concepts—Change and Transport Management, Lifecycle Management, and Solution Management—are also introduced.

Chapter 3 provides you with the necessary foundations for optimizing existing system landscapes or implementing new ones. We describe different optimization approaches and provide explanations indicating which approaches are best used in which particular cases.

Chapter 4 describes the optimization of your Service and Support organization. We first outline the method of optimization, later identify factors for good support, the processes that need to be optimized, and possible support tools. The Best Practices for Service & Support Processes from ITIL form the main thread in this chapter.

In **Chapter 5**, we provide you with different methods to use in order to optimize your business processes: general performance optimization, system landscape optimization, business workflow, Reverse Business Engineering (RBE), SAP XI, and generic business process redesign.

Chapter 6 deals with real-time business monitoring. The possibilities and limitations of RBE are compared with the alternative of using business intelligence tools for analysis.

Chapter 7 provides a summary of the individual chapters.

In **Chapter 8**, we provide you with an overview of the optimizing strategies presented.

Lastly, in the appendices, you'll find a list of references and suggested further reading, as well as a brief biography of the authors.

1 Overview of SAP Solutions and Their Optimization Potential

In this chapter, we provide you with an overview of the SAP NetWeaver components and the solutions in the mySAP Business Suite. We also outline where any potential for optimization lies.

During the last five years, SAP has developed numerous solutions—in addition to its core products of SAP R/3 or SAP R/3 Enterprise—and launched them on the market with great success. Furthermore, during the same period, SAP has changed from a vendor of pure solutions to a vendor of technology.

Before delving into the subject of optimization, we will discuss the range of SAP products while considering the optimization potential of each. Then, we'll provide a brief summary of the functions and technical components of the different products and product groups and indicate where the potential for optimization lies.

1.1 The SAP Range of Products

Over the years, the range of SAP products has grown continuously and diversified. The numerous elements of the SAP product range are presented in Figure 1.1. The following SAP products are the most important:

- SAP NetWeaver
- mySAP Business Suite
- SAP Solutions for Small and Midsize Businesses (SMB)
- SAP xApps
- Industry Solutions

mySAP Business Suite

The mySAP Business Suite includes almost all the cross-industry SAP solutions such as mySAP ERP, CRM, and so on, which are based on the technical platform SAP NetWeaver (see Section 1.2). It also includes parts of the range for small to medium enterprises— mySAP All-in-One. This product provides cost-effective preconfigured solutions (both hardware and software). Consequently, the implementation time and cost is considerably reduced, which is important to cost-conscious midsize companies that don't need adjustments made to the standard configuration. The All-in-One solutions are preconfigured both by SAP and by its partners.

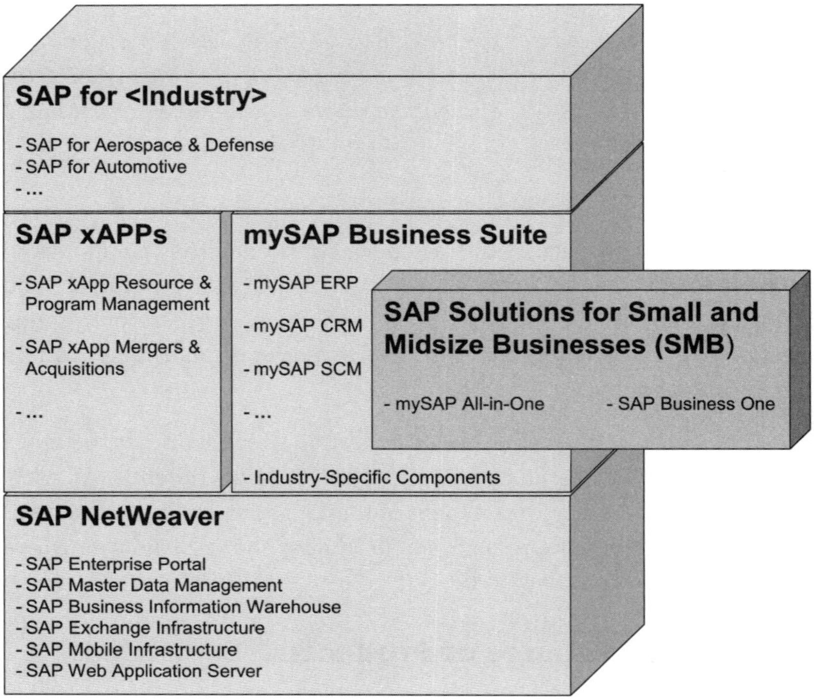

Figure 1.1 SAP Product Range

In contrast to the mySAP All-in-One solutions, the SAP Business One solution is not based on SAP NetWeaver. Rather, it is for small customers with only a few employees.

Industry Solutions The mySAP Business Suite, previously referred to under mySAP.com for licensing reasons, also includes all of the SAP industry solutions (currently 23, see Figure 1.2), which are designed to meet the special requirements of individual sectors, such as banking.

xApps Since 2002, the overall SAP product range also includes the Cross Applications (xApps). These are cross-component applications that use the functions of different SAP solutions and usually employ the SAP Enterprise Portal (EP) for front-end formatting.

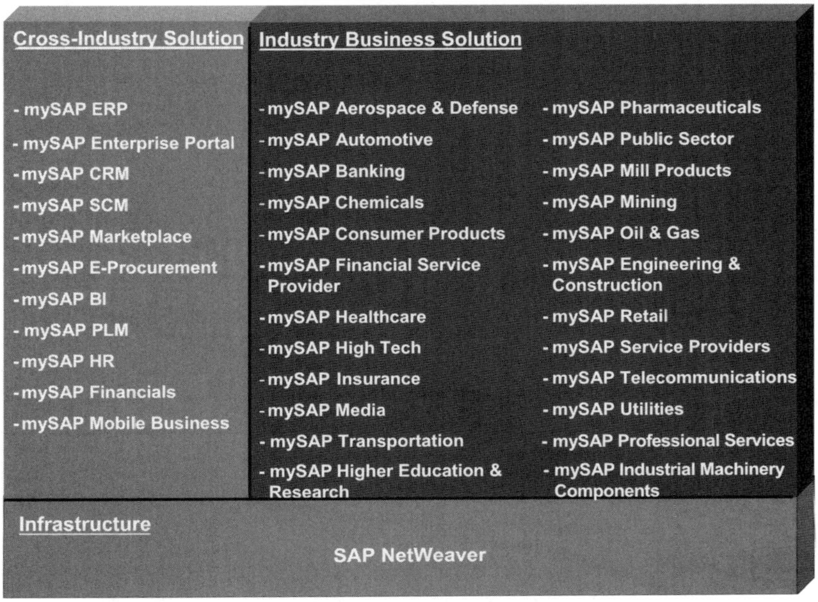

Figure 1.2 SAP Solutions

Recently, in addition to the industry solutions (which we will address later), SAP also offers solutions for specific branches of industry (*SAP for Industry*), which unite sector-specific software products with service and implementation. The following hierarchical diagram (see Figure 1.3) shows the configuration of the best known SAP components.

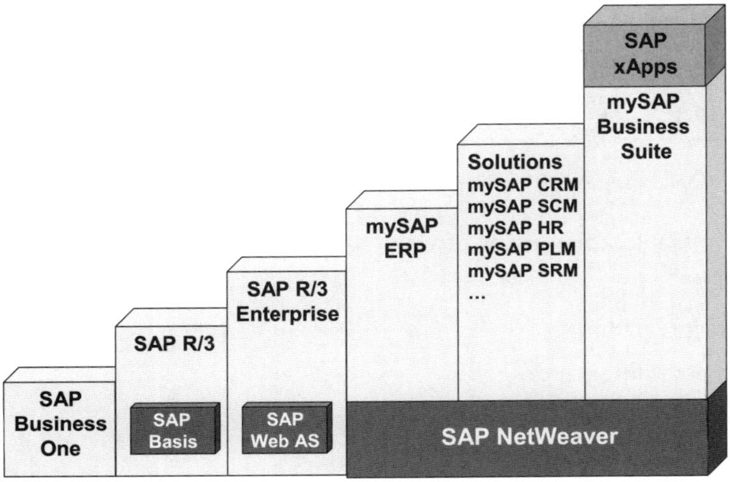

Figure 1.3 Structure of SAP products

All new SAP products are based on SAP NetWeaver as shown in Figure 1.3. The structure and technical components will be explained in greater detail below.

Subsequently, the individual modules of the SAP R/3 core system will be presented in detail.

1.2 What Is SAP NetWeaver?

Technology Platform

Since 2002, SAP has used the term *SAP NetWeaver* to refer to an overarching technological concept that comprises the different SAP technology platforms that henceforth will be merged. The focus of this new platform is the integration of people, information, and processes in one solution.

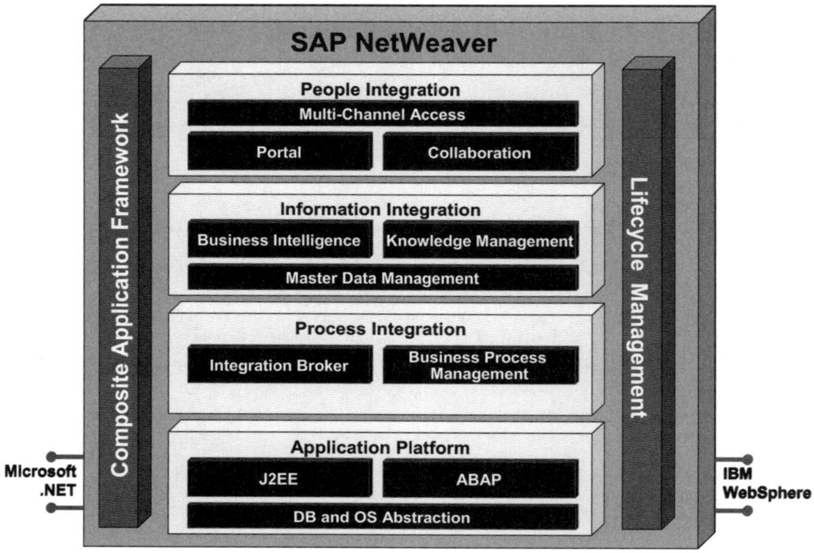

Figure 1.4 The Core Areas of SAP NetWeaver

Four Key Areas

From an organizational point of view, SAP NetWeaver consists of four core areas:

- People Integration
- Information Integration
- Process Integration
- Application Platform

These four key areas are described in more detail in the following sections.

1.2.1 People Integration

The integration of people is attained via a portal solution and a platform for working together in teams collaboratively. In an increasingly mobile world, end users must have access via different channels.

Technically, this solution currently involves SAP Enterprise Portal, Collaboration Package for SAP Enterprise Portal, and the SAP Mobile Engine (see also Section 1.3.).

1.2.2 Information Integration

Localization of relevant information—structured and unstructured (currently around 14 Exabytes worldwide)—is becoming increasingly laborious and more time-consuming for users. Converting information into knowledge is equally problematic.

One of the goals of *Business Information Warehouse* (BW) and *Knowledge Management* (KM) is to convert information into knowledge faster and with fewer complications than is being done today. In the area of information management, the problem of consolidated master data management beyond system boundaries is becoming increasingly important. From an organizational and technical point of view, the new SAP product *Master Data Management* (MDM) offers a solution to address this increasing demand.

Business Intelligence and Knowledge Management

The term *Business Intelligence* in the world of SAP refers, in the first instance, to SAP BW (currently Version 3.2). The SAP KM components mentioned, for the handling of un-structured data, is represented technically by the CM components of the SAP Enterprise Portal and the TREX (*Text Retrieval and Information Extraction*). The TREX is always directly visible in the SAP Enterprise Portal, but it is also increasingly used in other components, such as the *Knowledge Warehouse* (KW).

1.2.3 Process Integration

The new SAP products *Exchange Infrastructure* (XI) and *Business Process Management* (BPM) form the basis of optimized process management. BPM is technically based on the SAP XI.

1.2.4 Application Platform

The SAP *Web Application Server* (Web AS) is used as a basis for all SAP applications (currently Release 6.20). Release 6.40 of SAP Web AS will probably be available in the third quarter of 2004.

At the core is the old SAP Basis, which is independent of the database and operating system. It has been enhanced by the integration of the SAP J2EE Engine. The degree of synthesis of these two very different elements was continuously improved since the launch of the Web AS in Release 6.10.

The SAP J2EE Engine can be traced back to the In-Q-My product, which has been available for years and has been enhanced, adjusted, and made J2EE-compliant.

These main components have been enhanced with a Composite Application Framework, which provides numerous open interfaces (APIs), and Lifecycle Management—an extension of the previous Transport Management System (TMS)—in all components of SAP NetWeaver.

1.3 The Components of SAP NetWeaver

In Figure 1.5, you can see which technical components have been assigned to which areas of SAP NetWeaver. These components will be described in the following sections.

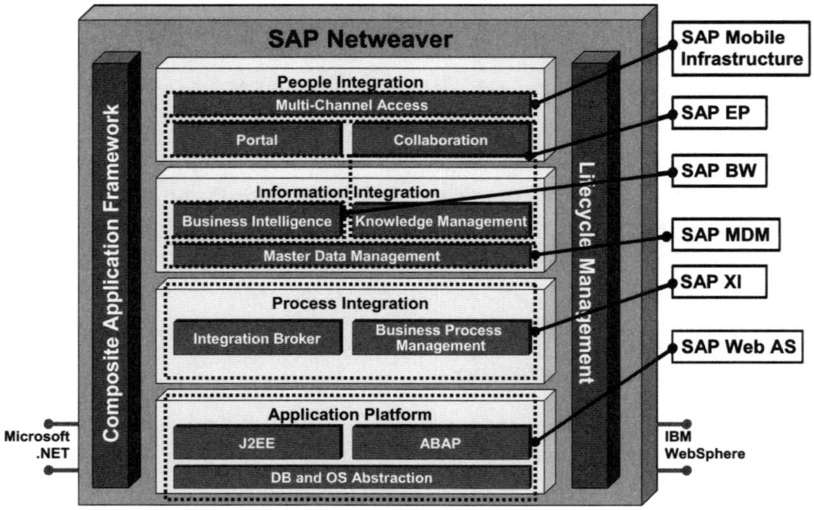

Figure 1.5 Technical Components of NetWeaver

1.3.1 The SAP Web Application Server

The SAP Web Application Server (Web AS) has been the application platform for all SAP products since 2002. It represents the logical development of the previous SAP Basis.

ABAP and Java

The current SAP Web AS still contains what is known as the *ABAP Personality* (ABAP development and runtime environment), with the dependability, scalability, and independence of an operating system and database. However, these basics have been enhanced with the SAP J2EE Engine including a Fast RFC connection between the Java personality and the ABAP personality and with an Internet Communication Manager (ICM), which is used for handling and distributing Internet queries to the individual components.

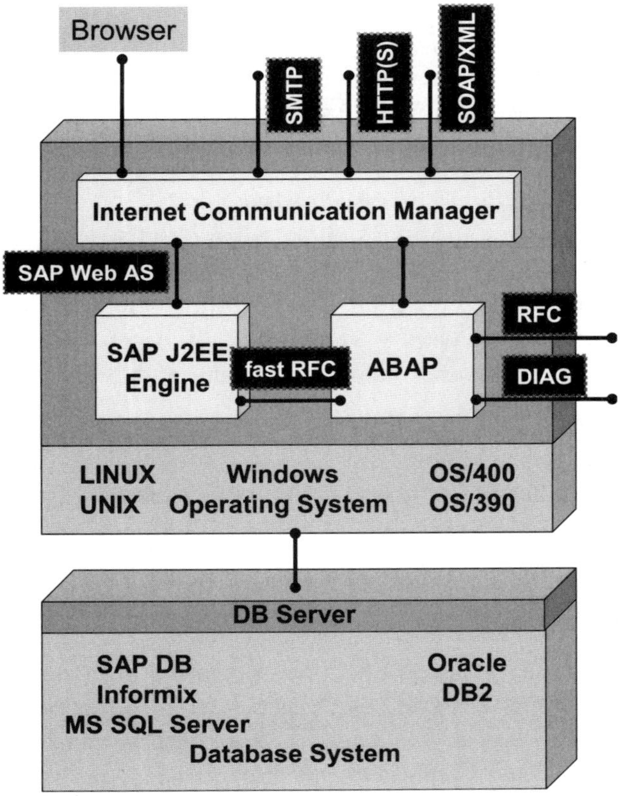

Figure 1.6 The Components of the Web Application Server

Supported Standards In addition, the openness of SAP to technical standards has been clearly expanded, for example, the following standards are supported:

- HTTP(S)
- SMTP
- WebDAV
- SOAP
- SSL
- SSO
- X.509
- Unicode
- HTML, XML, WML

1.3.2 SAP Enterprise Portal

In the age of the Internet, with browsers available on every desktop and multiple mobile devices, accessing an SAP system using an SAP GUI will not be a state-of-the-art scenario, but a common theme.

However, portals—and specifically the SAP Enterprise Portal—offer a uniform and personalized access to various different back-end systems via browsers. Combined with the Single Sign-On (SSO) function and a powerful Content Management System (CMS), together with numerous other features, SAP provides users with a Single Point of Access (SPoA). Together, these features enable users to work more efficiently.

Drag and Relate Other forward-looking functions of the portal are Drag and Relate, the transfer of Drag and Drop to business processes, and the linking of business objects between different SAP and non-SAP systems with adjustable functions.

In the overall landscape of future SAP architecture, the SAP Enterprise Portal represents the frontend for the end user.

Technically, the Enterprise Portal consists of previous components (Basis was the TopTier Portal 4.5) and many technically different components that contribute to move SAP to the Web and link the Java and .NET world. This balancing act must unite different programming worlds and philosophies in a single product.

Browser Frontend The portal uses as a frontend a browser in the form of Microsoft Internet Explorer, Netscape Navigator, or modified variations for mobile end devices such as PDAs, cell phones, or hybrid devices.

Portal technology is therefore possible for the end user to present and logically link relevant content from various different data sources on a single unified interface, in addition to all SAP products and numerous third-party applications such as PeopleSoft, Baan, or J.D. Edwards, data files (including Microsoft systems) and Internet information (e.g., from Yahoo).

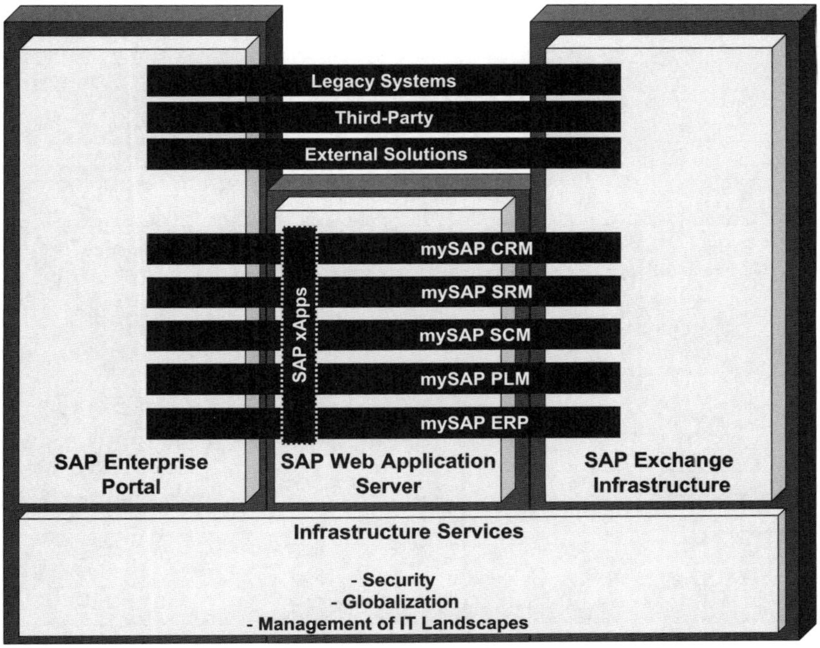

Figure 1.7 The Integration Possibilities of SAP Products

Portal Components

The Enterprise Portal consists of the following components:

- Page Builder and iView Server
- User Management
- Persistence Layer
- KM (Knowledge Management)
- Unification Server

Technically, the Page Builder and iView Server are currently made up of Microsoft's Internet Information Server (IIS) with additional filter components and the J2EE Engine, which should be familiar to you if you worked with SAP Web AS. For EP 6.0, you will also be able to use the Apache server as a Web server.

LDAP The user and authorization management of the portal currently consists of different LDAP products (for example, Novell eDirectory, MS ads, and so on). Starting with EP Release 6.0, use of the directory service will be optional.

The persistence layer currently consists of a file system storage and a database (MS SQL or Oracle) and in addition to content (pages, iViews and so on), it also contains personalization data.

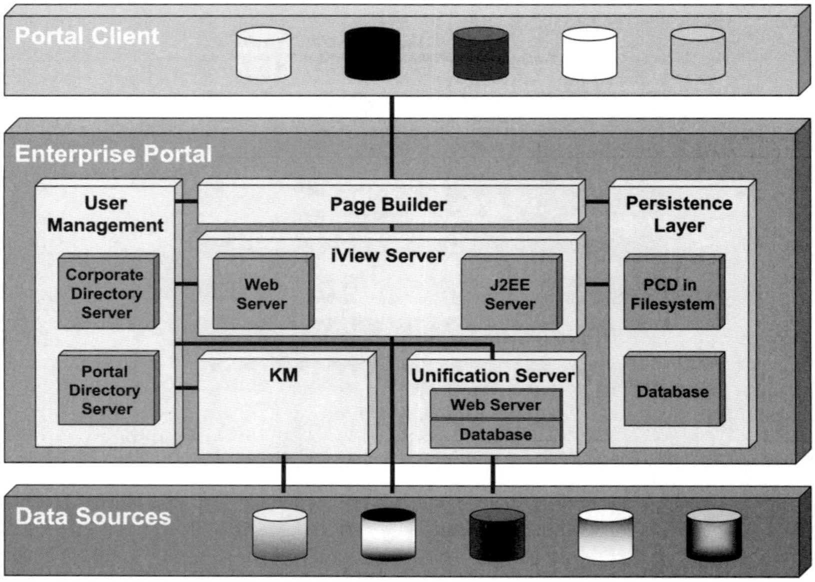

Figure 1.8 Structure of the SAP Enterprise Portal

Unification In addition to these essential components, you can implement two additional components. The Unification Server, based on the unifier for different back-end systems, permits Drag and Relate functions. In this way, business objects can be linked between back-end systems and provided with additional functions. A simple, common example is the linking of a purchase order in the SAP R/3 system with the FedEx delivery number so that by "dropping" the "dragged" order number on the link with the FedEx Web site, the order can be located. As a technical prerequisite, the unification server currently still requires an MS SQL database as a basis and its own IIS.

The Knowledge Management component consists of:

Knowledge Management

- Content Management
- TREX
- Collaboration

The Content Management component and the TREX are currently delivered as additional components and the Collaboration part is available as what is known as a *Business Package*.

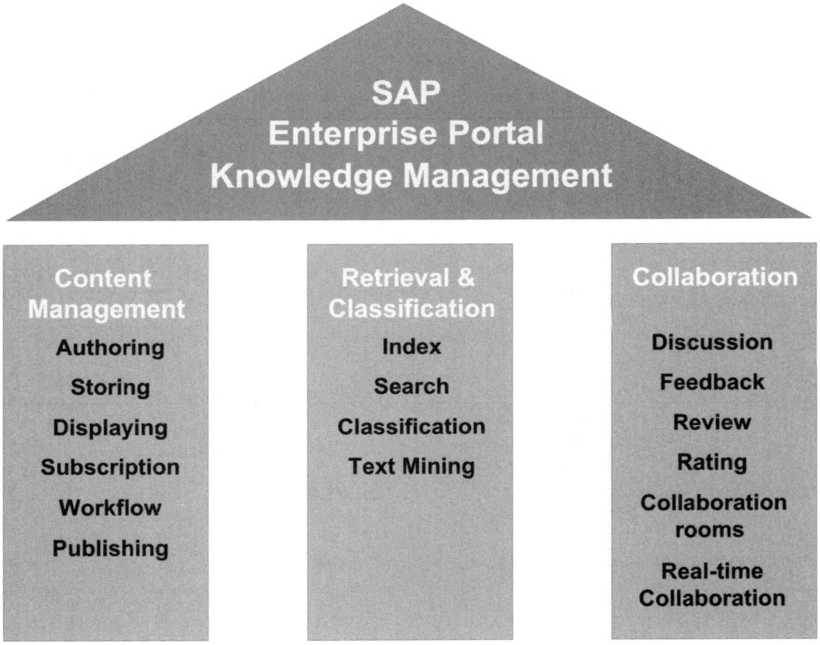

Figure 1.9 Knowledge Management in SAP Enterprise Portal

Figure 1.10 shows an example of the overall functionality that can be achieved with these components.

Given the backdrop of very different repositories, publishing and search mechanisms and collaboration can all be represented in real time.

Lastly, the Enterprise Portal as a whole offers the following features:

- KM
- Collaboration
- Personalization

- Unification (Drag & Relate)
- SSO
- Eventing
- Complete integration
- Openness
- Scalability

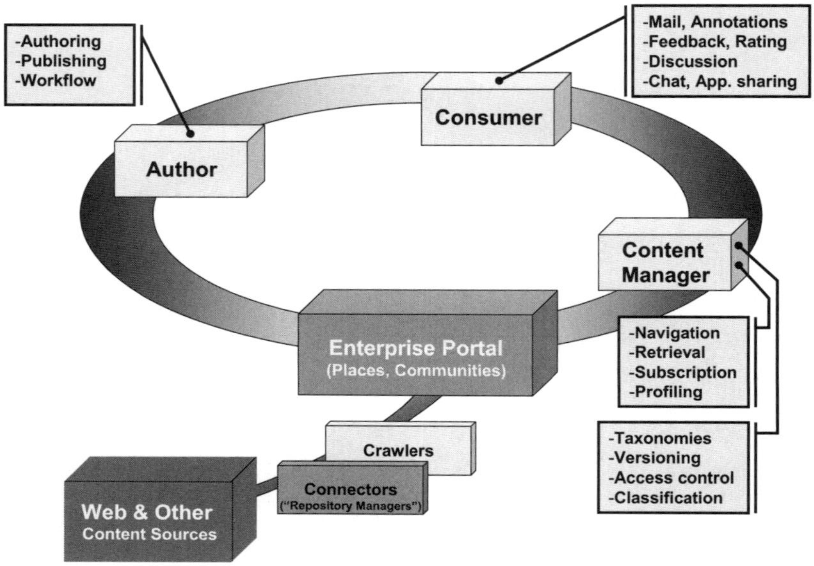

Figure 1.10 Content Management with the SAP Enterprise Portal

Business Packages Business Packages enhance the Enterprise Portal for the SAP Enterprise Portal solution. They provide SAP roles, pages, iViews; that is, interfaces and links compiled from a business perspective, which provide real added value for the customer and circumvent the need for numerous developments, so prevalent in other portal environments. Many Business Packages are already available.

The Enterprise Portal itself can be used to optimize system landscapes and especially processes. The greatest added values for existing customers are improved and accelerated processes and the KM component, which enables users to locate relevant documents faster.

1.3.3 SAP Exchange Infrastructure

The *SAP Exchange Infrastructure* (XI) acts as a pivot between SAP and external systems. It is SAP's answer to previous attempts to definitively resolve the problem of *Enterprise Application Integration* (EAI) with different products from various manufacturers, often in combination.

Technically, SAP XI is based on Web AS. From an organizational point of view, SAP XI comprises the following components: Integration Repository, Integration Directory, and Integration Server.

Architecture

Information about the overall system landscape is incorporated in both the Integration Repository and the Integration Directory. The *Integration Repository* is used to design the data exchange processes while the *Integration Directory* is used to save and administer the exchange information of daily operations. The *Integration Server*, which is available for data exchange between systems, provides the runtime environment.

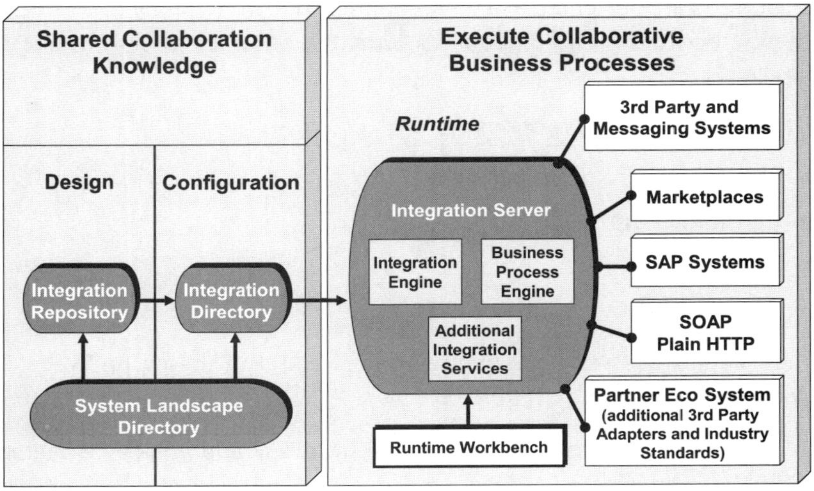

Figure 1.11 Components of SAP XI

Application Adapters

As in SAP Enterprise Portal, the idea of optimization is of course inherent to the SAP Exchange Infrastructure. Apart from providing the necessary exchange mechanisms and data between SAP components on the basis of Business Logic, SAP also provides *Application Adapters* for XI for the following products (XI Release 2.0):

- Baan
- Broadvision

- IDE World Software
- Oracle Applications
- PeopleSoft
- Siebel

This range will be expanded further with the XI Release 3.0.

1.3.4 SAP Business Information Warehouse

In today's rapidly changing world, management decisions based on substantive data and well defined information are required. Decisions based on instinct or intuition are no longer sufficient. The SAP Business Information Warehouse (SAP BW) can help you to select and present relevant information required for management decisions. It is the technical basis for the mySAP Business Intelligence solution. The functions and content of SAP BW are provided for mobile end-devices by the SAP Mobile Engine and are presented in a uniform interactive frontend by the SAP EP. These three technical components form the basis for mySAP Business Intelligence.

BW Processes

The most important processes in a BW system are:

- Extraction from the source system
- Transformation
- Loading
- Converting data into information

These four processes are supported by the SAP BW (based on Web AS since Release 3.0, current Release 3.2).

In addition to data storage and retrieval from SAP and non-SAP systems (Data Warehousing), SAP BW, as an OLAP system, offers extensive already prepared Business Content that enables fast and efficient implementation. Apart from standard reporting options using MS Excel, Web-based reporting is also an option. Today you can run high performance, complex analyses using huge databases and do so efficiently and expediently.

The fusion of NetWeaver components can be seen in many ready-made analyses in business packages, thus, representing the integration in the SAP Enterprise Portal.

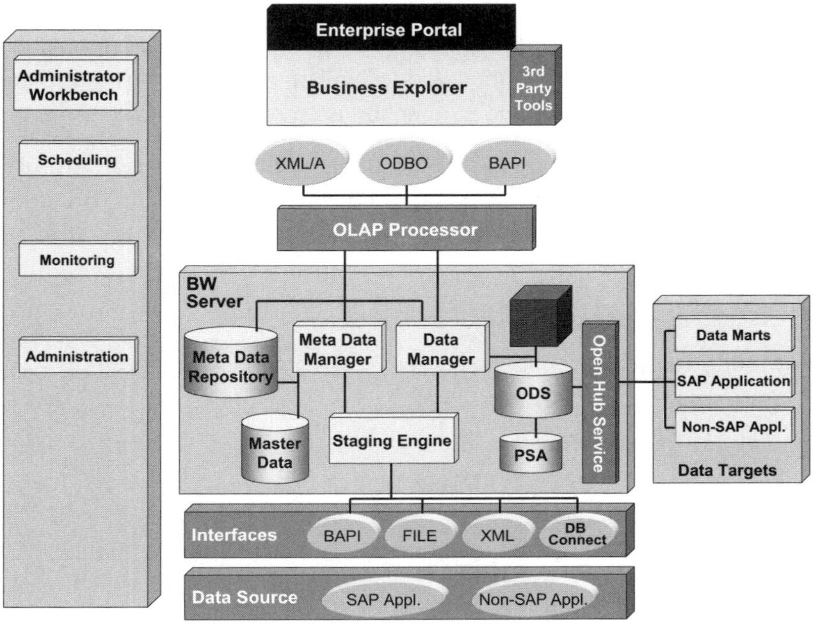

Figure 1.12 Technical Overview of SAP BW

As an OLAP system, high requirements are made on the BW, especially regarding the quick evaluation of data. This is a key area for optimization potential and that potential can be realized through clever database design and the targeted creation of indices (also to aggregates). Other possible areas for optimization can be found within the process of loading master and transaction data into a system via a transfer from non-SAP systems with the help of ALE functions.

1.3.5 SAP Mobile Infrastructure

SAP Mobile Infrastructure enables mobile access to all components of the mySAP Business Suite. One of the main features of the SAP CRM system—and, increasingly, of other components too—is that information can be accessed in real time, even when traveling.

The sales team or service technicians of modern enterprises should have permanent access to correspondence with their customers or access to information regarding the availability of replacement parts. The SAP Mobile Infrastructure provides the optimal technology platform for such tasks.

Mobile employees can be provided with information from SAP systems within companies via wireless LAN connections, or outside of companies via Wide Area Mobile Data Networks. Similarly, the offline use of many functions is also ensured if no connection is currently available.

Besides this basic package, SAP also offers the following ready-to-use applications, which are technically based on SAP Mobile Infrastructure for the mySAP Mobile Business solution:

Mobile Applications

- **Mobile Service for Handhelds**
  CRM solution for service and field sales employees
- **Mobile Sales for Handhelds**
  CRM solution for sales personnel
- **Mobile Time and Travel**
  ESS for time and travel management
- **Mobile Procurement**
  Mobile procurement
- **Mobile Asset Management**
  Management and updating of asset data
- **Mobile Supply Chain Management**
  Mobile integration in a company's logistic chain

Using SAP Mobile Infrastructure can help you to optimize business processes, for example, mobile employees can have access to relevant and up-to-date information at all times and from any location (without telephone queries). Another critical benefit is the vast improvement in service quality and customer care.

The success of these solution-based technologies depends on the use of appropriate end devices and networks (internal and external) and powerful and stable SAP systems or system groups.

1.3.6 SAP Master Data Management

Components of MDM

Heterogeneously, distributed IT landscapes can still be found in many companies, evermore so now because of the increasing number of new SAP applications. All of the systems in an enterprise must frequently access the same master data, such as names of business partners, addresses, warehouses, and so on. Many complex distribution processes were developed to ensure the consistency and the existence of this data. This problem is tackled by the latest SAP product, *SAP Master Data Management* (MDM).

SAP MDM consists of the following components:

- ▶ Content Integrator
- ▶ Master Data Server
- ▶ SAP MDM Adapter

The MDM also needs the SAP Exchange Infrastructure as a prerequisite technical component (and as a technical basis).

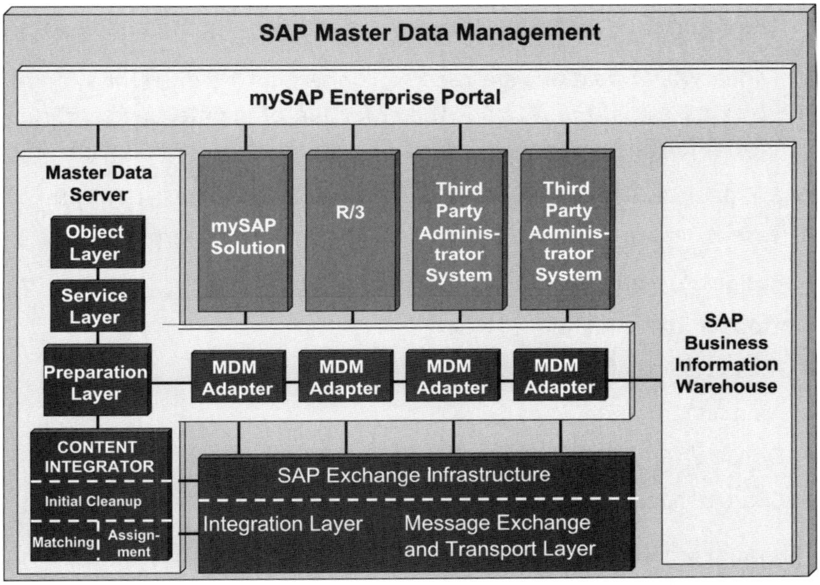

Figure 1.13 MDM Components

SAP XI is the technical foundation for SAP MDM. The MDM provides SAP XI information for the actual publish and subscribe mechanisms for the end systems. Changes to master data are sent, via open standards, to the backend systems for which the data is relevant or for which the enterprise has subscribed to these systems. SAP XI oversees the necessary data conversion and ensures the consistent transfer of data to the systems involved.

The *Content Integrator* links master data objects in different systems via object reference characteristics. Therefore, the identification of identical master data objects in the database, and subsequently, the elimination of the duplicates are ensured.

The *Master Data Server* (MDS) is the central component of the MDM. It administers the master data of the entire enterprise and therefore facilitates the consolidation, alignment, and distribution of master data. The MDS consists of three layers:

Layer Model

1. Object layer
2. Service layer
3. Preparation layer

The *object layer* provides predefined master data object types, while the *service layer* looks after management The *preparation layer* is responsible for the connection with SAP XI and the distribution of the master data.

Individual MDM adapters are used to connect to the different systems. The primary use of the MDM is the reduction of maintenance and running costs for the use and processing of master data.

The following preconfigured master was established for the MDM Release 2.0 ramp-up phase, which began in the third quarter of 2003:

Preconfigured Master Data

- Business partner
- Product master data
- Technical installations
- Product structure
- Documents
- Change management

This range will be dramatically enhanced in the next release.

MDM is also an optimization product in itself, which, in combination with SAP XI, allows for the central management of master data.

1.4 The mySAP Business Suite Solutions

1.4.1 mySAP Enterprise Resource Planning (ERP)

ERP Components

mySAP ERP is the central and most important solution in the mySAP Business Suite. It is based on SAP R/3 or its successor, SAP R/3 Enterprise. It is enhanced with SAP NetWeaver components and with additional functions for collaborative business (see Figure 1.14). SAP R/3 Enterprise is still at the core. It is made up of the Web Application Server, SAP R/3 Enterprise Core, and the Extension Sets. These extension sets (with their own release cycles) will mainly add new functions to the core application (see Figure 1.15).

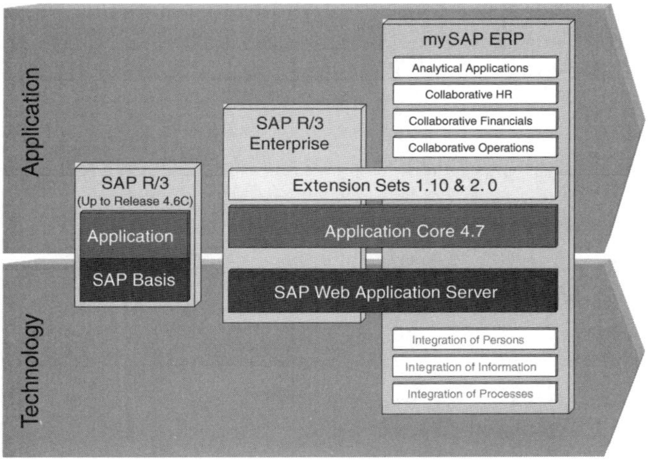

Figure 1.14 The Path to mySAP ERP

Before mySAP ERP, the term *module* was commonly used in the SAP environment. Now, this will change. The central system of an enterprise is hereafter separated into functions, for which SAP provides independent (sub-)solutions:

- mySAP Financials
- mySAP Operations
- mySAP Human Capital Management
- mySAP Analytics
- mySAP Corporate Services

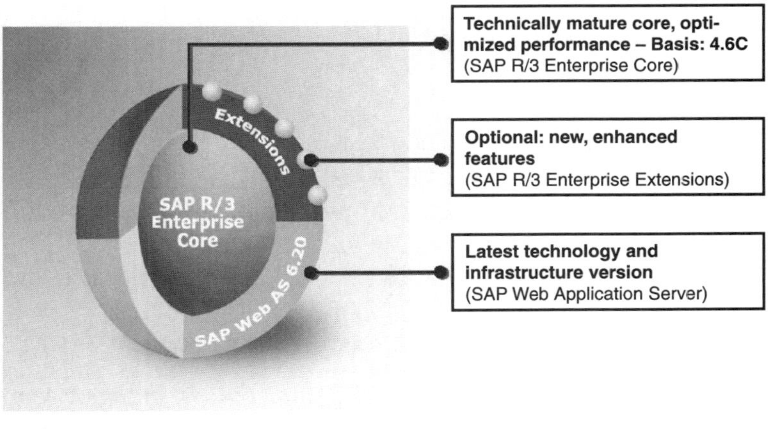

Figure 1.15 Architecture of SAP R/3 Enterprise

As previously mentioned, the technology platform that is behind these functions is the SAP NetWeaver.

The functions are made up of the following components:

Function	Component
Financials	▶ Financial Accounting ▶ Management Accounting ▶ Corporate Governance ▶ Financial Supply Chain Management
Operations	▶ Purchasing ▶ Inventory Management ▶ Production ▶ Project Management ▶ Plant Maintenance ▶ Quality Management ▶ Distribution ▶ Sales Order Processing
Human Capital Management	▶ Employee Relationship Management ▶ Employee Lifecycle Management ▶ Employee Transaction Management
Analytics	▶ Strategic Enterprise Management ▶ Financial Analytics ▶ Workforce Analytics ▶ Operations Analytics
Corporate Services	▶ Travel Management ▶ Environment, Health & Safety ▶ Provisions Management ▶ Real Estate Management
SAP NetWeaver	▶ Integration of people ▶ Integration of information ▶ Integration of processes ▶ Application platform

Table 1.1 Components of mySAP ERP

1.4.2 mySAP Customer Relationship Management (CRM)

After some early difficulties, the *mySAP Customer Relationship Management* (CRM) solution is gaining market share, although it is competing with well known rivals. During the years of economic crisis, many companies realized that they could not only manage their customer data; they could also use the data to help them better manage the relationship.

Three CRM Areas

The SAP solution encompasses all three facets of CRM:

- ▶ Operative
- ▶ Collaborative
- ▶ Analytical

The *operative* aspect forms the core of CRM. Processes related to the subjects of marketing, sales, enterprise management, service and support are mapped. The *collaborative* part focuses primarily on cooperation with partners and customers via the Internet, while *analytical* CRM supports the processing and evaluation of customer-related data. Such analysis is used to determine future interactions with the consumer. From a technical point of view, mySAP CRM is based on the SAP CRM server and SAP NetWeaver.

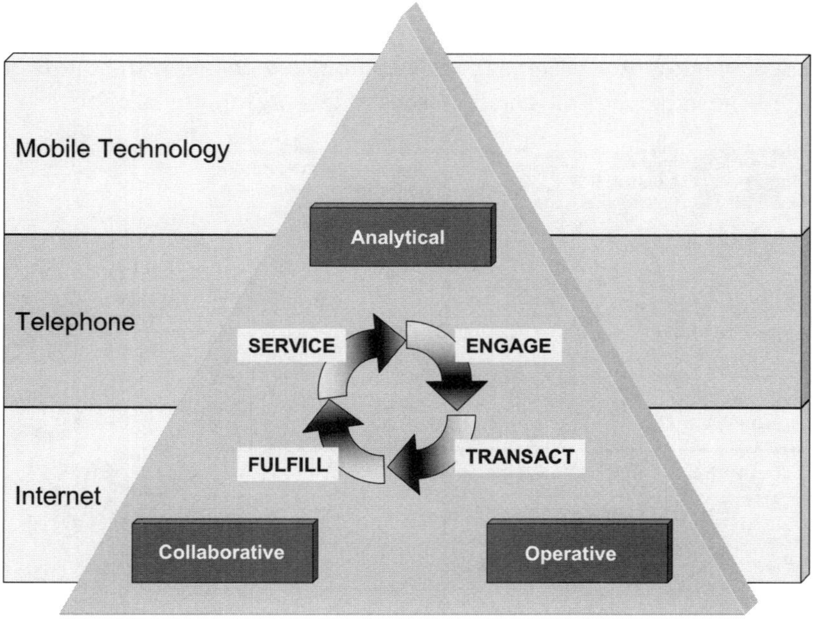

Figure 1.16 Core Functions of mySAP CRM

CRM is only as good as the data on which it is based. Apart from fine-tuning the implementation process, the potential for optimization exists primarily in high performance and prompt data exchange between all relevant systems (for example using XI or standard ALE technologies), and the mobile access to information, possibly improved with Push technology.

1.4.3 mySAP Supply Chain Management (SCM)

One universal goal in all manufacturing industry sectors is to have the lowest possible warehouse costs and warehouse stock by responding quickly and flexibly to customer needs. *mySAP Supply Chain Management* (SCM) fulfills the consumer demands because it includes all areas of a modern SCM system imaginable:

Areas of SCM

- Planning
- Coordination
- Collaboration
- Execution

Tier X suppliers and manufacturers can plan their activities together and therefore identify delivery bottlenecks early on and avoid them in the future. In addition, this type of procedure also results in long-term process simplification. Deliveries can be coordinated online, with no loss of time. The improved collaboration leads to less organizational effort.

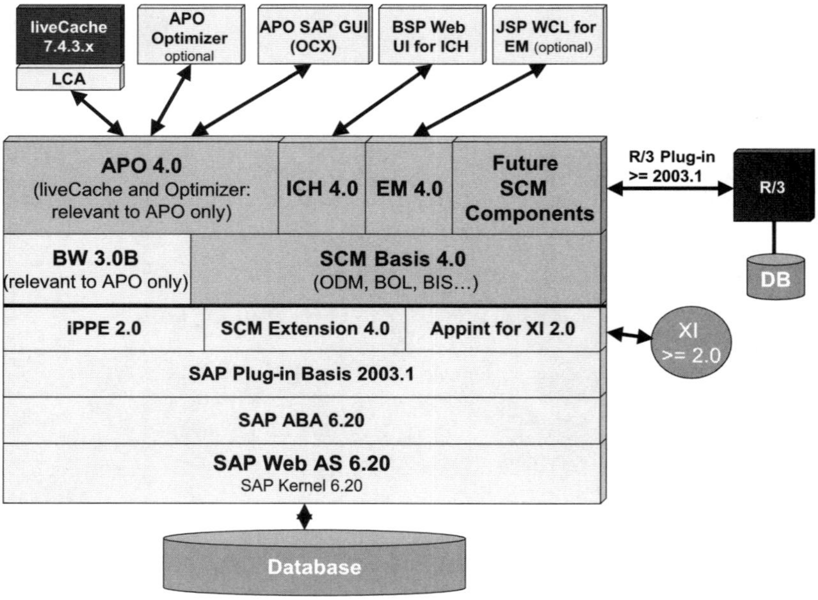

Figure 1.17 Technical Components of the SCM Solution

Industry Solutions SCM

Because different sectors also have different requirements to improve the logistic chains (e.g., single-part production versus batch production), SAP offers adequate solutions for different industries with special features. These industries include:

- Automobile industry
- Plant and machinery construction industry
- Processing industry
- Retail
- Consumer goods industry
- Logistics service agent
- Public service sector

Technically, mySAP SCM is based on numerous components, of which the *Advanced Planner and Optimizer* (APO) plays the most important role.

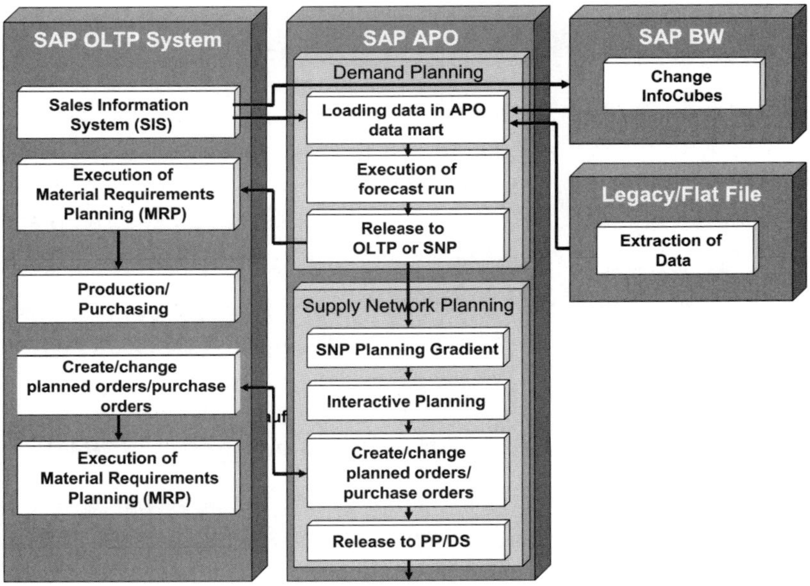

Figure 1.18 Typical SCM Planning Process

The online linking of suppliers, manufacturers, logistics service providers, and recipients is based on real-time access to relevant data. This aspect holds certain risks, because only released data may be visible and for the appropriate target group only. This places considerable demands on the security of the connections and systems.

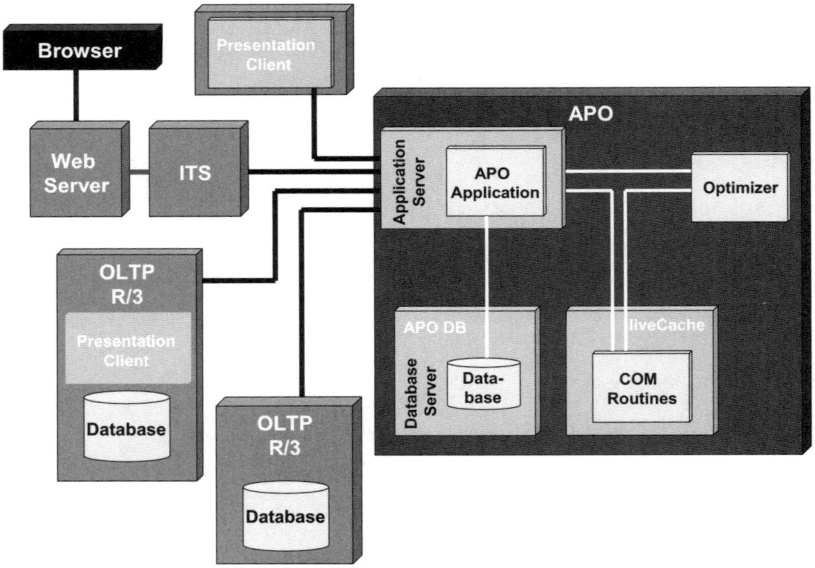

Figure 1.19 The Advanced Planner and Optimizer and Its Environment

The first goal of SCM solutions is to accelerate processes. They are efficient only if they are integrated with the relevant ERP systems in real time. Besides the purely technical performance of systems, the highest potential for optimization here is the association with other systems and people, in the SAP products SAP XI or SAP Enterprise Portal.

For more information on the administration of APO systems, please see *SAP APO System Administration* by Liane Will, which is also published by SAP PRESS.

1.4.4 mySAP Supplier Relationship Management (SRM)

In today's business world, direct communication and collaboration with customers (mySAP CRM) are indispensable, but so is contact with (Tier X) suppliers. The SAP solution *mySAP Supplier Relationship Management* (SRM) is designed to address this requirement. It allows you to link suppliers collaboratively into the relevant procurement process and therefore achieve cost savings or greater added value in the following areas:

- Optimized selection of suppliers
- Shorter procurement times
- Reduced process costs
- Precise procurement strategies

This is achieved technically in mySAP SRM by the following components:

Technical Components

- SAP Enterprise Buyer Professional
- SAP BW
- SAP User Management Engine
- SAP Content Integrator
- SAP Bidding Engine 1.0
- SAP Supplier Self-Services 1.0 (based on SAP XI)
- SAP Exchange Infrastructure
- Requisite BugsEye 3.5
- Requisite eMerge 3.5
- SAP Enterprise Portal 5.0

In addition, SRM facilitates collaborative business ideas by optimizing collaboration between suppliers and manufacturers.

In this solution, potential for optimization lies in the high performance integration of all components, in addition to the pure business process optimization.

1.4.5 mySAP Marketplace

Core Functions

With mySAP Marketplace, SAP offers a market solution with the following core functions:

- Business partner management
- Dynamic auctions
- Self-service procurement
- Supplier enablement
- Marketplace analytics
- Content management

The mySAP Marketplace solution based completely on SAP NetWeaver is scheduled for release in 2004.

Technical Components

The mySAP Marketplace solution currently comprises the following technical components:

- SAP Enterprise Buyer Professional
- Requisite BugsEye
- SAP BW

- SAP Marketplace Order Management (MOM)
- SAP Marketplace User Management
- SAP Marketplace Connector
- CMRC Catalog Publisher
- CMRC Trading Partner Connectivity
- CMRC eMarketplace Catalog

The main purpose of marketplaces is to optimize the procurement process. Therefore, you should consider network load and system connections, while not forgetting security aspects.

1.4.6 mySAP Product Lifecycle Management (PLM)

The aim of *mySAP Product Lifecycle Management* (PLM) is to help you bring products to market faster. To achieve this goal, mySAP PLM provides the following functions:

- Customer service and plant maintenance
- Product data and document management
- Program and project management
- Quality management
- Environment, health, and safety

mySAP PLM is mainly based on mySAP ERP with an additional extension set (ramp-up for PLM Extension Set 2.0 due in March 2004).

The effective use of PLM requires the high-performance, complete integration of *Computer Aided Design* (CAD) products, *Supervising Control and Data Acquisition Systems* (SCADA), and geographical information systems, collectively with other SAP solutions.

There is optimization potential in both the business and the technical site, in the areas of integration with standard ERP systems, and in the data exchange with third-party systems.

1.5 SAP Solutions for Midsize Enterprises

Contrary to public opinion, SAP has also gained market ground with midsize businesses. Over 50% of SAP customers are classic midsize enterprises. After unsuccessful attempts with the Ready-to-Work and Ready-to-Run solutions, SAP now has two new product lines for these customers. They should be of interest to small or medium-sized enterprises in search of a simple standard solution and to midsize companies that expect a high degree of flexibility from their central administration systems.

1.5.1 SAP Business One

SAP Business One is an ERP solution for small and midsize enterprises. It includes the following features:

- Administration
- Financial accounting
- Sales
- Purchasing
- Business partners
- Bank processing
- Warehouse management
- Final assembly
- Controlling
- Reporting

The SAP Business One solution is not based on SAP NetWeaver. It is designed for sales-oriented distribution and service enterprises with few employees. There is only limited room for optimization, which is not a problem because the solution can be used with standard means. Therefore, we will not prolong our discussion of SAP Business One in this book.

1.5.2 mySAP All-in-One

Unlike SAP Business One, *mySAP All-in-One* is based on standard SAP technology and consequently, offers a small, but sound introduction to the world of SAP.

Until now, the high costs for implementation and maintenance and, in particular, the high adjustment costs, have deterred many midsize businesses from making the leap into the world of SAP.

A typical midsize business expects an ERP system to reproduce its core processes without needing much adjustment. In collaboration with its partners, SAP can fulfill this need in approximately 80 sector-specific adjusted All-in-One solutions for retail, services, and industry.

To date, the most important target groups have been in the following areas:

- Automotive
- Service providers
- Engineering and construction
- Retail

mySAP All-in-One is reduced to the core processes and requirements of the individual sectors. The potential for optimization rests predominantly with the technical area; however, it also exists at the organizational level as well.

mySAP All-in-One is expandable and can also be transferred to the mySAP Business Suite.

1.6 SAP xApps

What Are xApps?

The term *xApps* initially caused a certain amount of confusion in the world of SAP. Are xApps pure Java developments without a database? Are they completely new products? Or, are they a link between old SAP components?

Since 2002, SAP has provided this powerful tool in order to use formerly separate processes across systems. This was possible because of the new Web-enabled SAP products, particularly when combined with a successful data exchange within heterogeneous system landscapes: NetWeaver enables the use of purely system-linked SAP components in integrated processes; Exchange Infrastructure oversees data exchange; the Enterprise Portal is responsible for presentation; and the Web AS provides the technical base.

Therefore, xApps are cross-system applications that implement processes using the technical possibilities of SAP NetWeaver. They are based on SAP process knowledge that goes beyond system boundaries. To achieve this, xApps access the different components of mySAP Business Suite and link the individual functions to produce an effective totality.

There are currently two SAP xApps available:

SAP xRPM

1. **SAP xRPM (SAP xApp Resource and Program Management)**
   This xApp controls and manages research and development processes in IT projects.

2. **SAP xMA (SAP xApp Mergers and Acquisitions)**
   This xApp focuses on takeovers and mergers and helps to accelerate these business processes, control them, and make them more transparent.

SAP xMA

1.7 Industry Solutions

SAP currently offers 23 industry solutions. The standard functions of the SAP R/3 system were not improved for many sectors and reflected only their needs to an unsatisfactory degree.

This development can trace its roots back to 1988 and the needs of utility companies (electricity, gas, and water providers) to map their consumption calculation in today's SAP R/2 systems. Over the years, many specialist solutions have emerged. These solutions have been developed in collaboration with customers and, consequently, even in those sectors with a high degree of specialized proprietary development, such as banking, they have increasingly gained acceptance. Within the context of this book, we shall choose only a few solutions as examples.

1.7.1 Industry Solutions for Banking

Heterogeneous Systems and Proprietary Development

The world of banking has become one of the most interesting customers for SAP. This group of customers is characterized by very heterogeneous system landscapes with numerous highly specialized proprietary developments. SAP has managed to penetrate this market increasingly since 1998.

The core products are the *Bank Customer Account* (BCA) and *Account Management* (AM) for processing and controlling checking accounts. BCA is for banks with a lower number of accounts; AM is particularly designed for mass processing. The next key banking area, loan management, falls under the responsibility of the area of *Consumer Mortgage Loans* (CML), formerly known as TR-LO (Treasury-Loan). These three products, integrated into the mySAP ERP solution, have been successfully used for years.

The *Payment Engine* (PE) is used for carrying out payment transactions. A more recent addition is the *Collateral Management System* (CMS), the development and preparation of which is currently being advanced in collaboration with some partner banks.

Additional banking functions, in particular, in the area of securities during trade, are currently addressed by partner products.

While the core functions of the SAP banking solution have proven stable, and to a large extent, capable of handling mass data, the Enterprise solution has also gained market share in the banking sector. In addition, the SAP XI, with its numerous interfaces, will arguably be integral to data in the banking sector.

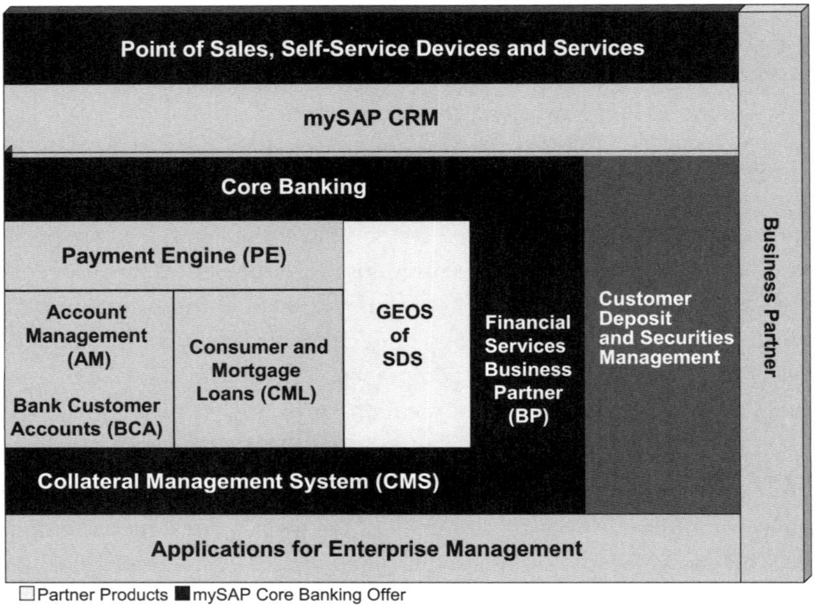

Figure 1.20 SAP Products for Banks

Bank Analyzer

Basel II determines new equity capital requirements for banks, which make considerable demands on data retention and data quality, and on the integration of data. These demands can be met with the SAP solution *Bank Analyzer*, in connection with other SAP or external systems. Bank Analyzer, currently at Release 2.1 (Release 3.0 will be available in January 2004), has also been intensively advanced with some partner banks.

The system architecture of the bank analyzer is based on two BW systems (*Tool BW*, *Reporting BW*) communicating via RFC, one of which is enhanced with add-ons. The Tool BW also contains a limited client capability, while the Reporting BW can also be used for other Business Intelligence functions apart from the Bank Analyzer (see Figure 1.21).

The Bank Analyzer comprises numerous overall bank analysis functions, which also enable the simulation and creation of consolidated financial statements, based on *Internal Accounting Standards* (IAS) (see Figure 1.22).

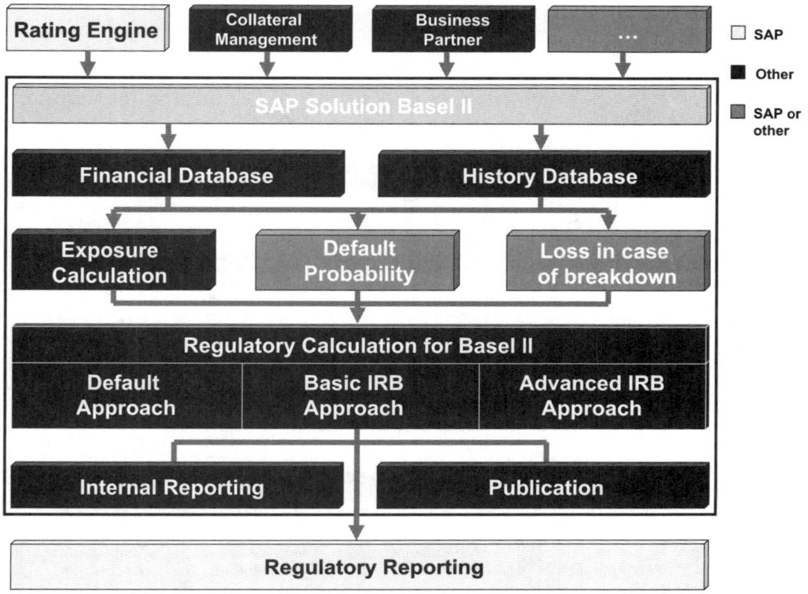

Figure 1.21 The Basel II Solution for Banks

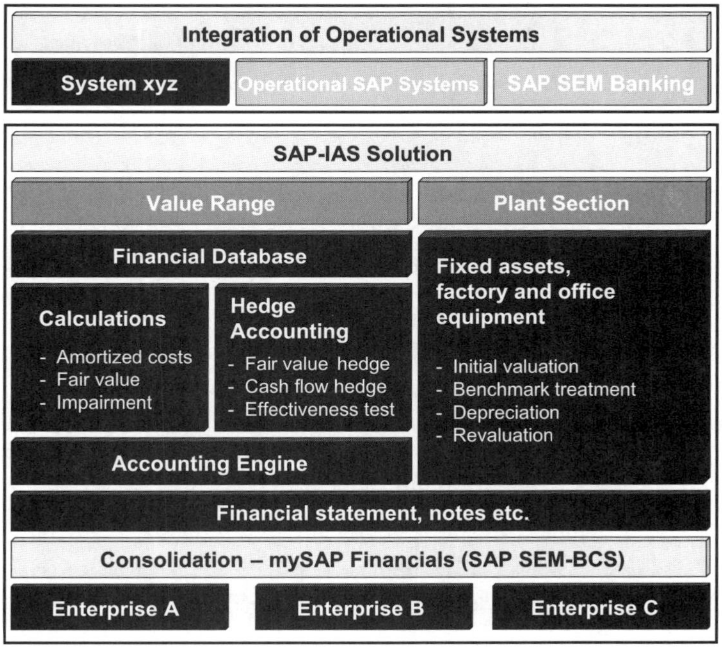

Figure 1.22 The IAS Solution for Banks

1.7.2 Sector Solutions for Insurance

As is true in the banking sector, SAP solutions for the insurance industry are also constantly being enhanced and adjusted, depending on the market requirements.

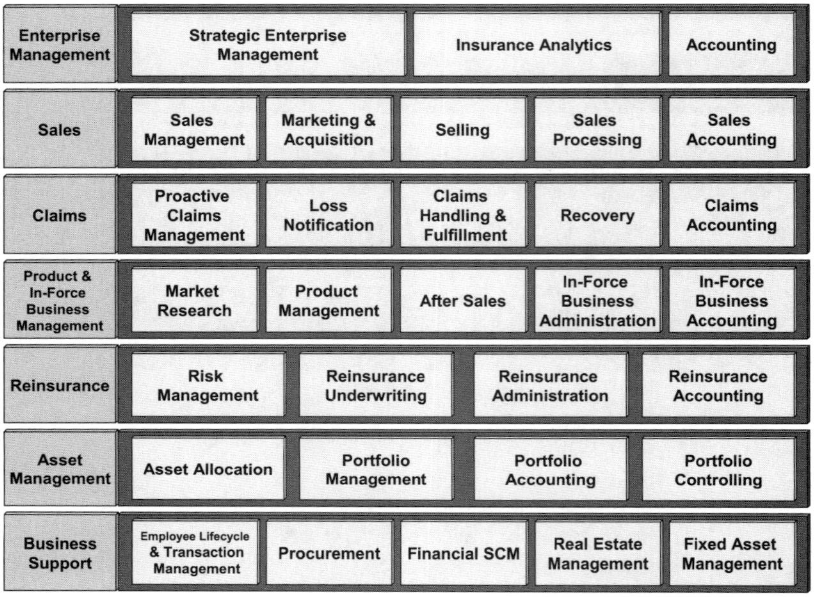

Figure 1.23 Insurance Solution

Apart from standard SAP functions, which are also of use and of interest to insurance companies, solutions adjusted to specific processes are developed—usually in collaboration with large customers—and brought to the market.

Optimization potential in the area of banks and insurance companies lies, on the one hand, with the implementation of ERP systems, that is, with the actual sector-adjusted processes, and, on the other hand, with the unification of the infrastructure or interface landscape using the *SAP Exchange Infrastructure* (SAP XI). Provided there is heterogeneity in the IT landscape of the banking and insurance sector (SAP doesn't yet have appropriate solutions for all requirements), in addition to central interface management, the option to align the user interfaces using the SAP Enterprise Portal also exists.

1.8 SAP Solutions for Optimizing the SAP Landscape

SAP offers numerous solutions for optimizing SAP systems or landscapes regarding performance or handling. We will describe these solutions in the next sections.

1.8.1 Archiving

Improving Performance

Productive SAP systems generate increasing volumes of data in their respective databases. The resulting huge dataset leads to increased access times for individual tables. Because this can have an impact on the quality of database and R/3 buffers, it can negatively impact system performance. To avoid this possible degradation in performance, you can remove data that is not currently needed, but should remain available, from the database and archive it. The archiving of data and the deleting of data from the database later on will ease the load on the database and consequently improve system performance.

The archived data must be stored for a long time according to legal requirements (10 years). It must also be available online for editing for a reasonable period of time.

Info structures

SAP info structures, in the form of an index, can be created in the SAP system to enable selective access to archived data. The creation of archived info structures creates additional entries in the database, however, you should select the number and complexity of the info structures carefully and therefore ensure that archiving does not create extra load on the database instead of relieving it.

Archiving print lists

Besides SAP archiving, you can also archive print lists from the SAP system. This relieves the load on the TemSe database or the corresponding file system (depending on settings). Print lists that are no longer needed online can be made accessible via archiving them and then deleting them from the database. In this way, you can improve print operations over time.

Using optical archives and linking them with the corresponding SAP system leads to a high load in the SAP system, or in a dialogue between document management and the SAP system.

The paperless office is a classic example of process optimization, in particular, when dealing with the SAP workflow, in which document-supported work processes can be carried out in real time.

1.8.2 Modern User Administration

In the ever-increasing world of SAP system landscapes—with its numerous systems and clients—user and authorization management has become harder to manage, from both a technical and an organizational perspective. The implementation of the SAP Enterprise Portal adds another administrative layer. Hence, if user and authorization administration are not semi-automated, it will be almost impossible to deal with this administrative albatross in a large system landscape over the long term.

Central User Administration

SAP Central User Administration (CUA) provides relief in sub-areas. If administration is centralized, then pure user administration is decidedly reduced, in particular, since CUA has overcome its teething troubles. For the productive use of CUA, we recommend that you pay close attention to the monitoring of ALE distribution processes by which the user changes are transferred to associated systems.

To make the allocation of authorizations in an enterprise more flexible, the allocation of SAP roles must be role-based. Ideally, these SAP roles should be linked with SAP organization management in order to circumvent the need for changes in authorization whenever there is a reorganization in the enterprise.

Directory Services

You can also use the authorization role approach outside the world of SAP. You can do this via exchanging data between the SAP system and directory services, which can be accessed by many systems via the LDAP protocol.

With SAP Enterprise Portal Release 5.0, you can use a shared enterprise LDAP, which processes this information directly to the EP. In future, this will be an option for linking different systems via an LDAP protocol and therefore will lead to the optimization of both the user administration and the authorization distribution for several different systems in an enterprise.

1.8.3 SAP Solution Manager

Solution Manager for Operations

Central system management solutions can be used to monitor and maintain SAP system landscapes in a meaningful and time-efficient way. In addition to numerous third-party vendors (IBM, HP, BMC, Realtech), SAP also offers a solution in the form of the *Solution Manager*.

Based on the *Computer Center Management System* (CCMS), available since R/3 Release 4.0, the system administration assistant and the Note Assistant, the SAP Solution Manager offers central monitoring for an SAP system landscape, including the ITS server, the SAP J2EE Engine, and Web servers. SAP existing solutions are used to monitor the operating system and the database.

Central Monitoring

The first release of the SAP Solution Manager still exhibits some handling problems. However, Release 3.1 of Solution Manager, due in early 2004, should bring a marked improvement.

Solution Manager for Implementations

Since the SAP initiatives ASAP and ValueSAP are now obsolete, SAP now offers several tools to implement SAP components and landscapes with the SAP Solution Manager. Besides complete process-oriented and therefore cross-system ASAP documentation, there are project control mechanisms, documentation possibilities, and customizing distribution beyond system boundaries—all helpful options for accelerating and coordinating SAP implementations. However, you should note that the customizing distribution can be *misused*, for example, to adjust authorization roles.

1.8.4 SAP Support Desk

With the *SAP Support Desk*, you can reproduce your support organization on a workflow basis in a *central administration system*. If you involve SAP support, you can edit error messages quickly and under supervision. These trouble tickets are automated intelligently, given the most important information on the errors is listed first, thus making the search for a solution easier (see Figure 1.24).

Central Administration System

You can also support this effort via the customer's own database with solutions for previously resolved problems. You can include external Trouble Ticket Systems.

1.8.5 Co-Hosting

Today, computers enable you to operate several instances on the same hardware without encountering any problems. This may be done in association with a dynamic allocation of memory and a CPU load between instances. Due to this so-called *co-hosting*, you can operate several systems, usually in the area of consolidation, test, and development and therefore, use hardware resources more efficiently.

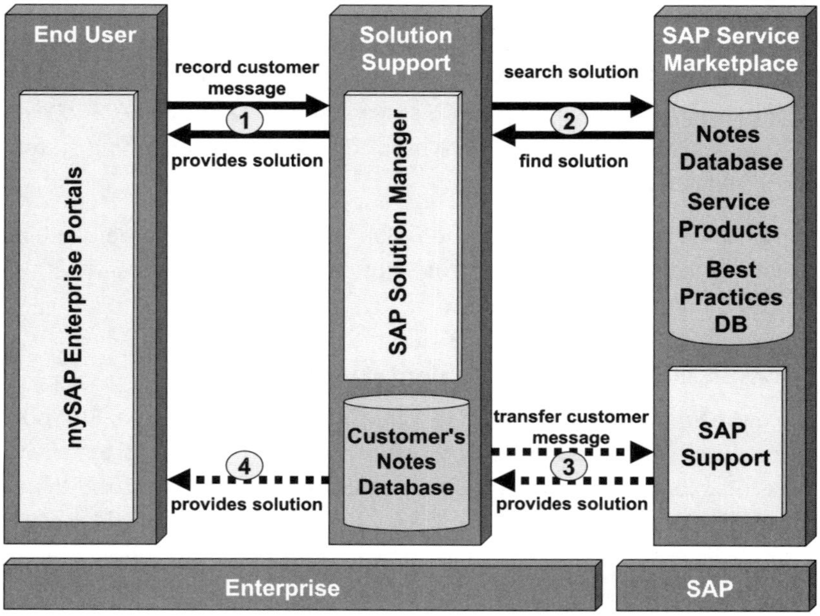

Figure 1.24 An Overview of the Online Support Process

If using two SAP instances on the same hardware, however, you should note that a kernel update will immediately have an effect on two or more systems. You should take this into account when planning the installation of the systems. SAP architecture, in which the SAP Basis—Web AS—is separated from the business part, allows for this type of procedure.

Frequently, however, development and consolidation systems, or several test systems with the same software versions, can be run on the same hardware. In this way, you can save on license and maintenance costs at the operating-system level.

1.8.6 Multiple Components on One Database

The *Multiple Components on One Database* (MCOD) technique means that you can operate several SAP systems on a single database.

Options 3 and 4 in Figure 1.25 are based on the MCOD technique and allow you to reduce operating and maintenance costs at the database level. In this case, the optimization potential is given in the area of saving memory space, back-up costs, and operating costs.

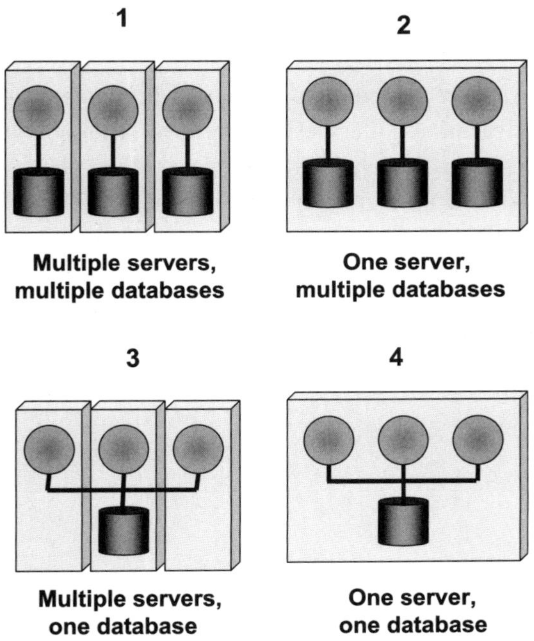

Figure 1.25 Possible Scenarios for Distributing SAP Systems on Servers and Databases

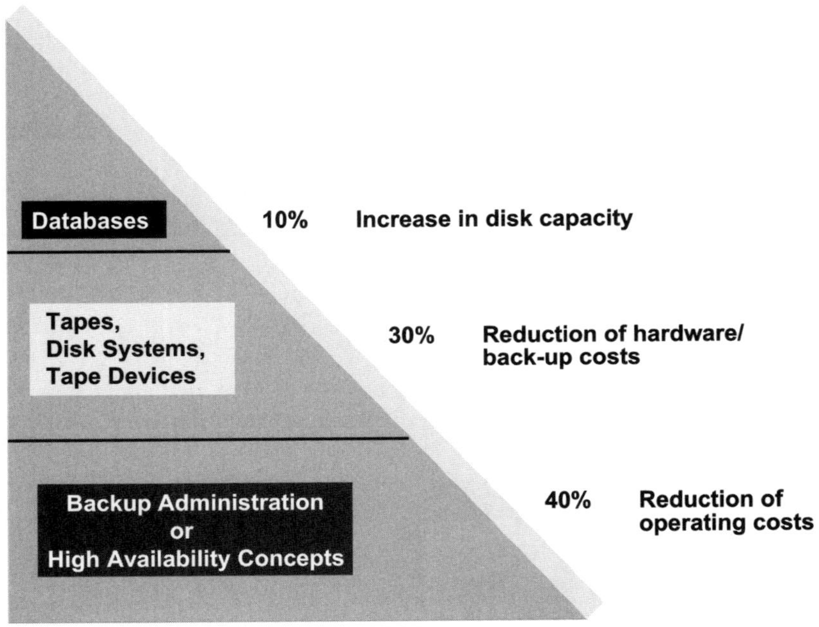

Figure 1.26 Saving Potential with MCOD

An additional effect is combined backups for related systems such as Enterprise and CRM.

It is possible to migrate to or from a shared database, which also enables you to control database release-dependencies. In any case, if designing an MCOD landscape, you should bear in mind the release dependency, performance criteria, and different DB parameterizations for OLTP and OLAP systems.

2 SAP Architecture Concepts

The central task of IT infrastructures in enterprises is to provide seamless support for value-added chains, within the company and beyond system boundaries.

The information necessary for the operative business and strategic development of a company can usually be found in different IT-supported areas, and is stored and processed in different systems. However, in many large firms, an exchange of data between the central IT systems and those of customers, business partners, or external employees is not uncommon.

You must consider these different requirements when designing system architecture, which should be flexible enough to allow for changes that can be integrated without too much effort.

2.1 SAP System Architecture

Many enterprises currently use SAP products to control production planning, purchasing and logistics, warehouse management and inventory management, production, vendor management, customer service, finance, personnel management and other basic business activities. As mentioned in Chapter 1, the mySAP Business Suite includes various business modules and numerous sector and cross-sector solutions.

System Architecture

A distributed system of this nature requires a common infrastructure, which is provided by SAP NetWeaver and, in particular, by the SAP Web Application Server (Web AS)—the successor to SAP Basis. This type of system architecture is subdivided into three layers, which make up the basic services of a business application system: the presentation layer, the application layer, and the database layer. Each of these layers performs certain functions and constitutes a part of the overall system landscape.

The *presentation layer* enables the user to interact with the relevant application. This interface is typically called the GUI (*Graphical User Interface*) and it is used to execute the application logic, utilizing the other layers in the combined infrastructure. Applications are executed in the *application layer* while the data to be processed is managed by the *database layer*.

The distribution of system functions over several layers means that an SAP system is extremely scalable. The separation into layers means that the overall load can be distributed over several servers. The functions of a single layer can also be distributed over multiple servers. This is made possible by, among other things, the network communication of the participating servers.

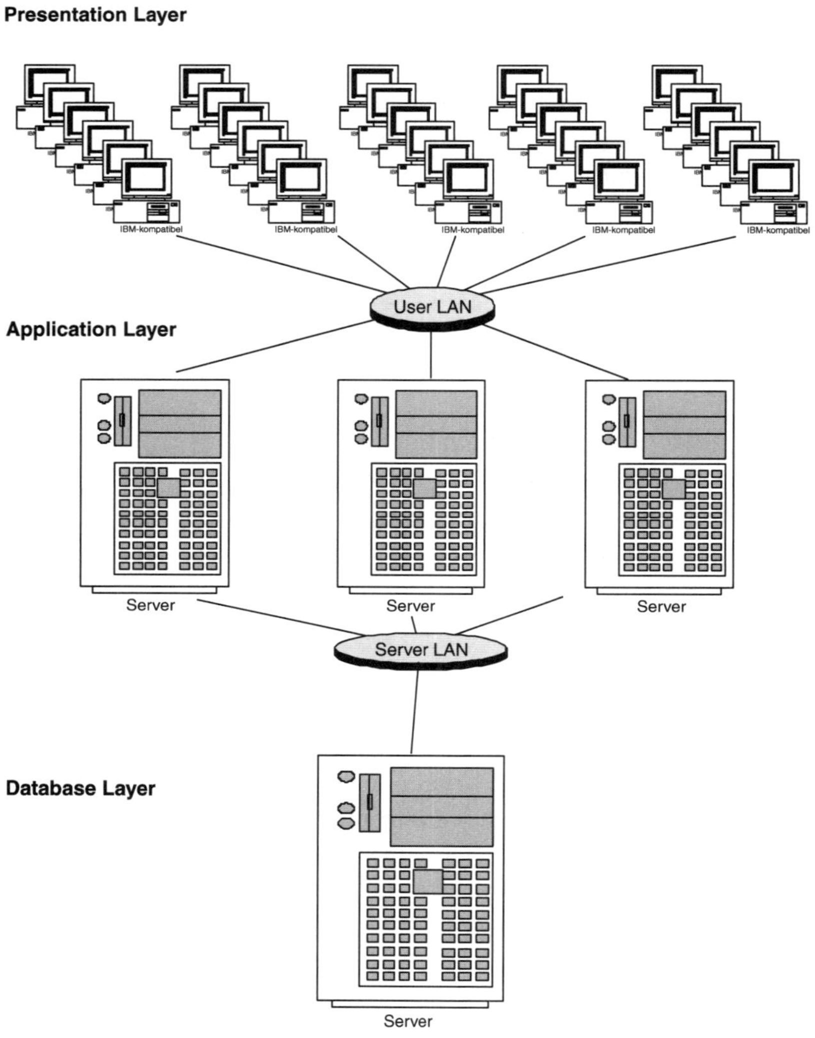

Figure 2.1 Three-Layer Model

In the days of SAP R/3, we spoke of one-, two-, or three-level architecture, depending on whether the services of the SAP R/3 system ran on one, two, or more servers. With one-level system architecture, all processing tasks occur on a single server. Two-level configurations are usually implemented with special presentation servers, which are responsible for preparing only the graphical interfaces. This is usually performed in such a way that the end users use their workstation (usually a Windows PC) as a presentation server via which they can access data that is stored and processed on a separate server. With a three-level configuration, a separate server is used for each service, that is, the presentation layer, the application layer, and the database layer run on different machines. The application layer, in particular, can be distributed over several application servers to counteract a possible high load caused by end users, data-exchange processes, or background processing.

Another prerequisite for the layers is that they should offer a high degree of flexibility with regard to hardware and operating-system environments. mySAP Business Suite is a standard software, so you must be able to use it on different platforms. Because the SAP system architecture supports a wide range of operating systems and hardware platforms, SAP tries to remain as platform-independent as possible. A Java version has been written for the SAP GUI, for example, which means that it can be run on almost all operating systems.

The application logic of mySAP components can run on numerous operating systems and hardware platforms. It should be noted, however, that the application programs cannot be run on different platforms without some amount of customization. An environment must be created that will allow for programs to be independent of the operating system. This is achieved using the SAP Web AS, or its predecessor, SAP Basis.

SAP Web Application Server

SAP Web AS is a later development of the SAP Application Server technology. New technologies were added to process or forward HTTP requests, for example. This is the task of a new process—the *Internet Communication Manager* (ICM). It can communicate via the Internet as a server and as a client.

Figure 2.2 shows the architecture of the earlier SAP Basis compared with the new SAP Web AS architecture. You can see the Internet communication enhancement in the form of the ICM.

Like SAP Web AS, SAP Basis provides the runtime environment for all SAP applications and ensures that the application is optimally embedded in the system environment. It defines a stable architecture framework for system enhancements and includes tools for the administration of the entire system. Additional tasks include the distribution of resources and providing system interfaces.

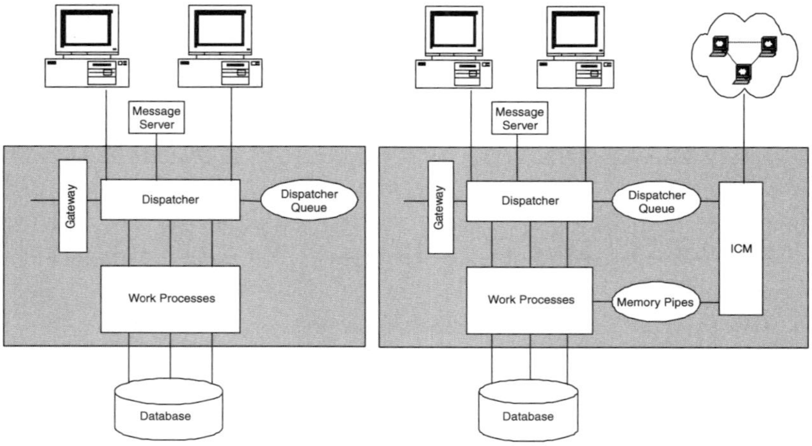

Figure 2.2 The Architecture of the SAP Web Application Server

Processes In contrast to the operating system, this runtime environment is a mass of parallel cooperating processes. On each application server, these processes include the dispatcher and a number of work processes, depending on existing resources. Special work processes can be defined according to the services for which the application is to be used, for example, an application server can be used exclusively for dialog processing. Therefore, we will define only dialog work processes on this server. You should use a different application server for background processing. Batch work processes are defined there for background processing. Communication between the dispatchers of an SAP system is done via the message server. There is always only one message server per SAP system. Communication between systems (R/3, R/2, external systems, and so on) is made possible thanks to the *SAP Gateway*.

The *SAP Internet Transaction Server* (ITS) is used for communication between an SAP R/3 system and a Web server. The ITS changes SAP screen images into HTML format and provides specific Web applications, which are known as *Internet Application Components* (IACs). You can also use SAP ITS as a gateway between a mySAP component and a Web server.

As previously mentioned, since the introduction of the SAP Web AS, new technology has been used to process HTTP requests (or other protocols) directly from the Internet, or send them to the Internet as HTTP client requests. To support this new development, another process has been added to the SAP kernel, namely, the ICM, which we already described.

Therefore, the definable processes available for the SAP Web AS are the message server, the dispatcher, work processes, the gateway process, and the ICM.

Standard Web protocols such as HTTP, HTTPS, Web DAV, SOAP, or SMTP are supported with the ICM. Output is in standard formats such as HTML, XML, or XLST. Requests and responses from the Internet with a specific URL (server/port combination) are processed with the ICM. The ICM process uses what are known as *threads* for parallel processing. Different threads have different tasks that can be carried out simultaneously. Thus, for example, the `Control` thread takes incoming requests and forwards them to the `Worker` thread, which processes a connection's requests and responses.

Instances

The services that run on a server are merged and managed together by an administrative unit, the instance, which is formed for this very purpose. Instances can carry out different tasks, depending on the configuration. If only one instance is connected to the database of an operative SAP system, it is referred to as the *central instance*. The central instance must be able to carry out all necessary services and should be configured appropriately. If an application server is defined with dialog work processes, this server is referred to as a *dialog instance*.

In large SAP systems, you can distribute the application layer over several instances. By distributing the load over several servers, you can improve the performance. Alternatively, you can run time-critical or load-intensive tasks on separate servers. If, for example, several hundred end users will be working with the SAP system, you can define different dialog instances to be used to achieve an evenly distributed load via logon groups. Should you need to output certain printouts—such as account statements or dunning letters by a certain date or time because they are a prerequisite for further procedures—you can define an application server so that it is available only for these tasks.

Buffer

Each of these instances offers *buffer* areas for different objects, such as for programs, dictionary objects, screen structures, or table contents. These buffers are built up while the instance is being used and are constantly being optimized. Different algorithms are used to organize the buffer so that it can store frequently needed data. If the buffer is not large enough (a typical scenario), existing entries are removed from the buffer to accommodate new entries. Instances are also used to configure high-availability solutions, for which you will need special HA software (High-Availability software, provided by third-party vendors) that automatically stores services and functions on another instance if the central instance fails, thereby ensuring the continued operation of the SAP system.

The best way to see how the different layers (presentation, application, database) are interconnected is to take a look at the process flow of an end-user request.

Request Process Flow

The *dispatcher* is the central process on the application layer for processing SAP transactions. Its main functions are to distribute the request load to the individual work processes, establish connection to the presentation layer, and organize communication between work processes. When an end user makes processing entries from his or her workstation, using his or her user menu (presentation layer), these entries are converted into a special format (SAP GUI protocol) and forwarded to the dispatcher. The dispatcher places this request in the dispatcher queue. The queue is then processed following the "first-in, first-out" principle. The dispatcher distributes queries to free work processes that carry out the processing. SAP transactions are usually implemented in several worksteps. A query is created for each workstep and is assigned to a free process, enabling each transaction to be processed by several work processes until that transaction is complete. The result of the processing is then returned to the presentation layer via the dispatcher, whereby the SAP GUI interprets the data received and generates the output screen.

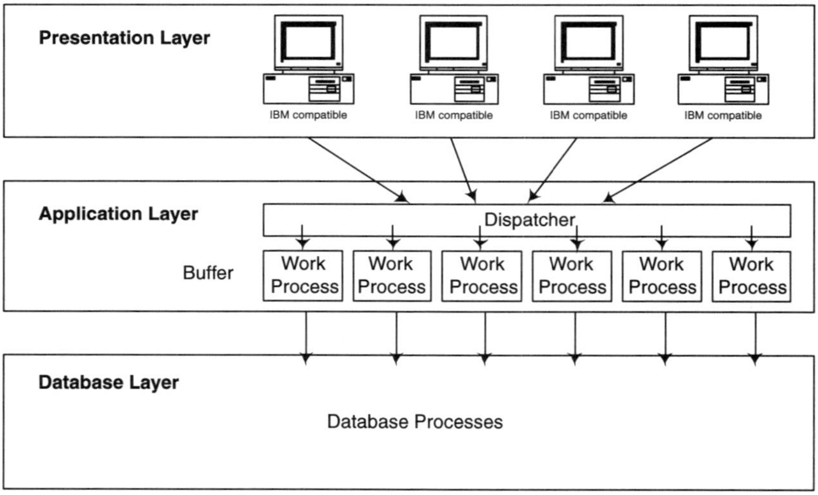

Figure 2.3 Processing a User Request

After we present an overview of the SAP system's architecture, we will examine the individual steps in greater detail.

2.1.1 Presentation Layer

SAP GUI

The *presentation layer* allows the end user to interact with the relevant application. This layer is presented in the form of the SAP GUI. The *SAP GUI* is a universal client for accessing SAP R/3 or mySAP functions. The SAP GUI works as a browser. It receives information on the "what, when, where, and how" from the SAP server and displays the content on the user interface.

The SAP GUI offers easy access to all SAP functions including application transactions, reports, and system administration functions. Thanks to the clearly defined menu structure, navigation is simplified. The SAP GUI is available in over 20 languages, which is integral to the development of international business processes today.

SAP has optimized the protocol between the presentation and application layers with regard to network load. When a user makes an entry, only the necessary data is sent via the network to the client. This also means that communication between the clients and the application server can also be produced within a WAN without additional loss. Therefore, for example, companies with several subsidiaries can use a central SAP system to handle business processes and users can access the system from their local sites.

The SAP GUI family comes in three different formats, each of which has its own unique selling point and is suited to a particular user group.

Extensive Integration

- **SAP GUI for Windows**
  The SAP GUI for Windows has been specially designed for Windows operating systems. It provides an environment similar to that of Windows applications and also offers integration with other applications in the same way as the Windows environment (using OLE interfaces or ActiveX controls). In addition to the standard functions offered by all members of the SAP GUI family, SAP GUI for Windows offers extensive integration with Microsoft Office and links with mySAP components such as mySAP SCM.

Access Using the Web Browser

- **SAP GUI for HTML**
  The SAP GUI for HTML allows access to certain transactions using a Web browser. For this access, however, you will need the SAP Internet Transaction Server (ITS), which controls the actual conversion to HTML. Using the services of the SAP ITS and HTML templates, screen elements of SAP transactions are converted to HTML. Not all elements can be converted to HTML, but all standard elements such as tables, lists, menu trees, and so on can be displayed. The use of SAP GUI for HTML is therefore best suited for occasional users. Access to SAP functions using the

SAP GUI for HTML doesn't require a separate client on the end-user's desktop, just a Web browser, for example, Microsoft Internet Explorer. To develop a business process with the help of a Web browser, you need *Internet Application Components* (IAC). IACs are SAP transactions that have been specially developed for execution via the Internet or intranet. They are based on *Business Application Programming Interfaces* (BAPIs), which use objects and methods to access SAP processes and data. IACs are addressed by the SAP ITS with the help of the SAP GUI protocol.

The SAP ITS acts as a gateway between the HTTP, the SAP GUI, and the Remote Function Call (RFC) protocol. Basically, the ITS is like a layer between the presentation layer and the application layer in SAP architecture, which means that the three-layer architecture becomes a four-layer architecture.

Platform-Independent and Direct

- **SAP GUI for Java**

  The SAP GUI for Java was developed to achieve platform-independence in the area of the SAP frontend. The SAP GUI for Java is a uniform SAP frontend for many platforms, providing front-end functions with the help of JavaBeans. The technology behind it is a combination of Java and C++. The ActiveX controls, which are used in the world of Windows, are written as JavaBeans. Existing C/C++ libraries on the desktop in question are used by SAP GUI for Java to provide functions such as network communication, data transfer, or others. The SAP GUI for Java is installed on the desktop as an application (browser-based installation) and communicates directly with the SAP Web AS.

Summary

The presentation layer of the SAP system implements the GUI and therefore allows the end users to work with the application software. We can differentiate between different implementations of the user interface: SAP GUI for HTML, SAP GUI for Windows, and SAP GUI for Java. With SAP GUI for Java, you can use the GUI on almost all platforms, thanks to the Java Virtual Machine (JVM). The SAP GUI for HTML also enables you to interact with the application logic, regardless of which platform is used, provided the client is a current Web browser. The SAP GUI for HTML is implemented on the server side, however, it can be used only by end users. Only SAP GUI for Windows and SAP GUI for Java provide a development environment. Another restriction with the Java or HTML execution is that there is no integration with MS Office.

Web Dynpro

Web Dynpro technology is a new development. It can be used for programming the user interfaces. Web Dynpro technology provides a development and runtime environment for Web applications, based on server-side scripting. Java Server Pages (JSPs) and a tag library are used for the interfaces. The Web Dynpro technology closes significant gaps between the typical Web development tools and the need for a cost-efficient, easy to adjust, manageable professional user interface for business solutions. It adheres to guidelines that also apply to SAP dynpro technology.

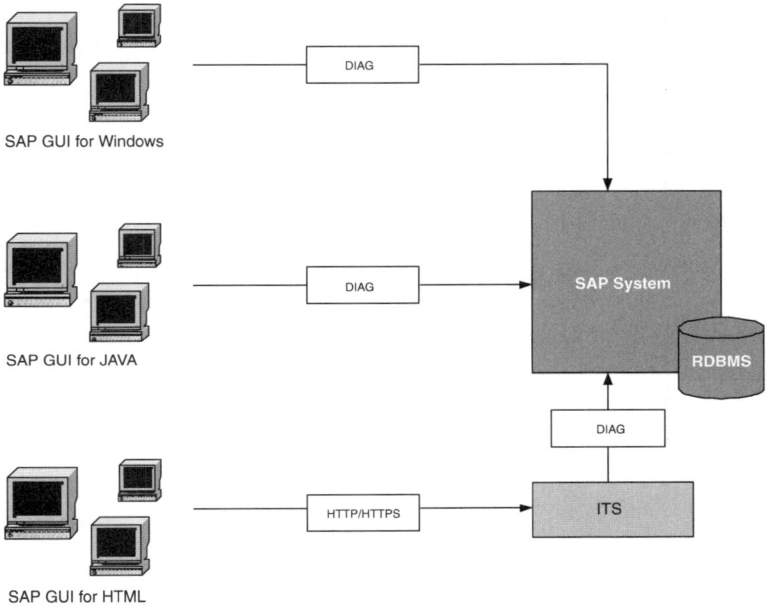

Figure 2.4 SAP GUI Family

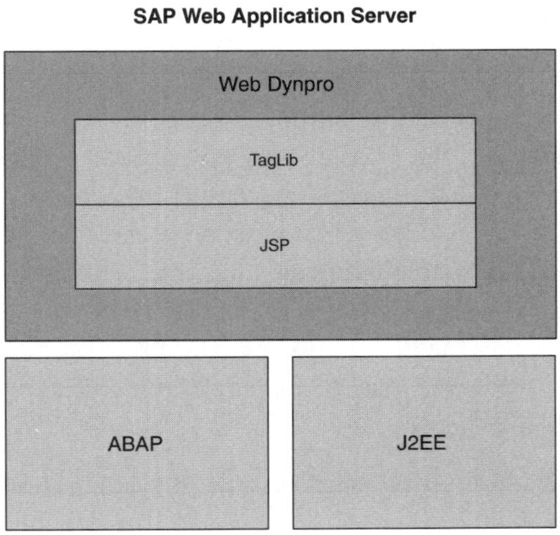

Figure 2.5 Web Dynpro

2.1.2 Application Layer

In recent years, the development of business software has grown to unforeseen proportions. Increasingly, you can integrate more business processes and show how business processes can work outside the realm of the company. This means that the potential usefulness of this type of software to an enterprise has grown enormously. Higher demands are made on planning, maintenance, and administration, however, mainly due to the integration of the Internet. Requirements such as platform-independence, security, development versioning, multi-user possibility, internationalization, and so on, are becoming increasingly important, and therefore, the underlying system environment must conform to these requirements.

SAP Web Application Server

The *SAP Web Application Server* (Web AS) provides an environment in which all applications, in addition to the particular characteristics of the underlying operating system, can be developed, managed, and executed. SAP Web AS offers a platform for efficient development and for using Web applications and is a component of all mySAP installations. The server contains the presentation and application layers in its environment and ensures the independence of the database system used. It combines reliability, scalability, international language support, and connection to the *Change and Transport System* (CTS) with open standards such as HTTP, HTTPS, SMTP, WebDAV, HTML, XML, and server-side scripting. With SAP Web AS, SAP offers a uniform infrastructure for J2EE- and ABAP-based applications (*ABAP Personality* and *Java Personality*).

Internet Communication Manager

The SAP Web AS enhances SAP's application server technology (SAP Basis) for the Internet world and is therefore fully integrated into the SAP environment (development environment, user administration, authorization concept, system monitoring, communication protocols). Another process added to the SAP kernel is the *Internet Communication Manager* (ICM). It uses threads to communicate via the Internet. If the incoming HTTP request is processed by a work process, data exchange occurs using what are known as *Memory Pipes* in the shared memory. The ICM distributes user requests to the presentation layer or sends Web service requests to the integration layer. If the ICM is addressed by an application or a client, it acts as a server. If the SAP Web AS initiates communication, however, then the ICM acts as a client.

Within a work process that oversees different tasks in the application layer, the *Internet Communication Framework* (ICF) provides the environment for handling HTTP requests. The ICF is the layer between the ICM and the processing of requests in the work process. This makes it possible for work processes to generate Web-compliant content, which is forwarded to a browser via the ICM. One option for creating this content is to use applications with *Business Server Pages* (BSPs), which have been developed in the SAP system using the *Web Application Builder*.

To ensure a high degree of flexibility, the SAP Web AS is functionally divided into different layers.

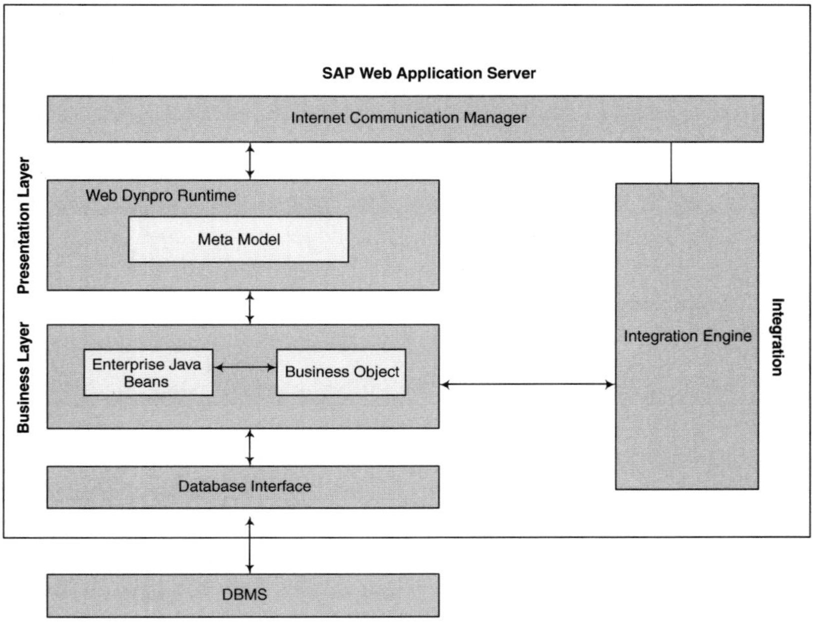

Figure 2.6 SAP Web Application Server

In the presentation layer, you can develop user surface for a Web application directly using JSPs or BSPs and the corresponding JSP tag library or using the new Web Dynpro technology. The underlying business layer provides content in Java or ABAP.

Business Process Logic

The most important function of an application is the *business process logic* that processes business-critical data. This logic runs in the application layer of the SAP Web AS and can transfer the results to a user interface or an external application. It can be written in ABAP or in Java, based on the J2EE standard. This offers greater development flexibility. The application layer of the SAP Web AS makes up a fully functional J2EE-certified runtime environment that processes the requests sent by the ICM and delivers dynamic results. New application programs, based on a component model for application logic, can be developed with *Enterprise Java Beans* (EJBs). You can also access application objects written in ABAP. The conventional functioning of BAPIs is further supported. In addition, the SAP Web AS supports standards such as XML, SOAP, WDSL, UDDI, and so on to allow for the development of and access to Web services. These Web services can be used within an enterprise or outside the realm of the company, with different SAP or non-SAP applications and entirely platform-independent. Enterprises can therefore use Web services to help define business processes that affect several business partners with different application systems. To help you react quickly and flexibly to market requirements, you can use the following tool—ABAP Workbench.

ABAP Workbench

The development environment of the SAP Web AS, the *ABAP Workbench*, is a strongly integrated environment for developing application objects. Over the years, the ABAP Workbench has proven to be extendable and reliable, so the concepts underlying this development environment are also applicable to the Java environment. This ensures that the robustness and reliability integral to developing enterprise-critical application programs is also inherently true for the Java personality.

Database Layer

The *database layer* of the SAP Web AS offers many outstanding features. Thanks to Open SQL, it ensures optimal access to data via the ABAP environment. Optimizing functions, such as buffering SQL statements or data buffering, are used. This interface ensures that the business processing logic can be developed independently from the underlying database and the operating system. The database interface monitors the conversion of Open SQL statements—from the ABAP statements to the appropriate database statements. When interpreting the Open SQL statements, the interface carries out another syntax check and ensures that the capacity of the SAP buffer, which is used to process any statements in the SAP system, is used optimally. Then, SAP transfers experience gained in the ABAP world to the J2EE development environment. Database independence is also ensured, for example, via the use of open standards such as *Java Database Connectivity* (JDC). The functions of Open SQL for ABAP are transferred to an Open SQL for Java and a range of *Application Programming Interfaces* (APIs) is provided for Java development.

The SAP Web AS forms the basis of any mySAP component system, be it mySAP Customer Relationship Management (mySAP CRM), mySAP Supply Chain Management (mySAP SCM), or others. Besides the open, integrated development environment, concepts such as connection standards, platform-independence, scalability, high availability, globalization, manageability, change management, and even security and performance are also considered critical.

Connection Standards

Several connection standards, such as J2EE Connector Architecture or Microsoft.NET Connectivity, are supported. In this way, you can mix different products and applications so that non-SAP applications can also be integrated with the SAP Web AS. To ensure that it's possible to communicate with all possible applications, many protocols and formats are supported, such as COBRA, FTP, SMTP, or RFC as SAP standard protocol. XML documents can also be interpreted.

Connection Technologies

The technical foundation of the Business Framework consists of the different connection technologies provided by SAP Basis or the SAP Web Application Server. These standards mean that you can integrate the different SAP functions, programs, objects, and so on, outside system and platform boundaries. *Remote Function Call* (RFC) technology and *Intermediate Documents* (IDoc) form the basis for executing SAP functions in distributed systems. This technology is embedded in the business process scenarios via the Application Link Enabling (ALE) distribution model, and via the definition of SAP business objects, known as BAPIs, which we already introduced and will elaborate on below.

Remote Function Call (RFC)

RFC is the SAP variant of the *Remote Procedure Call* (RPC). It allows functions to be executed in other programs. There are different remote function call procedures to satisfy the different requirements of individual applications and their business processes:

- With *synchronous RFC* (sRFC), function modules in external systems can be called in realtime. With this type of RFC, the client waits until the server has completed processing.
- Long-running processing can be split into different function calls using *asynchronous RFCs* (aRFC), which are then processed in parallel.
- If errors occur during the processing of aRFC or sRFC, it is impossible to detect if the error occurred before or after processing. It is also impossible to establish whether or not the RFC was even executed. With *transactional RFC* (tRFC), data consistency and unique execution is ensured. Transactional RFC is asynchronous and assigns a *Transaction Identifier* (TID) to ensure that if data is sent numerous times because of network problems, it is recognized by the server. This helps to avoid data being processed several times, which can lead to erroneous information

in the application. One condition of asynchronous processing, however, is that parameters can only be transferred from the client to the server. The direct return of information or status information is not possible.

- The *queued RFC* (qRFC) is an enhancement of the tRFC. With qRFC, the calls are placed in queues. This ensures that function calls are processed in a fixed sequence.
- Web-enabled exchange of information with XML is carried out by *HTTP-RFC* (xRFC). Function calls are sent via HTTP to an SAP system in the form of an XML document based on the SOAP standard.

ALE and IDocs

Application Link Enabling (ALE) is an interface technology developed by SAP to link application systems (SAP systems and non-SAP systems) to each other via a distribution model. ALE enables systems on different platforms to communicate with each other. Data is exchanged asynchronously using *IDocs* (Intermediate Documents), a data format defined by SAP. IDoc is an SAP standardized document format that allows you to link different application systems via a message-based interface. It is similar to a container used to exchange data between SAP systems, or between SAP systems and non-SAP systems, because it features a neutral data structure. IDoc types are assigned different message types that are linked to business objects from the *Business Object Repository* (BOR). Thus, IDoc types are assigned to specific business processes.

BAPI

Another important SAP interface is the *Business Application Programming Interface* (BAPI). BAPIs are interfaces based on real business process scenarios. The idea of the BAPI is based on an object-oriented modeling concept, which is converted in the implementation of BAPI as RFC-enabled function modules in SAP applications. Using SAP Business Connectors,[1] however, BAPIs can also be called via the Internet.

Telephone, Fax, and Email

SAP architecture offers many different functions to help provide fast and efficient communication for optimizing business processes within a company and between companies. The Internet is also increasingly being used to develop and optimize processes. There is also a need, however, for the exchange of unstructured information using media such as the telephone, email, and fax, and exchanging structured data such as XML documents, worksheets, or electronic forms. Many different services and interfaces are required for this, which are provided by SAP architecture via APIs, special user interfaces, or interfaces to partner products. These services can include:

1 The *SAP Business Connector* is a middleware product that permits the integration of SAP business process operation using open and non-proprietary technologies. It uses the Internet as a communication platform and the data format used is XML/HTML.

- Communication via the SAP Enterprise Portal
- Sending and receiving documents via email or fax using SAPconnect
- Integration of groupware products
- Telephone integration using SAPphone
- Calendar and scheduling overview
- Generic object services such as SAP Business WebFlow or SAP ArchiveLink for integrating scanned documents with the relevant business processes.
- XML documents

Platform-Independence

The SAP Web AS is platform-independent. Consequently, enterprises enjoy great flexibility in the choice of their hardware or operating-system platforms, depending on their requirements or the existing IT infrastructure. To ensure this flexibility, SAP adheres to a strategy that supports all platforms that are persistent and have an adequate market share. Consequently, numerous combinations of hardware, operating systems, and database are possible. In discussing the SAP GUI family, we already described the necessity for the presentation layer to be platform-independent.

Scalability

Application server technology, which SAP has further developed as the SAP Web AS, ensures the high degree of scalability of an SAP installation. Consequently, the scaling of SAP systems—according to growing business requirements—is ensured and can process a growing number of business procedures. If you distribute the application layer over several application servers, offering additional resources to support the growing load, then you can easily expand your SAP landscape. There are also software-based possibilities to distribute the load evenly over several instances. Load distribution using the SAP Web Dispatcher can also be supported to process HTTP requests. The SAP Web Dispatcher acts as a "software-web switch" between the Internet and the SAP system, made up of one or more Web application servers. In this way, there is only one entry point for HTTP requests in the system. The SAP Web Dispatcher also provides load balancing by forwarding requests to the application server with the current highest capacity.

Globalization

The latest professional Web applications should satisfy different language and business requirements. To meet the requirements of globalization, the SAP Web AS offers a range of functions that support the expansion of business process flows. These functions address concepts such as internationalization, currency support, time zones, security aspects, and much more, with country-specific conditions and language differences also taken into account. The implementation of Unicode, for example, means that several languages can be supported concurrently.

2.2 Security

In a business environment in which there is an increasing use of open networks and cross-enterprise business relationships and processes, secure data transfer between the Internet and the company intranet is integral to doing business. The SAP Web AS provides an infrastructure offering far-reaching functions in the area of security in heterogeneous environments. Business processes and their data in applications and Web services are protected against unauthorized access and misuse. Access authorizations and roles can determine who may view and process data. In addition, security aspects regarding the operating system and the database can also be considered separately. The SAP Web AS offers various guidelines to ensure technical system security, which can be converted into enterprise requirements with the help of a security plan. The most important aspects of security that must be addressed include:

- **User Authentication**
  Only authorized users can have access to the system; unauthorized persons cannot copy an identity. Users can execute only those tasks for which they are authorized.
- **Protecting Integrity**
  No unnoticed changes can be made to data.
- **Protecting Confidentiality**
  Data and communication must be protected from unauthorized reading and eavesdropping.
- **Non-Repudiation (liability)**
  Reliability and legal liability must be ensured.
- **Checking and Logging**
  Activities and events must be recorded so that they can be accessed at a later point in time (for example, audits).

There are a range of mechanisms available for user authentication in the SAP system.

Authentication

- **User IDs and Passwords**
  To save passwords, the system converts a user's plaintext password with a one-way hash routine into an appropriate hash value that is stored in the database. The one-way hash routine guarantees that the original plaintext password cannot be evaluated from the hash value.
- **Secure Network Communications (SNC)**
  SNC is available for user authentication when the SAP GUI for Windows or RFCs are used. SNC uses an external security product for authentication between the communication partners instead of the conventional authentication (i.e., user name and password). If, for example, the security product Public Key Technology is used, then a *Public Key Infrastructure* (PKI) will be needed.
- **SAP Logon Tickets**
  After authentication on the SAP system, a user can issue himself or herself an SAP Logon Ticket to provide Single Sign-On (SSO) for several systems. The ticket can then be presented to other systems (SAP or non-SAP systems) as an authorization token. The user won't need to enter a user ID with a password, but can access the system once the logon ticket has been checked.
- **X.509 Client Certificate**
  As an alternative to user authentication with user ID and passwords, when using Internet applications via the *Internet Transaction Server* (ITS), the user can present X.509 client certificates. Here, user authentication is executed on the Web server using the Secure Sockets Layer protocol (SSL), where the transfer of passwords isn't required.

The individual functions can be supported by additional features. User administration can be supported via the use of a central directory service that would allow the company to maintain user roles and authorizations efficiently. In a distributed system landscape with several SAP systems, this aspect is also supported via the use of a central system for user administration. The SAP Web AS offers these *Central User Administration* (CUA) functions. They allow for several systems and their users, along with authorizations and roles, to be maintained centrally, and then automatically distributed to the systems in the system group using ALE. In addition to a defined organizational management and the Directory Service mentioned above, a certain automaticity of functionality can also be recorded.

Network The network infrastructure is of paramount importance to the security of a system. The network must support the communication needed by the company and its requirements excluding unauthorized access. A clearly defined network topology can help to avoid security risks based on software errors (at the operating-system level and at the application level as well), or access to the network, such as unauthorized eavesdropping.

The most important SAP services to ensure network security are the SAProuter and Secure Network Communications (SNC).

SAProuter The *SAProuter* is an SAP program for transmitting SAP system connections through firewalls. The SAProuter is a proxy in the network interface layer (NI layer)[2] of the SAP system. It can also log connection activities at various levels of detail. The SAProuter, alone, cannot control access to the network. Rather, it must be used in connection with a firewall system.

Secure Network Communications (SNC) *SNC* is a software layer in the SAP system architecture that offers an interface to an external security product. You can increase the security of the SAP system with SNC via implementing additional security functions not directly offered by SAP systems (for example, by using smart cards for user authentication). SNC offers security at application level. This means that a secure connection between the components of the SAP system (for example, between the SAP GUI and the SAP Web AS) is ensured, independently of the communication connection or the transport medium. Therefore, you can rest assured that the network connection between two communication partners protected with SNC will be secure.

Digital Signatures SAP applications can use what are known as *Secure Store and Forward (SSF) mechanisms* to ensure the integrity, authenticity, and confidentiality of data. If these mechanisms are used, then the actual data itself is protected if it leaves the SAP system. SSF uses digital signatures and digital envelopes to protect data. The *digital signature* is a unique identifier for the signer. It cannot be forged and it protects the integrity of the data. (The digital signature is not valid for any changes made to data after signing.) The digital envelope ensures that the data content can be read by the intended recipient only. SSF needs a security product to carry out its functions. Since Release 4.5, SAP delivers the *SAPSECULIB* (SAP Security Library) with SAP systems as the standard library of the SSF service. SAPSECULIB is a software solution especially devoted to digital signatures. An additional SAP-certified external security product is necessary to support cryptographic hardware (for example smart cards, security boxes, and so on) or digital envelopes.

---

2 NI is SAP's abstract network protocol based on TCP/IP.

2.3 Change and Transport Management

All enterprise applications require intensive maintenance throughout the software lifecycle. In order to customize an application to reflect business processes, the company must usually create its own application settings. To support this maintenance effort and stay current with all the changes, specially developed tools for the particular configuration settings are used and continual updates are made to the system landscape. However, for security reasons, changes should not be implemented in the business-critical productive environment; instead, they should be made in a separate development system of the productive system. In this way, changes can be tested before they are actually put into use. SAP recommends that you use a separate system or independent layer for each sub-task in the development or change procedure. Generally, a three-system landscape is constructed for each component system in a system group, consisting of a development, quality (test), and productive system. Changes or developments are executed in the development system and SAP mechanisms are used to transfer them to the test system for extensive testing. After successful testing, the changes are transferred to the productive system to be used for the relevant business procedures. For this, the SAP architecture offers a complete Change Management and Transport service that fulfills business-critical requirements.

The special data structure of the SAP system is decisive for handling changes. In addition to business settings (customizing), which are only relevant for certain SAP clients,[3] the SAP system always contains cross-application settings and objects, that is, client-independent customizing and the Repository.

ABAP Workbench

All development objects in the ABAP Workbench are stored in the central repository and are client-independent. These are mainly programs, tables, screens, function modules, classes, and so on, which are organized in *packages* (previously referred to as *development classes*). The packages contain semantically-related development objects. Changes can be made to the repository in different ways. Any necessary company enhancements to the standard repository are implemented with customer developments, therefore, new objects are created. The company uses the customer name range for these objects to differentiate them from the standard SAP objects, which is important for software upgrades. Modifications or customer enhancements, on the other hand, are changes to

3 A *client* is a self-contained unit within an SAP system, under commercial law and from an organizational and data systems point of view.

the repository via which standard SAP objects are changed or expanded with customer-developed objects (Customer Exit).

Customizing Via customizing, you can adjust the business settings in the system to meet the requirements of the business procedures. These settings must be carried out when an SAP system is first installed and can, if necessary, be adjusted during operation due to enterprise-specific or, for example, legal changes. Examples of customizing settings are company codes, plant, warehouses, and so on.

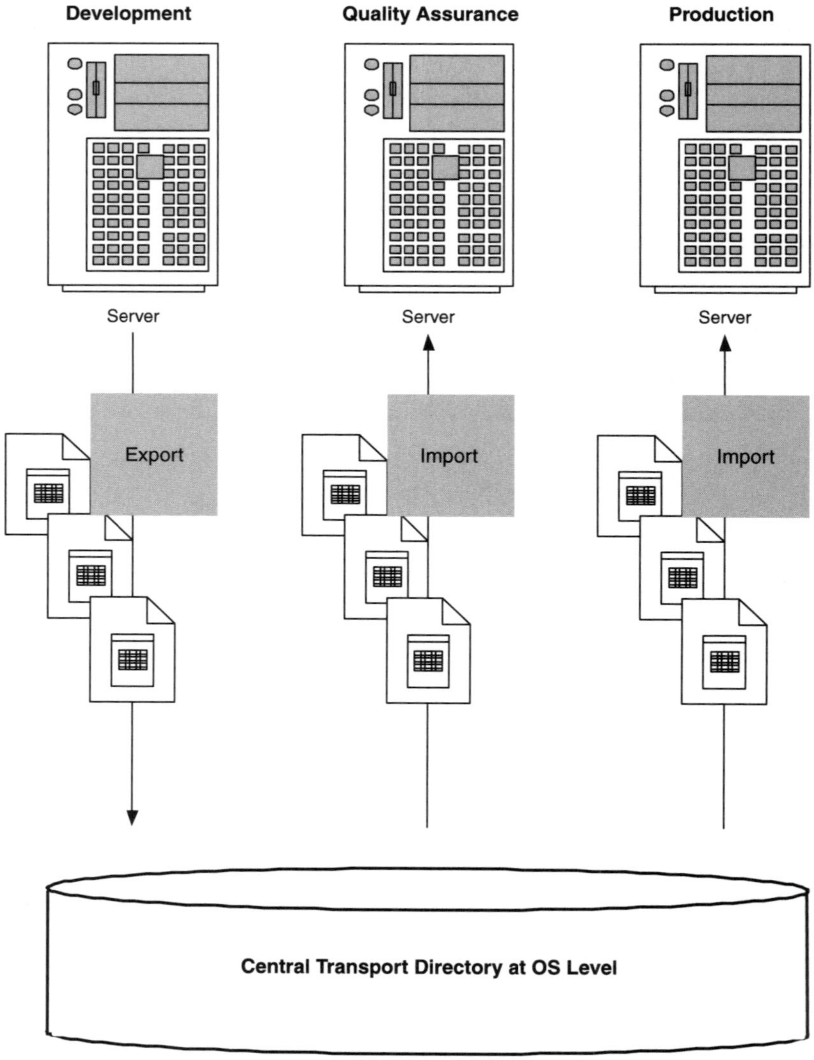

Figure 2.7 System Landscape with Transport Directory

Change Management and the necessary transport services, provided by SAP architecture, support the need for a company to execute, test, and use changes and developments on different levels. The recording and transport of object changes and settings is controlled by the *Change and Transport System* (CTS). Therefore, changes are transferred from one system to another system using transport and the export and import phases. The *Transport Management System* (TMS) is used for importing into the target system. It manages all import queues. Technically, a central transport directory is used for individual exports from and imports to the corresponding systems. All systems in the landscape have access to this directory, which contains the data and structural information of the changes.

Transport Requests

In the SAP system, changes to the repository or customizing are usually recorded in transport requests. This provides the following advantages, in the context of SAP software logistics:

- Change history at object level
- Centralization of project-specific changes to different objects
- Distribution of changes/settings/modifications beyond system boundaries

Transport Layers

The distribution of transport requests takes place along defined transport layers. All development projects carried out in an SAP system and transported via the same route to the target system (or systems) are brought together in a transport layer.

Transport layers are created before the start of the first development in the transport route editor in the TMS. This transport layer is assigned to the development system as a standard transport layer. The allocation of development objects to the relevant transport layer is done using the previously mentioned packages. Objects supplied by SAP belong to the SAP transport layer. Additional transport layers are then usually needed only if new development systems are integrated into the system group.

Transport Routes

We can differentiate between two types of transport routes:

- **Consolidation routes**
  To make changes transportable, you need a consolidation route for each relevant transport layer. The starting point of this consolidation route is the development system and the destination is the quality assurance system (in a two-system landscape, the production system). Changed objects, for which a consolidation route has been set up in the transport layer, are recorded in transportable change requests.

Once the request has been released from transport administration, the changed object can be imported into the consolidation system.

If objects are changed and no consolidation route has been defined for their transport layer in the current SAP system, these changes are automatically recorded in local change requests (or in customizing requests without transport destination). You cannot forward them to other SAP systems.

There can be one consolidation route only per SAP system and transport layer.

- **Delivery routes**

  Once developments have been imported into the quality assurance system, they must be adopted in the production system or in several SAP systems (for example, additional training systems), for which delivery routes must be defined. These delivery routes have a source system and a target system.

  By setting up a delivery route, you ensure that all change requests imported into the source system of the delivery route are automatically earmarked for import into the target system of the route.

  Depending on the existing system landscape, you can set up several delivery routes with the same source system and different target systems (parallel forwarding), or attached one after the other (multi-step forwarding).

Transport control in the CTS ensures that all requests from the development system for all other SAP systems are earmarked for import in the same sequence in which they were exported. The same repository object or the same customizing setting can be contained in different requests at different development stages and consequently, you can avoid a new version being overwritten by an old one.

Transport Request Types

Because changes to different objects are handled differently, they are also recorded in separate transport request types. As a result, there are workbench requests that are mainly used for recording changes to repository objects in the ABAP Workbench and to client-independent customizing. There are also customizing requests that record the client-dependent customizing settings from just one client (i.e., the source client of the request). Additional request types such as copies or relocations are used to transport complete objects to a specific system. With copies, the original system of the objects remains the same; with relocations, the target system becomes the new source system.

Separate tasks can be assigned to a transport request for different project employees. Each employee can release his or her assigned task after completion of the development work (customizing work). Once all tasks have been released, the transport request can be released by the request holder. If, for example, a repository object is processed by a developer and recorded in a change request, it is reserved exclusively for this change request for processing. This object can be changed only by developers who are also participating with a task in this change request. Until the change request has been released, the development or maintenance of development objects is locked for all other developers not working on it. These developers can view the objects in question only.

To simplify transport administration, the transport system can also be workflow- or project-driven. If the transport system is workflow-driven, a workflow, which controls the work process, is automatically started on release. The agents of the individual steps are automatically determined and a work interface is provided to allow them to carry out their tasks directly.

If the transport system is project-driven, developments and customizing activities are planned in project structures of IMG project management. Changes that are independent of one another can be separated into different projects and imported into the next system independently.

Transport Organizer

The *Transport Organizer* offers functions for the creation, documentation, and release of change requests during the customizing and development process and for reorganizing the development landscape. The Transport Organizer tools are primarily intended for the development team and those in charge of a development or implementation project.

Transport Management System

Whereas the Transport Organizer is helpful for the development team in the software development process until the release of a change request, the *Transport Management System* (TMS) supports the administration when importing the request into the target system. The TMS is started using Transaction STMS.

The TMS enables you to organize, execute, and monitor transports between different SAP systems. Because all necessary information and functions are reproduced in the SAP system, in most cases, no additional user action is required at the operating-system level.

The TMS offers the following functions:

- Configuration of transport routes with a graphical editor
- Display of import queues in all SAP systems in the transport domain
- Import of all requests in an import queue
- Import of all requests for a project
- Import of individual requests
- TMS quality assurance
- Transport workflow
- Transport between SAP systems that don't share a transport directory

2.4 SAP NetWeaver

Integrated business processes constitute part of SAP core competencies. In heterogeneous system environments, however, and in situations where many different solutions are replaced by a single integrated solution, there is a need for technology that supports enterprises with the integration and development of their software products. In a heterogeneous IT environment, you can now define integrated, self-contained business processes outside department and enterprise boundaries. You can also use an existing infrastructure that protects current investments and adds value to applications already in place. The key here is *Enterprise Services Architecture* (ESA), an SAP concept for designing business applications, which is based on Web service standards. SAP offers an open integration and application platform for the implementation of this concept: SAP NetWeaver.

Comprehensive Integration Approach

SAP NetWeaver uses the approach of integrating users, information, and business processes across technologies and organizations. It provides different technologies to support this integration. SAP NetWeaver is the successor to mySAP Technology and it expands on the functions of the latter, especially when it comes to *integration*. With this type of solution, all possible influencing factors associated with the areas of people, information, or technological processes such as infrastructure or heterogeneous components, must be considered.

The key words associated with SAP NetWeaver are People Integration, Information Integration, Process Integration, Application Platform, and Solution Lifecycle Management.

- **People Integration**
  The integration of employees in the enterprise process flows is made possible via different technical components:
  - *SAP Enterprise Portal* for uniform, personalized and role-based access to heterogeneous IT environments used for linking people and information
  - *Collaboration* for the advancement of communication and collaboration between different teams in real time. It has functions such as collaboration room, team messages, team calendar, task assignment, and so on.
  - *SAP Mobile Infrastructure*, which makes it possible to link up with the enterprise system via voice, mobile, or radio technology
- **Information Integration**
  The following areas contribute to the integrated processing of information:
  - *Business Intelligence* for the integration, analysis, and distribution of business-critical information to allow for informed decision-making
  - *Knowledge Management* for access to unstructured data such as text files, presentations, or audio files
  - *SAP Master Data Management* for data integration in heterogeneous landscapes—master data can be consolidated and aligned systemwide
- **Process Integration**
  Business processes can be unified and given an integrated design thanks to:
  - *SAP Exchange Infrastructure* for communication between application components of different origin; software components, interfaces, mappings, and content-based routing rules are defined
  - *Business Process Management* for the design and operation of business processes in a dynamic IT environment
- **Application Platform (i.e., SAP Web Application Server)**
  Important features of the application platform, which we addressed earlier in this chapter, are:
  - *ABAP Personality* for supporting ABAP
  - *Java Personality* for supporting J2EE
  - *Business Services and Features* for supporting business applications and procedures

- *Connectivity* for supporting connection standards and Web services
- *User Interface* for linking the presentation layer with the application
- *Database and operating-system abstraction* to ensure the independence of existing databases and operating systems

- **Solution Lifecycle Management**
  Solution Lifecycle Management supports the individual phases of the software lifecycle such as design, development, implementation, testing, or operation with the following core functions:
  - Customizing and testing
  - Data archiving
  - Hardware sizing
  - High availability
  - Installation
  - IT landscape
  - Performance
  - Software change management
  - System management
  - Technical infrastructure
  - Upgrade technology

SAP NetWeaver is the basis for different SAP solutions today. In future, all SAP solutions should be developed based on the concept of SAP NetWeaver or ESA.

The individual SAP NetWeaver components can also be integrated into the existing IT landscape by themselves. For example, SAP XI can be used as a solution for application integration or the SAP Business Information Warehouse (SAP BW; as the technical base of mySAP Business Intelligence) can be used for the integration and analysis of business-critical information. The SAP XI, for example, is a platform for the interaction of different application systems and therefore ensures the consistency of transactions.

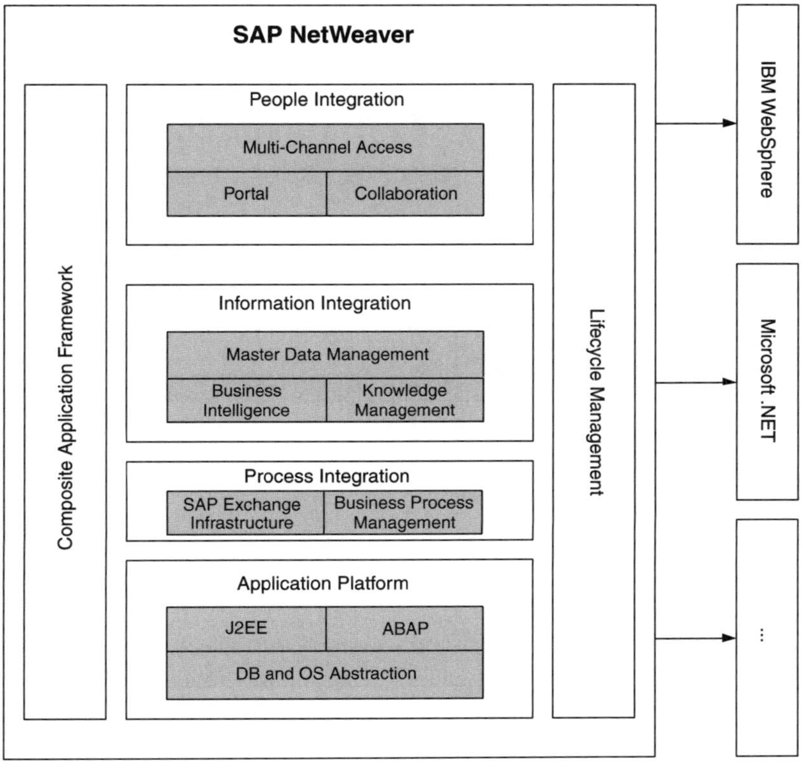

Figure 2.8 SAP NetWeaver Architecture

Predefined Integration

As an integration and application platform, SAP NetWeaver provides predefined integration and business content in one solution. This preconfigured content helps to accelerate integration and in this way, SAP NetWeaver helps to reduce costs. Business processes are becoming increasingly complex and are planned beyond system and technology boundaries. Therefore, SAP is currently providing a technology platform that offers the services necessary to meet these new requirements. Business process flows can be designed flexibly because open technologies, such as Web services, are used.

In the Internet age of cross-solution and cross-enterprise business, closed solutions are being replaced by an open IT architecture in which end-to-end business processes are represented by different Web services running on several distributed component systems. Each of the component systems is specialized in particular services. The use of different components helps to provide optimal support for enterprise business, but it results in complex IT system landscapes.

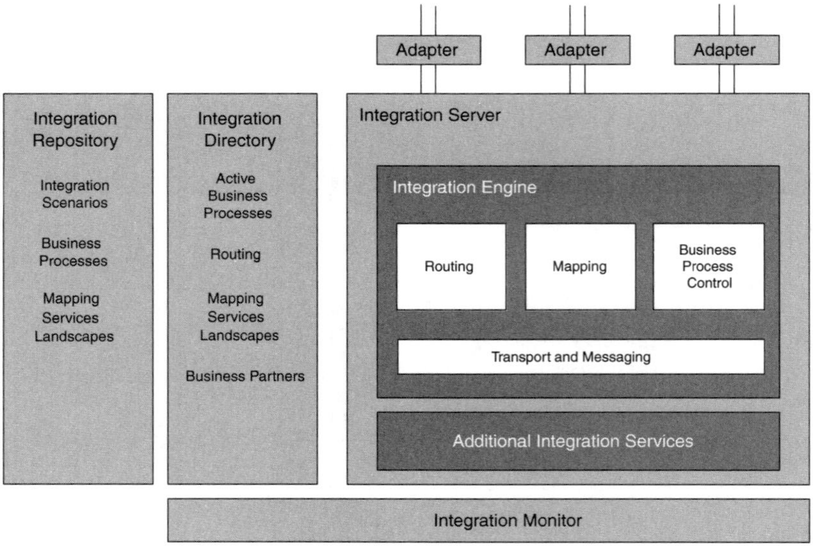

Figure 2.9 SAP Exchange Infrastructure

Adaptability

It is essential that the IT architecture ensures the reliable, cost-effective operation of distributed landscapes, while simultaneously offering the enterprise the option to adapt the IT landscape to reflect the changing business requirements. The architecture must be open and flexible to meet these requirements.

SAP NetWeaver offers possibilities ranging from simple, compact IT systems installed on one server to highly available, scalable, and secure configurations for critical applications.

The optimal technical infrastructure for a given business requirement is determined by factors such as landscape type (development, quality assurance, production), main business processes, transaction volumes, security, and availability.

Key Attributes of SAP NetWeaver

To ensure that key figures such as availability, performance, and *total cost of ownership* (TCO) represent the highest standards, SAP NetWeaver has the following key attributes:

- Multi-component architecture
  - Component-specific infrastructure
  - Component-specific upgrade, tuning, and availability strategies

- mySAP components are platform-independent
  - Component-specific performance improvement and scalability
  - Protection of existing investments in hardware, software, and IT know-how
- Platform topology specification

  Can range from maximum consolidation (single server, one database) to maximum distribution (multiple servers, multiple databases on different platforms).
- The ability to run several clients on one physical system
  This is particularly important for *Application Service Providers* (ASPs) that want to host independent customers on a single system.
- Migration tools to support platform changes
- Complete system management tools

A key factor for reducing overall operating costs over the entire lifecycle of an e-business solution is the ability to continuously provide an optimal IT infrastructure at each stage of the cycle and to customize the configuration to meet changing business requirements. Ultimately, SAP NetWeaver provides tools for the design, implementation, operation, and maintenance of IT landscapes. Predefined sample landscapes describe possible IT landscape configurations. Enterprises can use them as templates for designing their own IT landscape and then configure this IT landscape to best reflect their own specific business needs.

2.5 SAP System Landscapes

Several questions arise when planning system landscapes:

- What services do I need to execute business processes? What application components can I use to support these services?
- What type of data will be shared between these components?
- What additional technical components will I need?

You must answer these and many other questions during the first phase of an implementation project in order to define the system landscape. Depending on the enterprise- and business-specific requirements, these landscapes can differ significantly in structure.

In the next section, we present different example landscapes to illustrate the possible alternatives and their effect on availability, performance, scalability, and TCO.

2.5.1 Example Configuration: Internet Sales and Procurement

The infrastructure of SAP Internet Sales is based on an SAP CRM system and the SAP J2EE Engine 6.20. Almost all business processes are processed on the CRM system and some business applications also run in Java applications. mySAP CRM runs on the basis of the SAP Web Application Server (Web AS).

SAP Internet Pricing and Configurator (IPC) is used to configure products, process configurations, and determine prices. Special services for the area of e-business, such as search functions, are provided by the *TREX program* (Text Retrieval & Information Extraction). With TREX, simple text and HTML documents can be indexed and searched.

An *OLTP system* (Online Transaction Processing System), such as SAP R/3, is used as a back-end system for materials and finance applications. The SAP BW can be used to analyze business and draw up reports. It is an optional component, however, as is the *SAP Advanced Planner and Optimizer* (SAP APO), which is used for queries regarding availability in the e-selling scenario, in Supply Chain Management, Demand Planning, and other areas.

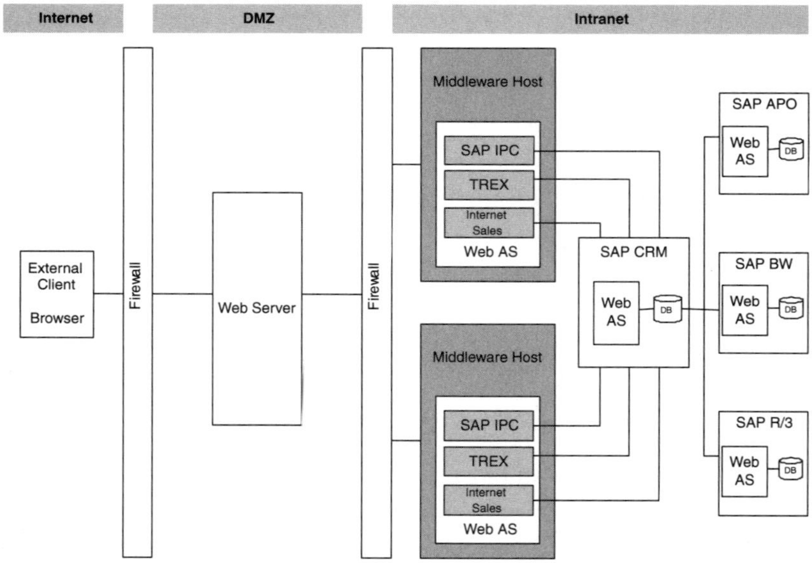

Figure 2.10 Internet Sales

Defining Requirements

The design of the technical system infrastructure has a direct influence on the cost-effectiveness of the implementation. For this reason, the demands made on the system must be clearly defined. You must consider different factors, the most important of which is what purpose will the system serve. This means that you must know if the system on which the critical business processes are to be run is a development system, a test system, or an actual production system. You should already have determined how many end users will work with the system. If you cannot calculate this figure, you must find some appropriate means in which to do so. Availability requirements must be defined, so that the necessary provisions can be made. You should note, however, that ensuring high availability is very costly. System security is another subject that you must consider as it too has a large influence on the infrastructure. The separation of different software components on a network and the use of firewalls does, of course, make the landscape more complex, something that also has an effect on landscape administration. When planning an IT landscape, a high degree of flexibility should also be a priority. Planning should be done in such a way that the landscape can be extended at any time and adjusted to fit new requirements.

The *Customer Relationship Management* (CRM) and *Enterprise Resource Planning* (ERP) *systems* are installed separately to ensure optimal performance and the appropriate choice of platform. The separation of Web services from the other components improves performance and scalability. A separate Web application server provides the runtime environment for these Web services.

A firewall separates the internal components from the external Web server, which can be accessed via the Internet using HTTP. Consequently, the application systems are protected from possible external access.

Availability

Each of the physical server platforms can be scaled independently. Companies can develop a separate high-availability solution for each software component, database, or host. It is important that all of the hardware and software is included in a high-availability concept. For each component, there is a special technology to provide for high availability. A redundant construction of network topology may be necessary for the network, while cluster technology can be used for the server and the operating system. Databases can be given high availability with the help of replication, for example, while the disk mirroring and SAN technology may play a role in the area of memory management. If there is a need for load balancing, you can do so using several application servers for middleware and the individual SAP component systems as well. In this way, the functions of the dispatcher or the SAP Web Dispatcher are used to distribute the load.

The overall e-business solution runs on separate servers and possibly on different operating system and database platforms. SAP XI, which forms part of the SAP NetWeaver, provides the system connections.

This clear differentiation between application and technical platforms ensures that companies can change or expand the platform without affecting the overall functional integration.

This setting can be used for productive systems with up to a few thousand intranet and Internet users.

2.5.2 Example Configuration: mySAP CRM Interaction Center

The interaction center is a key area for executing business procedures with customer relationships and offers a complex platform for the interactive processing of these business processes. In the interaction center, agents create the links between the business partner and the business processes. The customer information necessary for this is provided there. The following scenarios, among others, can be reproduced in the interaction center:

- **Inbound telesales**
  for customers who want to place an order; they can contact the interaction center
- **Outbound telesales**
  for the support of sales campaigns
- **Information help desk**
  for processing customer queries
- **Service**
  for processing service queries and requests
- **Complaint handling**
  for processing complaints

The mySAP CRM Interaction Center is based on the CRM server, which contains the *Interaction Center Framework* (ICF) and the components SAPphone and SAPconnect. With *SAPphone*, you can integrate telephone functions into the SAP application and with *SAPconnect*, email functions (with the help of a mail server). Additional external products are also required to integrate telephony functions, such as the telephony gateway, the telephony server, and the interface to the telephone system for *computer telephony integration* (CTI).

To create, check, and distribute messages and announcements, which a supervisor can delegate to individual agents, you will need the *Broadcast Messaging Server*. The messages will then appear at the appropriate agents' work centers. You can define the priority, language, and expiry date of each message. Products can be configured, configurations processed, and prices determined with the help of the SAP IPC. The TREX program supports flexible document searches and the structuring of accumulations of documents using automatic document classification. With TREX, simple text and HTML documents, providing necessary customer information, can be indexed and searched. As in the first example (Internet Sales), an OLTP system (such as SAP R/3) can be used for materials, management, and financial applications and to evaluate key figures from the different scenarios of SAP BW. SAP APO is necessary to monitor the availability of products.

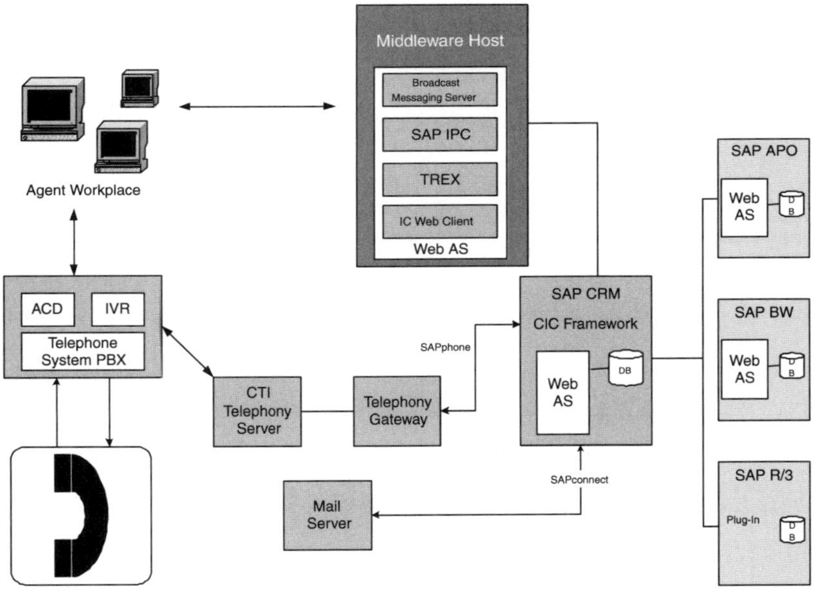

Figure 2.11 mySAP CRM Interaction Center

2.5.3 Example Configurations for System Landscapes and Client Strategies for Change Management

Multi-System Landscape

A system landscape always comprises all application systems involved and their corresponding SAP clients. Software logistics are used to coordinate and distribute changes made to SAP software. When planning this landscape, you must consider different requirements that include:

- The security of productive data
- Quality assurance
- Optimal system performance
- Development standards
- Upgrade strategy

Additionally, there are factors such as hardware and maintenance costs and administrative effort.

When putting together a system landscape, SAP recommends that customers plan for a three-system landscape, with separate systems for the development, quality assurance, and productive environments. Companies with a large international system implementation may need more systems for the different functions. There may also be, for example, training, load-testing, or sandbox systems. The three-system landscape applies to each component system within the system group, which means that a three-system landscape should be built for an SAP R/3 or R/3 Enterprise and also for each additional component system such as for each SAP BW or each CRM system.

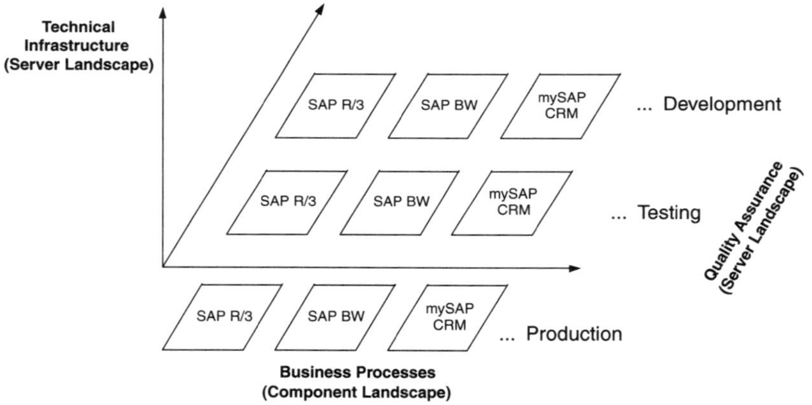

Figure 2.12 SAP System Landscape

Figure 2.13 shows a common landscape for quality assurance. The landscape consists of a sandbox system, a development and customizing system, a quality assurance system, a copy of the production system, and a production system. The sandbox system is used to test simple new functions without affecting development processes or planned test procedures. The development and customizing system is used for the actual development work or customizing settings, so that they are executed centrally according to their specification. These settings are transported to the adjacent quality assurance system where technical and functional tests are carried out on the new developments or settings. A copy of the production system is inserted to allow for integration tests in a production-like environment and under production conditions (interface tests, far-reaching changes, and so on). It is provided with all new developments to ensure that it is at the same development stage as the production system itself. Far-reaching tests can be devised that can, for example, also be used as load tests if you know that a high load will be generated, so you can see how the system reacts to certain load peaks. If all tests are successful and the settings or new developments generate the required functions, you can then import the changes into the production system where they will be available for the actual business processes.

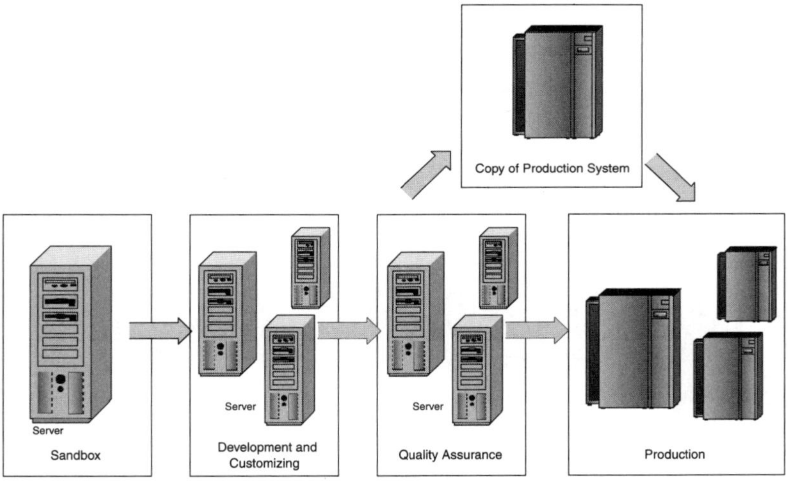

Figure 2.13 Quality Assurance System Landscape

You can differentiate between changes such as new developments or settings for new sub-processes and changes arising via end-user support. In the course of production support, small adjustments are frequently made to customize settings, or program errors are removed. This is necessary to ensure unrestricted production operation. These changes must be made available to the end users and at relatively short notice for their daily work. New developments or new sub-processes, however, are often scheduled for the long term, and are the result of temporal planning as part of the development and test process. They are transferred to the production system only at a specified time after the successful completion of development and test work. This scenario can occur with a graded multi-system landscape so that the different change processes can be executed independently of each other. A development thread made up of a development and a quality assurance system is used for new developments that provide the thread for production support: a preproduction system, final quality assurance, and a production system. This is referred to as a two-phase system landscape.

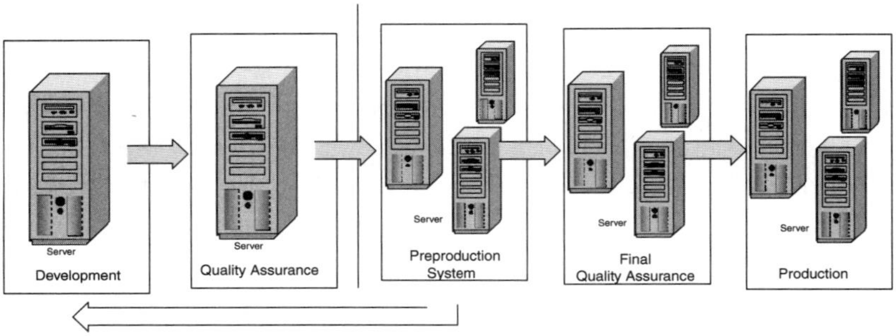

Figure 2.14 Two-Phase System Landscape

Client Concept

The functions related to the Change Management process can also be distributed on separate levels with the help of a suitable client concept. Clients can take on different functions, such as:

- Sandbox
- Blueprint demo
- Customizing master
- Quality assurance master
- Quality assurance test
- End-user training

SAP systems are client-enabled, therefore, multiple clients can be defined. This means that business units can be defined as self-contained, logical subsystems with their own master and transaction data. As you can see in the previously mentioned client functions, clients can also be used for technical and organizational purposes. Consequently, a client concept can be designed to determine how different clients are distributed to the development, quality assurance, and production systems. This makes it possible to separate the different sub-processes in an implementation technically and organizationally, by uncoupling development clients and customizing clients, or defining several clients on the quality assurance system for different locations or applications. On the production system, however, you should apply only those clients that are used productively.

Multiple production clients require increased administration. Therefore, try to implement the least number of production clients possible.

2.6 Lifecycle Management

Lifecycle

Distributed software solutions require more systems than do closed solutions. As IT landscapes grow, consideration of the TCO becomes an increasingly important factor. To lower the TCO, the IT landscape should be serviced, maintained, and extended throughout its entire lifecycle. Going live is not the key objective. A well balanced, well defined design prior to implementation and the constant improvement of the solution after implementation are equally important. The primary goal is for the solution to maintain a high value during its entire lifecycle.

The lifecycle of an IT landscape can be broken down into different phases:

1. Design
2. Installation
3. Implementation
4. Operation
5. Change management

While the goal of a software environment is to support the business processes of an enterprise, it undergoes all of these phases. As the system landscape grows, the phases become exponentially more complex.

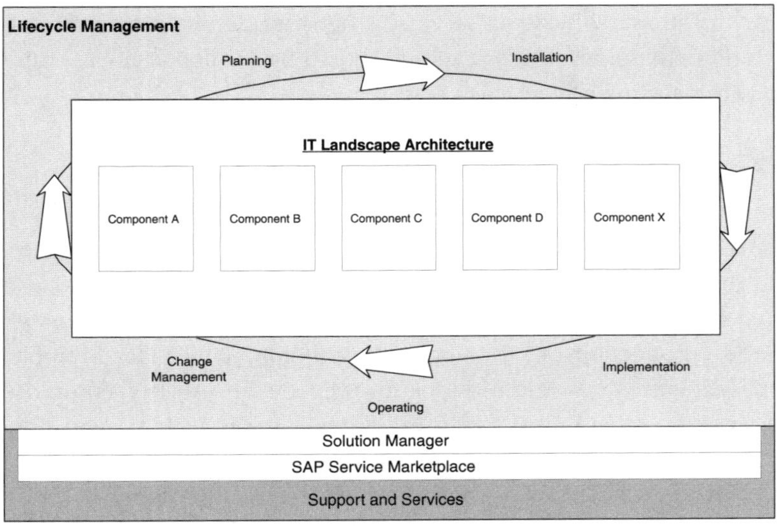

Figure 2.15 Lifecycle Management

2.6.1 Design

Formulating Requirements

During the design phase, the requirements that will shape the solution are discussed. These requirements are primarily determined by the business processes to be supported by the solution. To optimally translate the requirements, the appropriate component systems or non-SAP applications must be selected, the communication routes set down, and the structure of the system landscape planned. You must consider to what extent any existing system landscape can be extended. The platforms to be used are also selected. Issues such as the appropriate security strategy or high-availability requirements must also be considered.

Sizing

Once you have identified the necessary components to be defined for the system landscape, sizing must be carried out for the system. In sizing, you will determine how the individual systems should be designed so that the requirements for supporting business processes can be fulfilled in all situations. Realistic sizing must factor in hotspots and load peaks. This includes daily load distribution of, for example, end-of-day processing, monthly and yearly close, and seasonally conditioned load. During the sizing phase, you must estimate hardware requirements such as network bandwidth, main memory layout, processor performance, and so on. You should keep in mind various factors such as the number of users needed to work with the different applications, or the volume of data that will be created by this work or that must be distributed outside the realm of system boundaries. The estimated number of users should be determined by how much you think they will work with the system. Estimations made during this phase, which will serve as a basis for determining the hardware and network resources required, should be verified again at a later time with performance and load tests.

2.6.2 Installation

New Systems and Upgrades

After the design phase, you must install the defined component systems. Both new installations and system upgrades must be taken into account. It is also important that there is as little as possible user access and also limited system downtime (for upgrades). The launch of the SAP Web AS saw the introduction of new upgrade technology which, for example, greatly minimizes downtime during an upgrade to SAP R/3 Enterprise (latest version of SAP R/3) because different phases such as repository import or activation can be carried out while the system is online. Furthermore, the release strategy of SAP R/3 Enterprise is designed in such a way that the technological basis of the system—the SAP Web Application

Server—can be updated separately from the application functions (application core and enterprise extensions), thereby reducing the complexity of an upgrade.

In heterogeneous landscapes with different applications, it is critical that these applications can be integrated without too much effort. For this reason, SAP NetWeaver offers an *Application Programming Interface* (API) that can be used by other installation routines.

2.6.3 Implementation

The installation of individual component systems alone does not yet deliver the complete application functions needed to establish the business processes of an enterprise. To do this, the individual steps and functions must be adapted to the circumstances of the enterprise. With heterogeneous landscapes and cross-system business processes, you must map the process flow in software and in the system, and coordinate the individual sub-steps with each other precisely. During this step, external applications must be connected and the necessary data flows must be implemented using interfaces. It is often necessary to formulate extra developments to achieve the desired functionality.

Defining Business Processes in Detail

The success of this implementation phase depends to a large extent on how well the business processes are defined and documented. It is important to clarify how different procedures should run and what areas need to be considered during them. The more precisely these processes can be defined and the enterprise-specific conditions described, the more accurately the business process requirements can be reproduced in software components and program flows. New components and integration into existing systems must, of course, also be considered.

The implementation phase will be more complex if business processes that surpass system and enterprise boundaries are designed. With these scenarios, generally applicable requirements and component- or enterprise-specific prerequisites must all be considered. To a large extent, these settings depend on each other; they also influence the success of the software execution of business processes in detail. Settings for each component must be made depending on other components and in the event of adjustments; you must always remember that changes can affect other application areas and therefore, the business processes themselves.

Implementation Tools

Different tools are provided for the individual SAP components to support settings made during the implementation phase—from technical settings in the system to recommendations and templates for carrying out different processes. Among other things, all configuration settings are automatically connected to the previously mentioned Transport Management for software distribution. In addition, with the SAP Solution Manager, SAP provides a central platform for efficient solution management that supports individual processes from the implementation phase through system operation. The concept of SAP Solution Management will be described in greater detail at a later stage.

Testing Settings

Settings that go beyond the system landscape must be tested very carefully to ensure the precise functioning of the processes and the integrity of individual landscape components. This should be done after every partial implementation. It is important that the sub-processes of the individual application components are correctly planned, that interfaces to other systems—whether SAP or non-SAP systems—can ensure the desired data exchange, and that the process sequence as a whole yields the desired results. To ensure that these tests run smoothly, well defined test scenarios, which can always be restarted and easily adjusted to new constraints, must always be in place.

2.6.4 Operation

After converting the relevant requirements into an integrated, cross-system software solution during the implementation phase, new requirements are inevitably made on the IT infrastructure. This type of infrastructure should offer the following characteristics:

- **High Performance**
  A good overall system performance is a prerequisite for user satisfaction and for the effectiveness of the entire system solution.
- **High Availability**
  The systems (SAP and non-SAP) form the business framework of an enterprise. Each system failure inevitably leads to an interruption of business.
- **Low costs**
  The total cost of operation (TCO) of a system must be taken into account to keep the running costs of an application as low as possible.

The goal of running this type of infrastructure or its component systems is to support business processes; as such, it is essentially a service provided by the IT department of an enterprise for the other areas of business. It involves relevant processes and tasks, required on a daily basis, to ensure that the characteristics listed above are maintained. The individual levels of the system should be considered separately. Operation can be divided up between the administration and monitoring of SAP components and the underlying operating systems and databases, the middleware used for communication and data exchange, and the areas of network and non-SAP applications.

Service Level Agreement

The service to be provided by the IT department for other departments is usually described in *Service Level Agreements* (SLAs). An SLA should have a clear definition of the services to be provided and the criteria to gauge the quality of services. In addition, the method and type of reporting on service performance and necessary escalation levels—in the event of non-fulfillment of agreements—should also be defined.

Operating Concept

A generally applicable administration concept should be defined to support and align the individual tasks in systems operation. Such a concept would cover the organization of the tasks that form part of systems operation for an SAP solution and contain all necessary information for the successful administration and maintenance of the entire system infrastructure. It is necessary for you to differentiate between routine tasks carried out regularly to identify possible problems early and remedy them; reactive tasks that crop up in the event of failures; and proactive tasks that monitor and analyze certain key figures in an effort to avoid imminent resource bottlenecks, or, using support packages in order to avoid known problems in advance.

Necessary tasks for the execution of systems operation for an SAP solution may include the following:

- Monitoring the hardware resources of the entire infrastructure
- Monitoring system resources to ensure performance
- Checking manufacturer's notes on known problems with hardware and operating systems
- Maintenance and monitoring of the database and database backup
- Checking the SAP operating parameters such as work processes, buffers, security settings, and so on
- Checking SAP Notes
- Implementing and monitoring output management (printing, fax, email, and so on)

2.6.5 Change Management

Due to the fast moving, flexible market requirements, adjustments to the systems, the infrastructure, and the application-specific process flows are unavoidable. Every change is not without its risks, however, which can have a deleterious effect on the operation of the software solutions. Badly prepared changes are the primary cause of operation problems and can even lead to system breakdowns. It is therefore vital that each change to be executed is carefully planned. Matters such as the expected effects of the change, necessary tests, or emergency strategies should be included in these plans. Predefined Change Management can help you to minimize the risk of inconsistencies that can arise due to changes in an operative system.

Defining Processes

To reduce the potential for inconsistency, you should define the following processes:

- **Approval Processes for Planned Changes**
  Approval processes should, among other things, help to centralize Change Management so that all departments can check the influence of a change on their processes.
- **Risk Appraisal and Emergency Strategy**
  Possible risks must be defined from the outset and appropriate measures must be implemented in the event that these risks become real problems.
- **Informative Test Cases**
  Changes should not be executed directly on a production system; otherwise, you run the risk of permanently damaging productive operation. Adjustments must therefore first be transferred to a test system and tested thoroughly.
- **Documenting Changes**
  In order for changes to be carried out at any time and by anyone, you must log each correct setting.

SAP offers an integrated Change Management concept for SAP solutions containing different specifications of the software delivery: upgrade, support packages, and SAP corrections.

Support for Upgrades

Completely new release versions are delivered in the form of upgrades, featuring new or functionally enhanced versions of SAP standard programs or other repository objects. With SAP Web AS, SAP provides new system-switch technology that minimizes the system downtime required during an upgrade. In addition to the productive system, a temporary instance of SAP Web AS is installed that contains the new repository object. This means that most upgrade phases can be implemented while the productive system is online for the execution of business processes.

Support Packages

Errors in different software components are corrected with *support packages*. Support packages contain corrected SAP objects that replace erroneous objects. These packages are made available by SAP at certain intervals and can be implemented into the SAP system online, although this is not always advisable.

SAP Corrections

SAP corrections contain corrections for errors in individual objects, for example, ABAP programs that have been prepared by SAP because of problems in some application processes. These corrections can be implemented in certain actual cases.

With all methods of the SAP Change Management concept, modifications made by customers to SAP objects will be taken into account, because modifications come under the system change control and can therefore be harmonized. The Change Management process is supported in SAP systems by the Change and Transport System (CTS), as described in an earlier part of this chapter. The services offered by the CTS are extended with the SAP Web AS for the area of Java.

2.7 Solution Management

Due to the fact that the phases in the lifecycle of an IT infrastructure become more laborious to execute as openness and complexity increase, there is a need for functions and tools that will support these processes. System landscapes become increasingly more complex as the dependencies of different applications grow in importance, as a result of the pronounced dispersal of business processes beyond system boundaries. Increased integration due to technical and business-critical demands must also be taken into account, as well as the increased significance of the Change Management processes or support. Consequently, in addition to the tools provided by SAP NetWeaver, SAP also offers a solution management platform that supports the administration of complete IT landscapes.

SAP Solution Manager

The *SAP Solution Manager* provides tools, services, methods, technical, and application-related documentation and templates that can be used for implementation, for support and for the operation of complete IT solution landscapes. It should be used as the central infrastructure for solution management and provide the link between technical key values and the critical business processes.

SAP uses the following approaches in its Solution Management strategy:

- **Standardization**
  Consistency and clarity can be ensured by standardizing services, methods, and technologies. This is important to keep the total operating costs to a minimum.
- **Solution orientation**
  Since IT solutions (e-business solutions) are no longer made up of one system or one application, but of multiple applications of differing technologies, SAP uses a cross-system, solution-oriented approach to manage the entire infrastructure. The system solution is therefore considered to be a collection of integrated systems so that the dependencies of the individual systems and applications can be considered automatically.
- **Process Orientation**
  To achieve complete control over the system solution, you must look at the main business processes that are integral to the complete value chain of an enterprise. Therefore, the focus is on the most important business processes and their individual technical steps. Among other things, monitoring these processes is organized more flexibly and the correlation of systems and applications to problems is more easily identified.
- **Openness**
  To fully map the SAP administration solutions to the complete enterprise infrastructure, SAP targets its Solution Manager openly at all SAP and non-SAP applications. This ensures a complete overview of the software landscape to be tended to.
- **SAP integration**
  With the help of the SAP Solution Manager, SAP follows the approach of setting up a continuous support infrastructure, by integrating itself into the customer's support process. Thanks to a constant connection of the customer system to SAP, services can be updated and executed, or customer support messages can be forwarded to SAP for processing.

With the help of the SAP Solution Manager, you should be able to have full control of the entire IT infrastructure to support the phases of implementation, operation, and support over the entire lifecycle of a software solution. This necessary and extensive standardized help to implement complex administration strategies will enable the enterprise to reduce the TCO, or, at least, to keep it low.

SAP subdivides its concept of Solution Management into different main areas, each with a different bias (see also Figure 2.16):

- **Global Strategy and Service Level Management**
  This covers the complete strategic management of an organization. It provides know-how and services to support the strategic specification of operating processes, monitoring and reporting on SLAs. It is intended for decision-makers.
- **Business Process Management**
  This guarantees the smooth and optimal flow of daily business processes and offers help with business process monitoring, interface management, or job management. It is primarily intended for those responsible for business processes and application support.
- **System Management**
  System Management provides a central administration environment for the technical management of the IT infrastructure. Here, the technical tasks of system maintenance can be processed, such as performance management, monitoring, and so on. It is intended for technical support personnel and system administrators.
- **Software Change Management**
  The purpose of Software Change Management is to support the implementation of software changes such as release management or test management. It is used to standardize and automate software distribution and maintenance and test cases for a complex, distributed software landscape. This area is for project and development teams and application support.
- **Support Desk Management**
  The Support Desk provides a support environment. By integrating end users, application support, partners, and SAP support, it enables you to define an efficient, integrated problem-solving process.

The SAP Solution Manager is a central platform that provides all the necessary tools for implementing an SAP software solution, monitoring it, and ensuring system operation and support. It is completely solution-oriented, which means that it not only allows for the support of individual systems, but for the entire IT landscape. It covers the entire lifecycle of a system solution (see Figure 2.17).

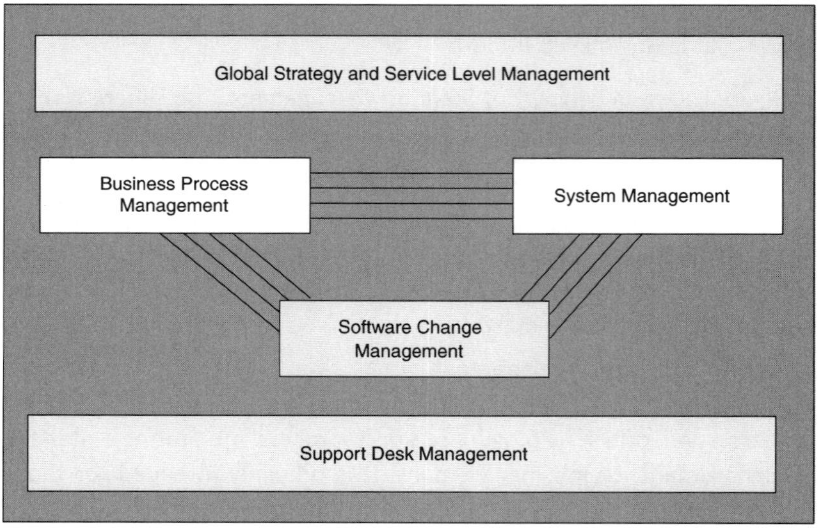

Figure 2.16 The Areas in SAP Solution Management

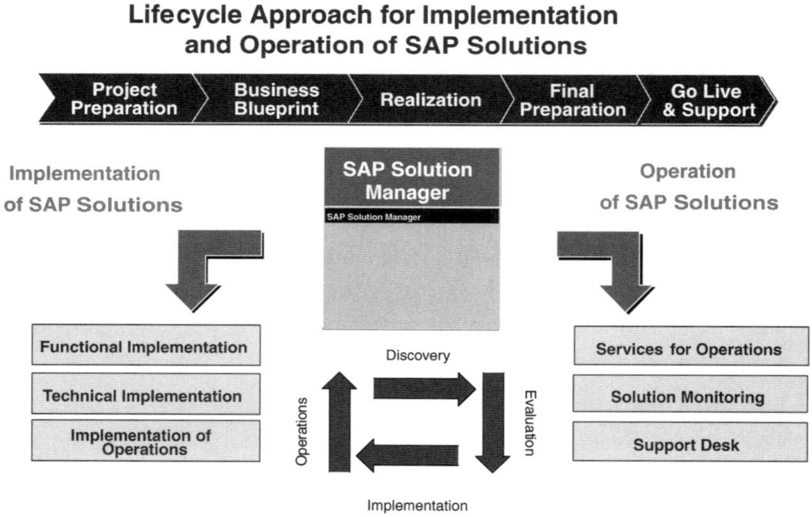

Figure 2.17 SAP Solution Manager Throughout the Lifecycle

SAP Solution Manager for Implementation

Basically, the SAP Solution Manager is divided into the SAP Solution Manager for Implementation and the SAP Solution Manager for Operation. The *SAP Solution Manager for Implementation* is an extension of the *ASAP method* (Accelerated SAP) and it offers functional and technical roadmaps for the support of implementation activities from the blueprint phase through system operation. With the help of what are known as Best Practices documents—documentation on specific application scenarios or configuration guidelines—content is provided that may be useful for the planning and implementation of software solutions and business processes. Customizing Distribution and the Test Workbench help you to set up application configurations and test cases in a process-oriented way.

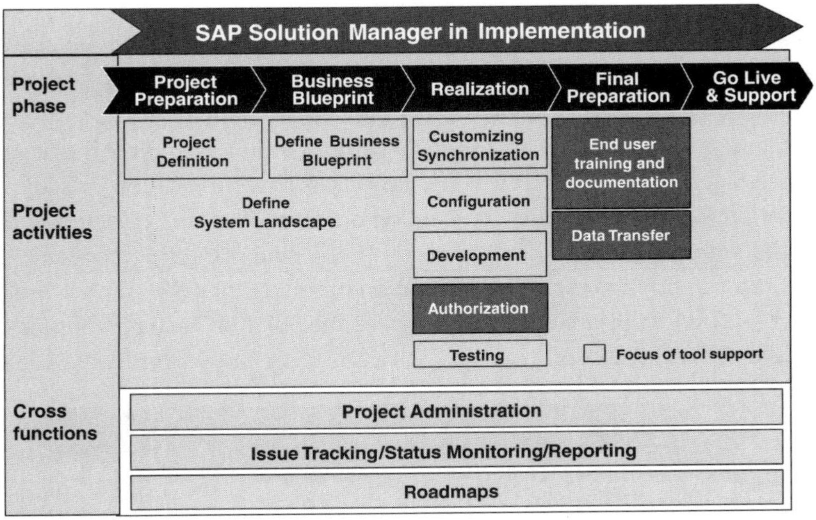

Figure 2.18 SAP Solution Manager for Implementation

SAP Solution Manager for Operation

The *SAP Solution Manager for Operation* offers functions for executing the complete system and application operation. It provides a platform for the provision and execution of SAP services for optimizing or securing SAP solutions and for monitoring the entire solution. Solution Monitoring is divided into Service Level Management, System Monitoring and Business Process, and Interface Monitoring. With the help of System Monitoring, the Solution Manager provides a central platform for monitoring the complete system landscape. This is based on the *SAP CCMS Monitoring Infrastructure* (Computer Center Management System). This infrastructure offers an object-based framework for monitoring components. Thanks to the CCMS, you can monitor all participating application systems because it provides a central view of the current system status. In addition to these mechanisms, analysis and reaction methods are also integrated. Business process monitoring maps the technical monitoring functions to business-critical processes via breaking these processes down into individual sub-processes and assigning them to software process flows. Therefore, you can assign a complete business process to different applications (cross-system) and monitor it centrally (interface monitoring).

SLAs, which define the services to be performed by an IT department, can be controlled via Service Level Monitoring. Defined key values in individual component systems are analyzed at certain intervals and summarized in reports.

Support Desk

In addition, the Solution Manager also offers the functions of the *Support Desk*. The Support Desk provides the environment of an extensive call center or message processing system. It offers functions for the efficient processing of internal company support messages, and evaluating and resolving them. SAP Notes are a big part of the Support Desk and are implemented with the help of the SAP Note Assistant. Complete message processing is also optimized with subjects such as escalation management, workflow integration, or solution database. Support does not end at the enterprise boundaries, however. If SAP support in the company is not in a position to resolve an application problem, then SAP Global Support (at SAP) is automatically involved via the Solution Manager/Support Desk.

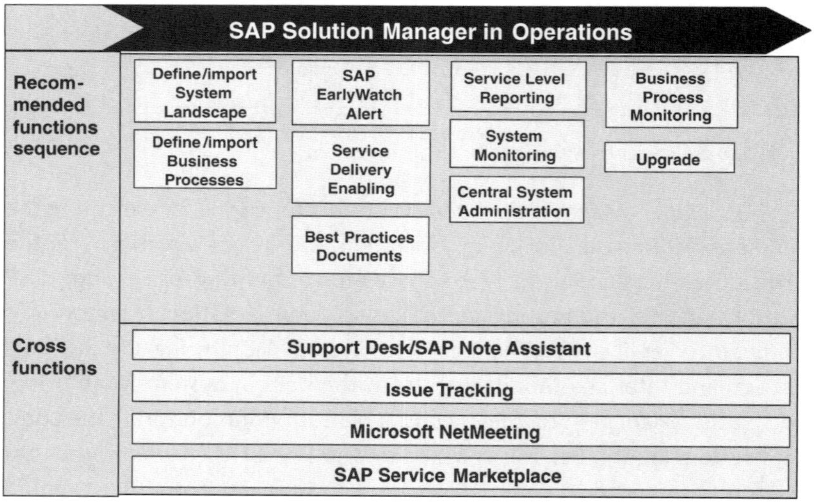

Figure 2.19 SAP Solution Manager for Operation

With the functions listed above, the Support Desk offers support for the construction of a user-driven support organization. This organization can be accessed directly from all connected SAP component systems. One particular advantage of the message creation is that the relevant system data for the system in question is automatically attached to the query, so that the message processor does not have to waste any time on the lengthy compilation of this data. Figure 2.20 shows a diagram of a possible workflow using the Support Desk.

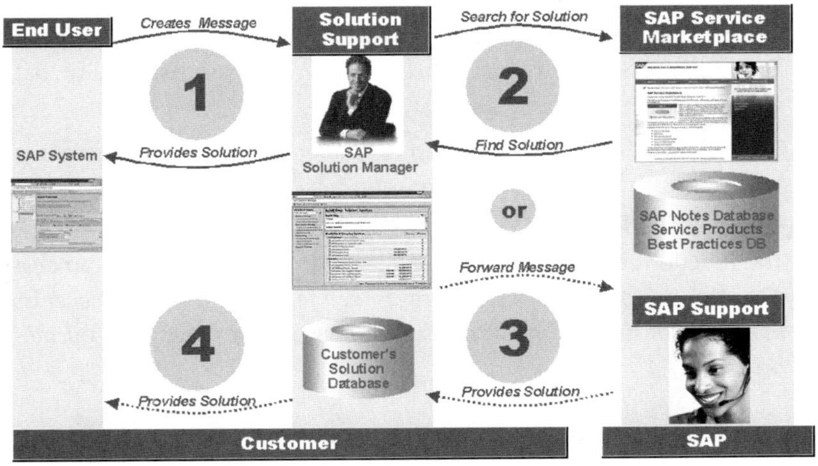

Figure 2.20 Support Desk – Workflow

2.8 Summary

SAP, when coupled with the different component systems (mySAP Business Suite), offers an integrated software system that addresses nearly all the business requirements of an enterprise. Software solutions that comprise multipart business-critical applications are designed in such a way that they implement and optimize the necessary business processes technically. Consequently, you must ensure the availability and performance of these solutions throughout the entire lifecycle. Different options are provided, based on the architecture of the SAP systems, to respond flexibly to the enterprise-specific and business requirements of a company.

The most important points regarding SAP system architecture are:

- The high scalability of SAP systems is ensured thanks to the use of client-server architecture (three- or four-layer model).
- All important component systems in the mySAP Business Suite are based on the SAP Web Application Server. This satisfies general requirements such as platform-independence, scalability, standardization, globalization, and so on.
- With the integration of new technologies, new standards are achieved in this Internet-driven world.

- With the advent of SAP NetWeaver, SAP offers an open integration and application platform for implementing the concept of Enterprise Services Architecture.
- SAP system landscapes are designed to meet the demands of the implementation of business processes, performance, availability, data security, and quality assurance.
- The SAP Solution Manager is used to support lifecycle management for an SAP solution. Its functions are used for all phases in the lifecycle—from the design phase through system operation.
- The functions of the SAP Solution Manager are solution- and process-oriented, resulting in the offering of services that address the entire software solution so attention can be focused on the critical-business processes.

3 Optimizing SAP System Architecture

In this chapter, we'll describe different approaches that you can use to optimize your SAP landscape. Then, we'll provide you with an implementation plan to put your optimization strategy to use.

"In order to see clearly, you often only need to change your line of vision."
(Antoine de Saint-Exupéry)

Continuous Task

By *optimizing* an SAP system landscape or SAP system architecture, we mean that you can adjust it to best meet the requirements that are demanded of it. You should not view this type of optimization task as a *one-time action*, but rather as a continuous and increasingly complex undertaking.

The reason for this approach is because of the ever-changing demands and consequently, the higher frequency of hardware and software upgrades designed to meet these demands.

Today, the IT infrastructure has become a decisive competitive factor for enterprises. In the past, restrictions in the IT infrastructure limited the mapping of enterprise requirements. Since then, the situation has changed dramatically: a modern, innovative IT infrastructure must fulfill varied, and sometimes conflicting, quality criteria. It must provide optimal support for the strategic goals and visions of an enterprise and be flexible enough to reflect future developments. High availability and scalability are also required.

Total Cost of Ownership

Given the economic developments of recent years and the associated financial insecurity, costs are becoming an increasingly important point of discussion. IT managers are faced with the challenge of meeting the growing demands on performance while at the same time reducing costs. The key issue here is to minimize the *Total Cost of Ownership* (TCO). To do so, we must use an integrated analysis procedure and consider the entire lifecycle of applications during strategic planning for the IT infrastructure.

SAP Components

IT landscapes today are dominated by *Enterprise Resource Planning* (ERP) software. As a market leader in this area, SAP is at the core of the IT infrastructure in most of the large and midsize enterprises. To address the issue of meeting ever-changing demands, SAP's current solution is *SAP NetWeaver*. It is the comprehensive integration and application platform for all SAP applications bundled in the *mySAP Business Suite* and the SAP platform for the realization of an *Enterprise Services Architecture* (ESA). Designed for smaller companies, the new *mySAP All-in-One* solution rounds off the range of SAP products. These new components enable SAP users to fulfill the requirements already mentioned.

The goal of this chapter is to provide you with the necessary ground rules to optimize existing SAP system landscapes and help you discern when it's best to implement new ones.

The following sections describe different approaches to optimization and recommendations for when they should be used. We have also included an overview of the factors that influence optimization and a procedure to help you develop your own optimization strategy.

3.1 Optimization Approaches

As we already mentioned, the optimization of SAP system architecture is a multifaceted, complex task and should be planned and implemented from time to time in the context of a complete optimization project. There are different triggers for the semi-conflicting optimization goals: flexible reaction to market changes; optimizing performance to improve response times; and, optimizing performance to reduce a consumption of resources. Depending on what triggered the optimization task or optimization project, different optimization approaches should be considered.

Business Requirements

In an optimization project, typical business requirements for an IT infrastructure can include:

- Agility in volatile markets
- Time-to-market
- Minimizing risks
- Achieving added value
- Reducing costs
- Uniform applications
- Integration

The following sections provide an overview of the basic aspects of optimization and the factors that are relevant to this type of optimization task. Subsequently, we shall present the different approaches or reasons for optimization and describe how to execute an optimization task.

3.1.1 Process Optimization

Business optimization is at the forefront of process optimization. The spectrum here can range from dealing with individual, limited sub-processes to comprehensive business process reengineering (BPR).

Objectives

The objectives for process optimization are:

- Reducing process lead times, thereby, for example:
  - Avoiding backlogs
  - Improving service quality
  - Reducing process costs
  - Reducing additional costs
  - Increasing customer satisfaction
- Improving user satisfaction
- Avoiding redundant data input or data retention
- Cross-system process integration
- Incorporating different user groups in the process

Workflow/ WebFlow

The conversion of process optimization requirements is ideally done using workflow-supported processing. The *SAP Business Workflow*, as an integral element in SAP Basis components, offers a functionally sound and stable base for this processing. With the help of the workflow-supported approach, a previously user-driven process now becomes a system-driven process. In this way, you can ensure that these processes will always be carried out consistently, following the stored process model. For example, by using automatic escalation procedures, you can keep to a maximum tolerable process runtime.

Thanks to the currently available SAP integration technologies, with Workflow you can control both same-system and cross-system processes. Both SAP systems and non-SAP systems can be involved in the process flow. You can use groupware integration or Web integration to incorporate new user groups. The Web integration technologies provided by SAP are particularly useful in the context of the growing importance of enterprise portals and collaborative process development. These technologies have been available since R/3 Release 3.1H. Today, this technological approach is referred to as *WebFlow*.

The incorporation of document management, desktop integration, and telephony integration offer additional possibilities for integration.

With the exception of additional new integration technologies, during process optimization, the IT infrastructure is only indirectly affected because it provides support for these new processes. This does not usually reduce IT costs, however, because although this type of saving is sustained, it can be realized only over a longer period of time.

For more information, see Chapter 5.

3.1.2 Optimizing System Availability

When optimizing system availability, you must consider the following two aspects :

- From the end users' point of view, the application system is considered available if they (i.e., the end users) can access it (i.e., they can log on to the system) and avoid encountering any problems in carrying out those functions that they're authorized to perform via their task profile. The necessary front-end infrastructure is also instrumental here, because if the SAP system is working perfectly but cannot be accessed due to a PC problem, or vice versa, this does not help the user.
- The response times or run times for certain functions, jobs, reports and so on must be within reasonable limits. For example, requirements might include the maximum response time for a call-center application: the goal being to achieve high throughput and therefore reduce waiting times for customers while simultaneously lowering the costs of processing customer queries. Furthermore, certain time targets must be adhered to for specific business procedures, for example, month-end closing and so on.

The first aspect addresses the *reliability* of the systems and the technical components involved; the second aspect addresses the *system performance* of the SAP application environment.

Performance therefore depends on availability, however, this doesn't mean that an available system is automatically a high-performance system. In short, availability is necessary for good performance, but it does not suffice alone.

Another important aspect in achieving high system availability is management. The best high-availability solution is useless if system administration is not suitably organized. We recommend that you structure administration as much as possible to ensure that all procedures, communication, and escalation routes to be used are documented in an administration manual. You must also ensure that all changes that affect this administration manual be updated in the manual; otherwise, such a document is useless.

Management

The following sections present the two aspects, reliability and performance, in greater detail.

3.1.3 Optimizing Reliability

Single point of Failure

As a client-server system, an SAP system covers an entire range of services. We can differentiate between services that are available multiple times, that is, redundant, and services that are integral to the system—if they fail, the whole system fails. The latter services are known as *Single Points of Failure* (SPoF).

They include:

- The database system (RDBMS)
- The enqueue service
- The message service
- The NFS service (Unix)

Planned and Unplanned Downtime

Increasing availability implies a simultaneous reduction of downtime. Downtime can be categorized into *planned* or *unplanned* downtime:

- *Planned downtime* refers to the controlled cessation of the system, for example, for hardware or software maintenance. Planned downtime is usually uncritical because measures requiring planned downtime can be planned in advance and communicated to users. Planned downtime is usually scheduled during times of minimum system activity. Thanks to redundant hardware components and components that can be exchanged during production operation, today, planned downtimes for hardware maintenance can be greatly reduced. Difficulties can arise if any problems occur during the scheduled downtime and cannot be resolved in a reasonable period. This will lead to unplanned downtime.
- *Unplanned downtime* means that a system component fails unexpectedly. Although high power servers can achieve 99 % availability today, which, with considerable effort can be increased to 99.999 %; com-

plete availability cannot be guaranteed. Logical errors in particular, caused by incorrect operation, cannot be offset with a high-availability solution.

Redundancy

The numerous possibilities for the redundant configuration of system services available in the SAP system allows for inherently high availability. Table 3.1 shows which services can be distributed and which services can be configured only once.

SAP Component or Service	Possible Number	System-wide SPoF?
RDBMS	1 per system	Yes
Enqueue service	1 per system	Yes
Message service	1 per system	Yes
Dialog service	2 – n per instance	No
Update service	0 – n per instance	No
Background service	0 – n per instance	No
Spool service	0 – n per instance	No
Gateway service	1 per instance	No
SAProuter	0 – n per system	No
NFS service (Unix)	1 per system	Yes

Table 3.1 SAP System Services and Single Points of Failure

High-Availability Strategy

To outline a high-availability strategy, you must first determine the maximum reasonable downtime periods and the maximum reasonable downtime frequency. Normally, the demands made at this point are too high, which results in excessive hardware costs. Availability costs go up in a fairly linear scale to an availability of around 95 %. Anything above that means an exponential cost increase.

Redundant Subsystems

One way to greatly reduce system-wide SPoFs is to encapsulate the entire system in redundant subsystems. Depending on the resources available for an SAP system, all non-SPoFs can also be configured as redundant. To achieve adequate redundancy for the SPoFs, and depending on the actual system configuration, the particular high-availability solution—adapted to the RDBSM used—must be developed in collaboration with the database and hardware manufacturer. For example, a cluster technology or a switch-over solution may be used.

For more detailed information on high-availability solutions, see SAPNet under *http://sapnet.sap.com/ha*.

3.1.4 Performance Optimization

Poor performance can have many different repercussions:

- Dissatisfaction on the part of end users
- Flow rates for accomplishing business processes are not attained, resulting in overtime, delays in production, and financial loss

In the opposite case, systematic, proactive performance optimization increases the value of the application system considerably.

Definition

When speaking of performance in the context of a data-processing system, we generally refer to the ability to meet requirements, measured in response time and data throughput.

Examples:

- Printing 5 000 invoices in 30 minutes
- Recording a sales order in one second

Performance is not an absolute attribute of an SAP system; instead, you should consider it in relation to the total load on the system. As business processes become more complex, it is important to take into account end-to-end processes. In other words, a process that runs over several SAP systems or SAP components, or even non-SAP systems, should be considered as a whole. Potential weak points here might be the system interfaces used.

Figure 3.1 shows an example of the relative optimization potential that can be achieved.

Classical System Monitoring

Conventional system monitoring—looking at a single system—is progressively reaching its limits. In addition to the SAP R/3 system, the mySAP system landscape is made up of a growing number of component systems (mySAP CRM, SAP BW, SAP APO, and so on), middleware components (SAP BC, ITS, CRM middleware, and so on) and portals (SAP EP or others), part of which is based on SAP Basis, part manages without SAP Basis and another part is made up of software products from third-party suppliers. Each of these components influences the overall performance of the system landscape in its own way and has its own administration and monitoring tools.

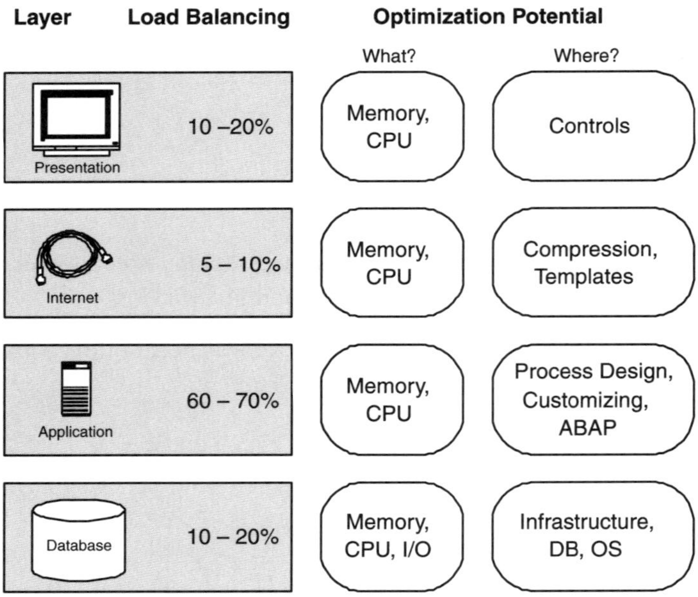

Figure 3.1 Potential with Performance Optimization

The cross-system or cross-component development of business processes that accompanies this expansion means that the separate monitoring of systems can no longer ensure the correct execution of business processes. IT departments are then faced with increasing fragmentation—additional and more intricate components need to be monitored, the know-how for developing and operating these components is more complex—all of this and a diminishing IT budget.

Consequently, SAP no longer speaks of System Management or System Monitoring but of Solution Management or Solution Monitoring. This concept includes the following key points:

- It is no longer sufficient to monitor only individual hardware and software components; the flow of information all along an entire business process, via several software components, is integral to monitoring and optimization.
- Availability, performance, correct execution, and security must be monitored.
- It is necessary to differentiate between real-time monitoring—spotting problems in good time via alerts, navigating to the source of the error, and eliminating the problem—and long-term monitoring (service level reporting, monitoring performance indicators, and so forth).

Solution Monitoring Tools

The central instruments for carrying out solution monitoring are the *Computing Center Management System* (CCMS) and the *SAP Solution Manager*. These instruments can be used to centrally monitor SAP systems and non-SAP systems (System Monitoring), business processes and interfaces (Business Process Monitoring), and measure them against pre-defined performance indicators (Service Level Reporting).

All monitoring data is recorded by the CCMS and can then be assigned to a system, an interface, or a process step. Therefore, in the SAP Solution Manager GUI, you can easily detect where a problem has arisen in the system landscape or the process chain. Monitoring data can also be imported from or exported to system management products from other suppliers, provided that the third-party supplier supports the interface to the CCMS. This does not mean, however, that system management tools from third-party suppliers can be completely replaced by the SAP Solution Manager. Instead, it means that these tools from outside vendors should be integrated.

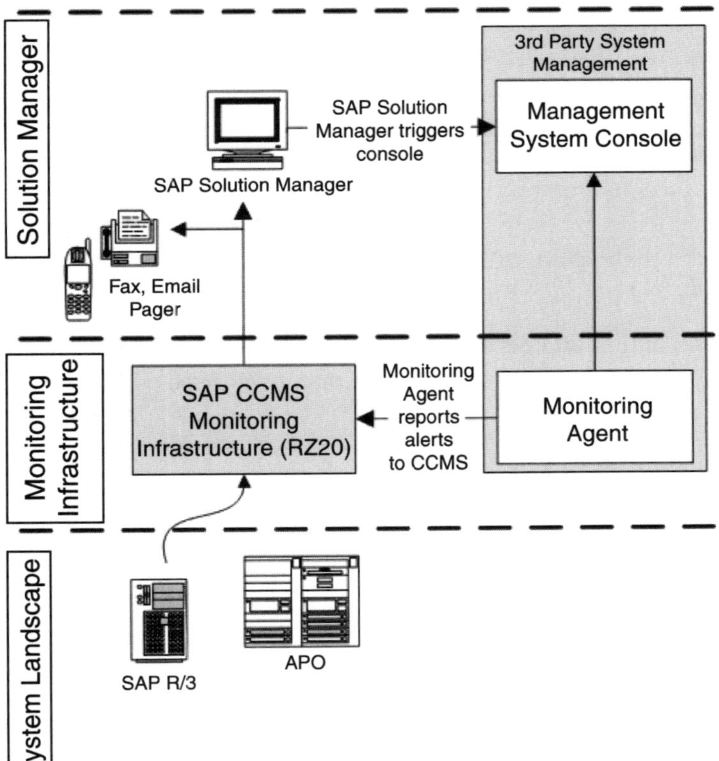

Figure 3.2 Interaction SAP Solution Manager with Third-Party System

Other possible uses for the SAP Solution Manager—such as the Solution Manager Support Desk for processing problem messages, or the Solution Manager for Implementation for supporting implementation projects—are discussed in Chapter 4.

Optimization Procedure

The following steps form part of the procedure for optimizing performance:

- Identification and analysis of problems
- Implementation of tuning measures
- Verification of results

We can basically differentiate between two areas of optimization here:

- **Technical optimization**
  Technical optimization refers to identifying, analyzing, and eliminating problems by combining or using individual components in an SAP system (SAP processes, SAP buffer, database processes and buffer, disk storage, and so on). Shortcomings in this area can have a negative effect on response time and throughput.
- **Application optimization**
  The goal of *application optimization* is to avoid unnecessary load caused by inefficient programs or the ineffectual use of programs.

In performance optimization, attempts are made to achieve the required performance levels by technical optimization and application optimization based on the existing system resources. If the measures implemented are not sufficient, resources must be upgraded accordingly.

Continuous Process

Performance optimization is a continuous process—attaining an acceptable level of performance is no guarantee that it will remain at this level. Some reasons for this are:

- Continuously growing datasets
- Constantly changing load profile (user behavior can only be approximated)
- Introduction of new functions
- Linking up additional users
- The installation of patches or support packages, or the implementation of upgrades

From past experience, we have learned that common causes of performance problems are customer-defined developments or changes to the SAP standard.

3.1.5 System Landscape Optimization (SLO)

The SLO approach is described at length in Chapter 5, therefore, we won't delve into great detail here.

Changes made because of business policy, such as globalization, mergers, spin-offs, or enterprise restructuring usually have far-reaching effects on the business processes and also direct and dramatic effects on the IT infrastructure.

Consolidating the IT infrastructure without changing the processes mapped in it is also conceivable. We would refer to this strategy as a technical SLO approach.

In general, an SLO approach requires comprehensive planning that also takes into account the system architecture, administration, and the support organization.

3.1.6 Cost Optimization

Cost optimization is another approach for optimizing IT systems. Recently, the costs arising from IT have come under close inspection. The reasons for this were cited at the beginning of this chapter. Although today's economic environment is very volatile and therefore much attention is placed on minimizing and/or avoiding risk, IT investments are critical to ensure the strategic future of an enterprise.

Investment Objectives

According to a survey on the most important objectives of the IT budget, published in *CIO Insight* magazine in June 2002, the most frequently cited reason for investment was to optimize costs. The distribution of investment objectives is illustrated in Figure 3.3.

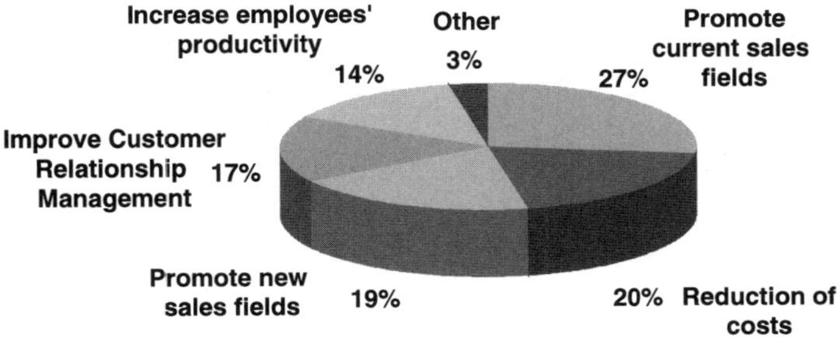

Figure 3.3 Reasons for IT Investments (CIO Insight: "Spending Survey," June 2002)

Calculation of Benefits

According to other studies, which have confirmed this trend, IT managers increasingly look for proof of the usefulness or cost-effectiveness of IT investments. There are different ways to calculate or analyze benefits, examples of which we have already given earlier in this chapter. The result also depends—to a large extent—on the direction and the scope of the cost factors included in the evaluation and the period over which the investments are in use. Therefore, in addition to seeking proof of usefulness, a uniform method to determine efficacy should also be sought.

A study by *CIO.com Research Reports*, dated June 2001, on the most frequently used method for determining the IT value chain gave the following results:

- 41% ROI (Return on Investment)
- 14% IRR (Internal Rate of Return)
- 29% TCO (Total Cost of Ownership)

ROI The *Return on Investment* is a key figure that provides information on the return earned on capital over a certain period of time. It presents the profit per unit of invested capital and therefore indicates potential for profitability. In practice, we can differentiate between two points of view:

1. Determining the advantageousness of a new capital commitment
2. Determining the profitability of previously invested capital

The oldest and most well-known key-figure system based on the concept of ROI was developed by the E. I. du Pont de Nemours (DuPont) and Company as early as 1919.

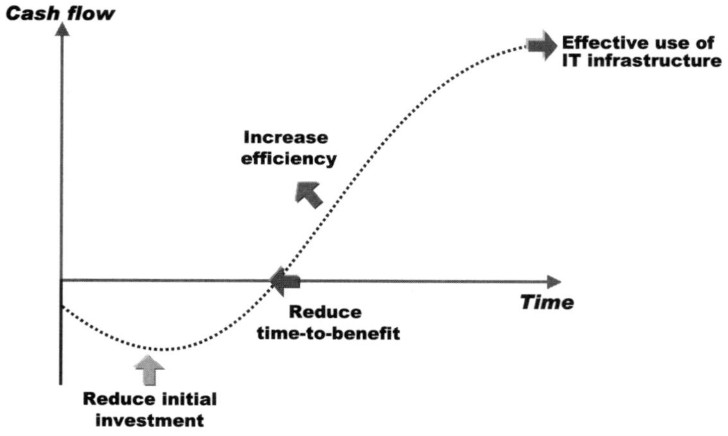

Figure 3.4 Increasing IT Profitability with ROI

The ROI is a central economic indicator. The assessment of success is made relative with the ROI and this allows for both comparison between business fields of different sizes and for the best possible use to be made of enterprise resources, both operatively and strategically, through the setting of a target ROI. For multifaceted international enterprises or corporate groups, the ROI represents an essential instrument for managing success.

By *Internal Rate of Return,* we refer to the interest rate that when applied makes the capital value of an investment equal zero. **IRR**

From this definition, we can derive the following:

- An investment that gives an IRR that is at least as high as the calculated interest is profitable.
- If the IRR is the same as the calculated interest, the investor gets the invested capital back and interest equal to the minimum required. Here, regardless of other factors, it wouldn't make any difference if the investment was made or not.
- If the return is lower than the calculated interest, the investor has not achieved the minimum interest required, and therefore, the investment is not viable.

Total Cost of Ownership is a method to identify the *total costs* of selecting and purchasing, implementing, using, maintaining, and managing a system over an extended period of time—usually the *lifecycle* of the system. By TCO, we consider the total costs, from planning to implementation through operation of an IT solution. **TCO**

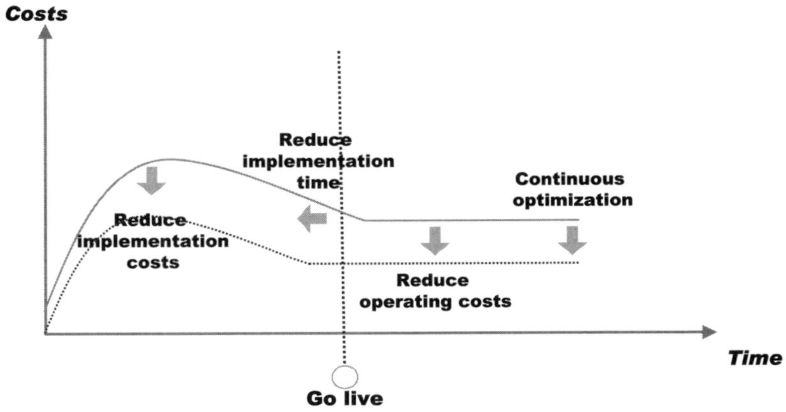

Figure 3.5 Reducing IT Expenditure with TCO

The basic idea behind the TCO approach is that not only should we compare purchase price; we must also consider all other costs that arise over an entire period.

Although the TCO approach seems plausible and you would expect that it's generally used to analyze IT investments, many studies show otherwise:

- Many customers don't know their TCO; they don't measure it systematically, regularly and correctly, and they don't disclose their public TCO or their real TCO.
- Many customers know even less about the usefulness achieved than the expense required.
- The real TCO surprises most customers because it appears to be too high.
- Frequently, the IT department is viewed as being an accomplice to the vendor (or vice versa) when trying to convince the CEO or CFO.

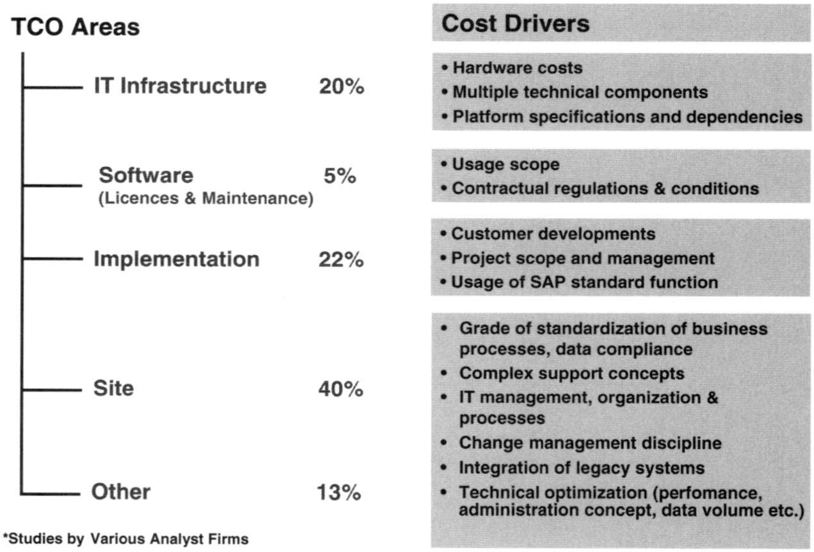

Figure 3.6 TCO: Areas and Cost Drivers

Cost Distribution and Cost Drivers

Figure 3.6 shows how costs are distributed and the cost drivers (originator) for each area, as determined by different studies. Much has been written on various TCO surveys, carried out with different methods. Because there is no standard for TCO-methodology, it's difficult to compare the results from one study with those of another.

The main differences in the methods used are:

- Differences in the cost factors considered
- Different time frame (2, 3, or 5 years)
- Different level of complexity of implementations (different number of countries, business locations, employees, and so on)
- Effects of different depreciation possibilities (purchase value versus current value)

Cost factors are usually split between direct and indirect costs.

Direct Costs

Direct costs are the budgeted costs that are directly related to an application. These include costs for:

- Hardware
- Software
- System Management
- Support
- Implementation
- Communication

Indirect Costs

Indirect costs are unbudgeted costs, such as costs for:

- Infrastructure support for end users (self-support, local data management, training, and so on)
- Planned/unplanned downtime
- Additional costs (savings that couldn't be made because optimization measures were not implemented)

Besides the pure assessment of the different cost factors, a TCO study should consider additional influencing factors, such as:

- Risk evaluation (high risk equals high cost)
  - Implementation risks (costs for failed projects)
  - Operating risks (system breakdown, loss of data, security aspects, and so on)
- The complexity of
  - Management processes (Change Management, Problem Management, SLAs and so on)

- IT infrastructure:

  Software (number of client-server applications, length of productive use to date, number of different operating systems, number of enterprise-critical applications, and so on)

  Hardware (number of mobile devices, measures for ensuring high availability, and so on)

Measures to Reduce TCO

From the cost factors and other levels of influence that we listed above, we can deduce that the TCO can be reduced via different measures:

- Reducing complexity
- Reducing risks
- Increasing the level of standardization
- Increasing the level of integration
- Improving training measures

A system assessment based purely on costs/TCO is too limited. Costs should always be considered in relation to the usefulness achieved.

3.2 Implementing an Optimization Concept

In the previous sections, we presented different optimization approaches. The following dictum applies to all these options: Optimization requires investment at first. Depending on the optimization variant chosen, the following range of measures can vary greatly—the associated analysis and planning effort, the costs arising, and the implementation times. You can differentiate between short-term objectives (quick wins, measures that form part of continuous optimization) and medium- to long-term objectives that strive for a redesign of the existing landscape.

Increases in value are achieved via target-oriented, top-down decisions and their consistent implementation.

Optimum Compromise

Because conflicting needs can arise at times, the results of optimization may not be optimal for *all* demands. Instead, there is typically an optimal compromise that takes into account all the influencing factors. To map the optimization result to the requirement profile in the best way possible, you must draw up a weighted catalog of criteria. Often, you will find that the optimization strategy can only be worked out via iterative approximation.

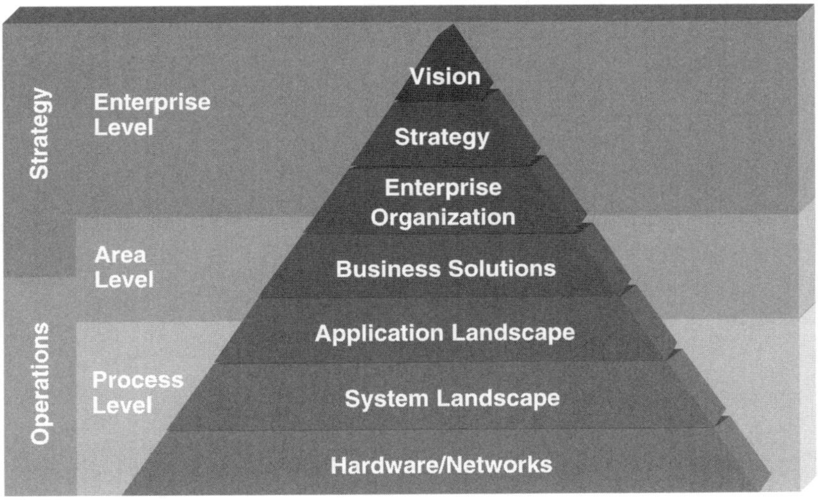

Figure 3.7 Implementing IT Usage from the Top Down

The following sections will explain how to create an implementation plan in greater detail. We won't discuss the formulation of enterprise objectives or vision here.

3.2.1 Development Plan

The first step in global implementation planning is to create a development plan that includes the following sub-concepts:

- The topology of the production landscape
- The realization strategy
- The topology of the development landscape
- The organization of implementation and support

All relevant alternatives must be determined for each of these four sub-concepts. You will need appropriate evaluation criteria to help you select from among the options in each case. The development plan is therefore the best combination of sub-concept variants, resulting from the total demands.

Integrated view

As you can see in Figure 3.8, the four sub-areas of the development plan cannot be considered separately from each other because there are dependencies among them. The sequence followed in creating the plan depends on the primary implementation objectives of the enterprise, for example, which country or which business unit will act as a pilot.

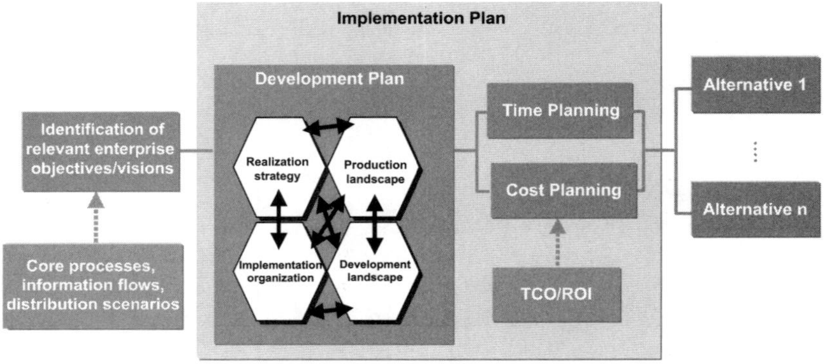

Figure 3.8 The Implementation Planning Process

The development plan provides information on:

- The total scope of functions on which it is based
- Which productive systems will be installed where and how they should be linked to each other
- Which systems will be required for project work, testing, and training
- Which template systems will be required and how the template components (specifications, reference settings and examples) will be transferred to other systems
- How upgrades and the release strategy will be addressed
- What implementation method and sequence will be used
- Which cross-system activities will be carried out
- How the project organization should be structured

The individual sub-components of the development plan will be dealt with in greater detail in the following sections.

3.2.2 The Topology of the Production Landscape

The topological model of the production landscape describes the SAP systems required and how they are interrelated. These dependencies are derived from the current and future business processes and from consolidation, controlling, and information requirements. Some of the criteria required for planning the production landscape are show in Table 3.2:

Enterprise-Specific Implementation Requirements	
▶ Changing organization structures ▶ Consideration of existing production systems ▶ Consideration of current projects	
Organizational Influencing Factors	
Central system	▶ All users directly affected by planned/unplanned downtime ▶ Short maintenance window makes maintenance difficult ▶ Central system management must support different languages and time zones ▶ More complex job management ▶ Highly-qualified support personnel needed
Decentralized systems	▶ Information systems required ▶ Redundant data maintenance and data retention ▶ Higher number of interfaces ▶ Higher number of systems to be monitored
Functional Influencing Factors	
Load distribution	▶ Separation of OLTP and OLAP functions (online transaction processing/online analytical processing) ▶ Data volumes ▶ Number of users
Requirements for functionality needed	▶ Industry Solutions ▶ mySAP components ▶ Non-SAP products
Integration scenarios	▶ Workflow/WebFlow ▶ ALE, EDI, SAP BC, SAP XI... ▶ Internet/intranet
Internationalization	
Languages	
Code pages	
Country-specific versions	▶ Standard country versions ▶ Non-standard country versions (modifications, add-ons)
Time zones	

Table 3.2 Criteria for Planning the Production Landscape

Flexibility	
Business flexibility	
System availability	
Release management	▶ SAP release strategy (mySAP Business Suite components, SAP NetWeaver components, country versions, and so on) ▶ Customer-specific developments
Physical versus logical system owners	
Security requirements	
Separation of strategic/sensitive data (personnel administration data and so on)	
Disaster recovery	
Geographical Spread of the Enterprise	
Business locations/ branch locations	
Computer centers	
Availability of support personnel	

Table 3.2 Criteria for Planning the Production Landscape (cont.)

The required evaluation criteria may occasionally differ. Sometimes, you need relatively little criteria to design a production landscape. In addition, the customer-specific prioritizing and weighting of criteria is also significant as they can differ greatly and even lead to conflicting specifications.

3.2.3 The Realization Strategy

The realization strategy highlights the different aspects of implementing new systems or functions. These include, for example, the sequence and the scope of the implementation steps required. The following points must be analyzed for the realization strategy:

- Transformation and migration strategy
  - SAP system → SAP system
  - Non-SAP system → SAP system

  Replacing a process in an enterprise area/over several enterprise areas
  Complete/partial/overlapping cover in the SAP environment

  - Heterogeneous landscape → homogenous landscape
  - Transformation of the organization structure
  - Transformation of the process organization
  - Transformation of the hardware architecture
  - Transformation of the SAP version
- Standardization, harmonization, optimization
  - Uniform reporting
  - Uniform chart of accounts
  - Harmonization of master data
  - Optimization of business processes
- Implementation
  - Drawing up studies (for example, for the harmonization of master data)
  - Preparation and execution of template projects for creating company-wide standards.
  - Preparation and execution of implementation projects
    - Pilot/master projects
    - Rollout projects (complete/partial rollout)
    - Autonomous projects

3.2.4 The Topology of the Development Landscape

In addition to the topology of the production landscape, you will need a topology for the development landscape to complete the total SAP system infrastructure.

The systems and clients required for a development landscape depend on the following important criteria:

- One development/test system per production system
- One quality assurance (QA) system per production system
- Training systems:
  - For the project team (for example IDES)
  - For end users (separate system or a client in the QA system)
- Client concept (number/distribution of clients needed; for example, customizing master, test clients for customizing, data transfer, developer test, and so on, training client and so on)

The development landscape is intended for the general support of the production landscape. It is by no means static however; during the implementation phase, it may be necessary to temporarily set up additional systems. For example, the need may arise for an additional development system to test critical developments separately, without restricting the entire project team. During the test phase, you may also find it necessary to set up additional temporary systems or clients for interface and high-volume testing.

As soon as part-volumes have been made productive, a maintenance system is prepared so that, in the event of errors in the production environment, a simulation and error correction environment—with the same software state as the production environment—can be made available.

3.2.5 The Organization of Implementation and Support

Another element in the development plan is the need to plan the staffing of the project organization and support organization defined in the realization strategy. Several factors influence this planning:

- The necessary qualifications, abilities, and skills
- Limiting the task area of internal/external project workers (consultants)
- The structure of internal competencies to operate the development and production system landscape
- Planning the structure of a Customer Competence Center (CCC), based on the support organization

You will find additional details on the last point in Chapter 4.

3.2.6 The Creation of the Global Implementation Plan

In addition to development planning, the implementation plan also includes the scheduling of individual activities and an estimation of costs. These two aspects are presented in the following two sections.

Schedule

Scheduling the implementation steps and the personnel required to implement these steps provides a basis for planning individual milestones, capacity planning, and resource allocation. You can calculate the total duration of the project based on the scheduling, which includes the following elements:

- The most important global milestones
- Scheduling personnel recruitment and material resource procurement
- Standardization and harmonization projects
- Redesign of processes
- Organizational changes
- Studies
- Training plan for the project team

Cost Planning

In the global implementation plan, cost assessment is still relatively sketchy. In some cases, it may be necessary to prepare a detailed estimation of costs. In Section 3.2.4, we introduced terms and methods related to cost optimization. The procedure used to estimate costs as part of the implementation plan follows along the same lines.

One possibility is to use a method to determine the TCO, which fulfills all of the requirements we just enumerated in the previous section. In this way, the most important cost aspects of a complex SAP infrastructure are addressed. Nevertheless, the TCO provides information only on those costs that actually arise; it doesn't shed light on the usefulness of the investment. To determine the proof of usefulness, you can estimate the ROI, the IRR, or the cost/usefulness ratio (Net Present Value, NPV).

- A positive IRR generally indicates a good ROI for the project.
- A positive NPV means that the project is worthwhile.
- An amortization period of a maximum of 18 months is a good guide value.

3.3 SAP's TCO Initiatives

For some time now, SAP has actively tried to support the reduction of the TCO for SAP implementations. We will end this chapter with a presentation of some, but by no means all, of the results of these efforts.

The TCO Service Map—Edition 2003—can be found on the SAP Service Marketplace under **SERVICESMAP · Customer Services Network · Total Cost of Ownership**. The TCO Service Map contains the services offered by SAP or SAP partners for the phases of IT strategy, implementation, and operation.

IT Strategy	IT Alignment	Value Assessment	Business Case	
Implementation	Implementation			
Operation	System Consolidation	Data Harmonization	Development	Optimization

Figure 3.9 The SAP TCO Service Map (Edition 2003)

Additional SAP measures to reduce the TCO:

- **Processes**
  - Providing Best Practices for various different sectors of industry
  - Providing preconfigured clients

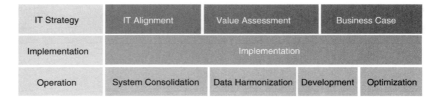

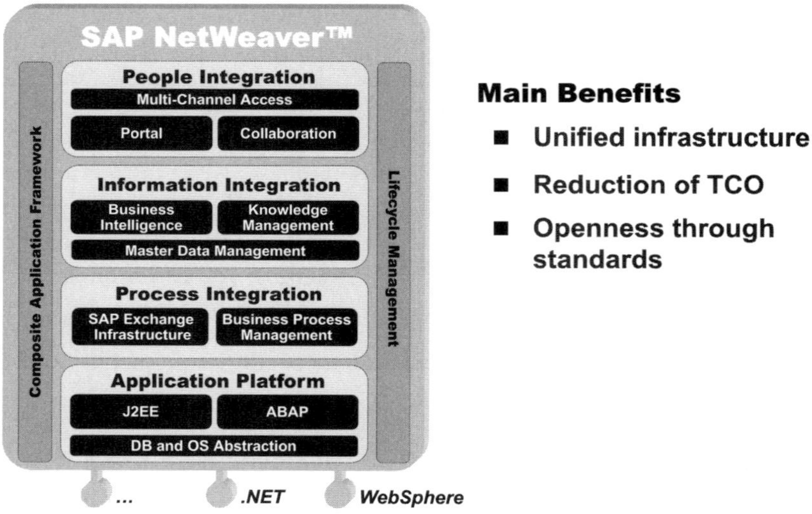

Figure 3.10 Business Value with SAP NetWeaver

- **Technology**
  - SAP NetWeaver as a central integration platform (see Figure 3.10)
  - SAP One Server (S1S), based on MCOD technology (Multiple Components One Database) provides IT consolidation for small and midsize customers
  - Downward-compatible SAP kernel
  - Downward-compatible SAP GUI

- **Tools**
  - SAP Solution Manager as the IT Service Management platform allows for central monitoring/system management, support for SAP implementation, ASAP methods, Customizing Scout (central customizing, maintenance, and distribution), test tools (Code Inspector, CATT/eCATT, Test-Workbench and so on), support for software maintenance
  - SAP Note Assistant
- **Upgrade tools/SAP release strategy**
  - Minimized downtime thanks to different upgrade methods
  - Repository Switch Upgrade enables a continuation of production operation during upgrade preparation and upgrade follow-up
  - Support for migration from SAP R/3, Release 3.11 or higher, to mySAP Business Suite
  - New software delivery concept since early 2002: first *ramp-up* with coaching and knowledge transfer (ramp-up knowledge transfer, RKT), later *General Availability* (GA) for which an upgrade process is no longer required, only the installation of support packages
- **Training**

You can find details on the individual points listed here and additional information, in particular, the latest version of release planning information, on SAPNet or in the SAP Service Marketplace.

4 Optimization of Service and Support

As IT landscapes become increasingly complex and exceed enterprise boundaries, Service and Support become more important as does ensuring the quality of the associated processes. This chapter describes procedures that you can use to optimize your support organization.

"Measure what is measurable and make measurable what is not so."
(Galileo Galilei)

Distributed Systems

Ever-changing demands on enterprises can lead to increasingly complex business processes. These processes, in turn, not only go beyond the boundaries of single software systems, but increasingly they also go beyond the boundaries of the enterprise itself. Added to this is the fact that as a result of growing enterprise structures, mergers, and takeovers, systems can be scattered around many locations and monitored from there by local teams.

Support for these distributed systems with their numerous interfaces and resulting dependencies is therefore evermore challenging and complex, especially when coupled with the escalating technical complexity of supporting the application.

Adjusting Applications

The challenge in supporting a heterogeneous system landscape with numerous applications lies not only in running it efficiently after it's conceived and built; it is also very trying to continuously adjust it to meet new technical and economical circumstances and demands. Support must ensure that all relevant processes, systems, and employees' skills are up-to-date and can respond quickly and flexibly to new requests. This is no easy task when working with distributed systems, applications, and support teams.

Furthermore, the increasing number of productive systems in large enterprises is multiplied by necessary development and consolidation systems, in addition to test and training systems and other systems, for example, for interfaces, data exchange, Internet applications, search engines, and so on.

Modified Support Demands

The demands made on support are progressively changing from being responsible for system availability to being responsible for only a multitude of complex business processes outside the system boundaries.

Due to the use of SAP Portals or SAP Workplace, users in today's SAP environment cannot often tell which system they are working on, or which application caused an error. This poses a big problem, because an imprecise or erroneous description of the error can prove very time-consuming.

Often, an employee manning a first-level Support Desk or Help Desk doesn't fully understand the problem (possible language difficulties aside) and is therefore not in a position to ask the right questions. A customer service representative at the Call Center, who typically deals with telephone inquiries from customers regarding PC problems, will also have difficulties, for example, isolating the complexity of an error on an SAP APO system, or figuring out with a SAP Portal user which application or which system is responsible for an erroneous function. Therefore, the problem cannot be resolved, but merely recorded. The result of this inability to resolve the problem is that the error message is usually forwarded directly to a higher level of support. Someone there must then contact the person who originally reported the problem to better understand it, or to determine that he is not responsible for this kind of problems and then send the error message back to the Help Desk. In large enterprises, this back-and-forth game can continue without anyone getting closer to resolving the initial problem. Ultimately, it soon becomes evident that a broad scope of knowledge is required even for classifying calls according to urgency and implication.

Integrated Solution

Service and Support Optimization must consider the kind of problems illustrated above and strive for a comprehensive solution. In this case, "comprehensive" means that a problem message is created in the right place, that it contains all the necessary data so that it can be directly forwarded to the appropriate level of support, and that the latter can, if necessary, add other support units without having to leave their support environment to notify the appropriate person via email or forward the necessary data over the phone.

Complete Documentation

Complete Documentation of the incident and problem management process is a prerequisite for the closely linked Change Management. Well organized Change Management is, in turn, a prerequisite for the optimal operation of complex system environments and business processes and for resolving—or even avoiding—breakdowns.

While more emphasis should be placed on optimizing business and technical requirements for the Service and Support area, you no longer need to take the "cost saving" spectre too seriously. If turnover cannot be increased, then costs should at least be squeezed; this is the simple formula for maximizing profit in many enterprises today and, of course, improving service all the while.

Challenges

Against this background, a typical SAP Customer Competence Center (CCC) is today compelled to set itself challenges and to constantly adjust and optimize the services offered to meet these challenges.

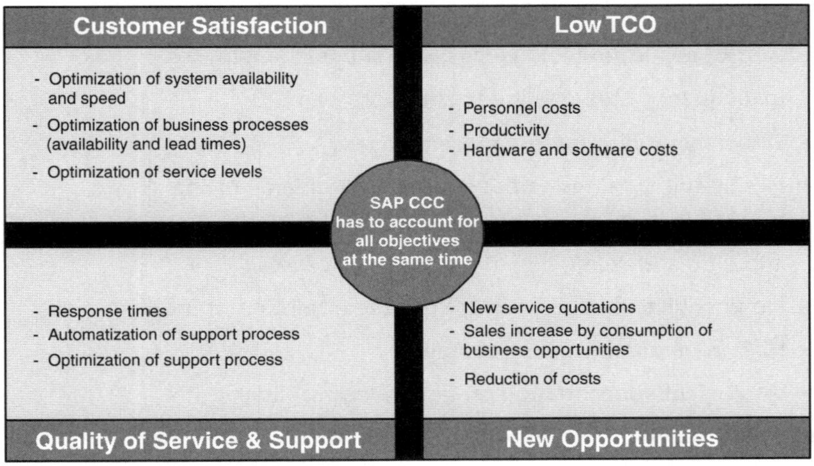

Figure 4.1 The Challenges Faced by an SAP Customer Competence Center

The task of increasing efficiency in the area of Support and Service is more complex than reducing costs. To initiate this change, you must first determine what level of efficiency you are presently at. Only by using this benchmark, can you measure improvements in the effectiveness of support processes. Identifying and measuring the important parameters is therefore the most important prerequisite to make the necessary changes. In short, you cannot improve what you have not measured.

Increasing the effectiveness and efficiency as well as the transparency of Service and Support processes in information technology are the themes for the following sections.

4.1 Service and Support Optimization

4.1.1 Triggers

The catalyst to improve processes is often triggered by problems in the current program flows. Due to the excessive demands placed on support, problems and failures are often only dealt with reactively and not proactively. Distributing roles and responsibilities over business locations takes up additional time and energy. Today, many enterprises and support organizations are faced with the following problems:

- Insufficient or absent structure in user and application support
- Lack of application knowledge with support employees
- Inadequate system behind the support team
- Difficulty monitoring support employees
- Firefighting used instead of structured problem-solving
- Repeatedly working with the same problems without investigating, and ultimately removing, the underlying causes
- No possibility for the interruption-free resolution of problems
- High dependency on key people
- Insufficient concentration on important problems
- Additional malfunctions due to a lack of coordination and not documenting changes
- Lack of investment in new business requirements, or they are viewed as an annoyance
- Support costs are not transparent
- Inconsistent quality of problem-solving and response times
- Little or no management information is available

Reducing Costs While Maintaining Performance

Frequently, the IT department is also required to make significant cost savings, while maintaining the same level of service. This paradoxical stipulation forces an IT organization to monitor all of its activities closely to see how the demands placed on their organization can best be met. Often, radical measures must be used if the IT organization is to achieve its objectives. Because IT organizations are generally overworked or develop a blinkered view, we recommend that you seek external assistance from Service and Support process consultants to help implement these fundamental changes.

There is often a demand for the outsourcing of services, because in-house performance is not transparent or cannot be measured due to a lack of service agreements. However, detailed service agreements must be agreed upon with the outsourcing partner. Because there is a clear assignment of costs, outsourced services appear to be transparent. But, there is no way to compare the outsourced services with one's own services beforehand, because these services that were outsourced were calculated at a flat, all-inclusive rate and not broken down into dedicated services.

Increased Transparency

Before you hunt for radical solutions, we recommend that you optimize existing processes and try to achieve more transparency in IT. Transparent IT services processes are necessary to identify problems—this is the first step in making improvements.

Change Management

In the SAP environment, with a rapidly growing number of systems and the complexity this entails, Change Management is another initiator of change. Established change processes quickly become insufficient for dealing with the complexity of the system landscape across countries, organizations, and systems. Today, even supposedly small changes can trigger system failures, or, even worse, erroneous data. Therefore, Change Management and its predecessor, Problem Management, must be granted greater importance.

4.1.2 Procedure

Figure 4.2 shows a general procedure and illustrates how it can be used to improve processes in a company. The model can be used generically for strategic, tactical, and operational changes, or even for benchmarking.

The illustrated procedure always compares the As-Is situation with Best Practice solutions and processes. The result of this comparison, when combined with the previously planned goals, defines the following change process.

You must change the planning needs to include the planned changes to the Service and Support processes and also the planned results of the changes.

By measuring the defined processes and evaluating changes in relation to the goals defined—via constant comparisons—the subsequent steps can be adjusted and the process can proceed on a course to long-lasting improvement.

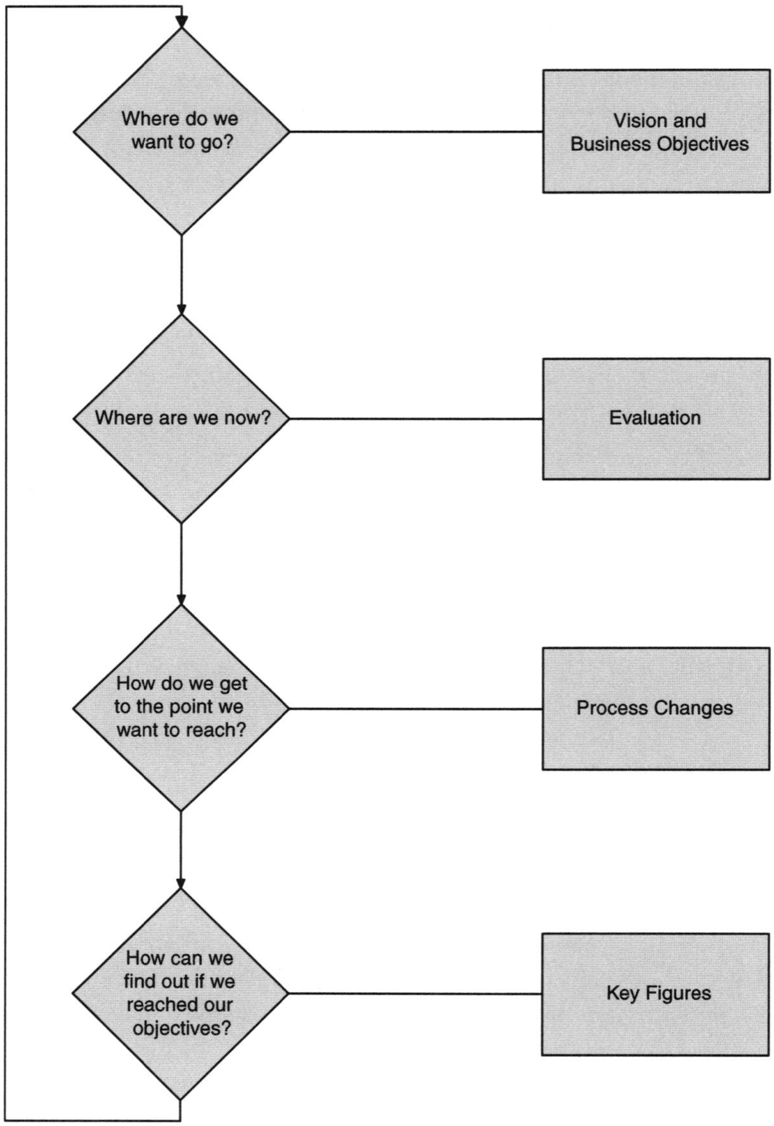

Figure 4.2 Procedure Flow in an Optimization Process

4.1.3 Factors

The introduction and optimization of support processes cannot be considered in isolation, rather, they are influenced by several different factors at the same time. The key to an integrated approach to change projects is to consider all of these factors simultaneously.

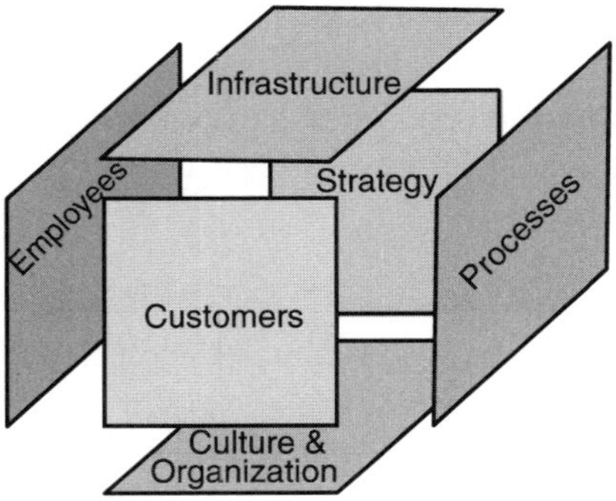

Figure 4.3 Key Factors in a Project

Processes

The key factors are obviously the Service and Support *processes*. The core essentials in an optimization project are the determination, evaluation, and prioritizing of the important processes.

Infrastructure

Service and Support processes are necessary for the optimal operation of the *infrastructure* and the applications in an enterprise. The processes also need a technical basis to store and process data and to map the necessary workflows.

Employees

Lastly, the Service and Support *employees* must implement the processes defined. For this to occur, you must define roles and responsibilities, as well as the locations and skills of the different employees. Regular appraisals and development plans are also necessary.

Customers

Ultimately, everything revolves around the *customers*. Business processes, the infrastructure needed for them, and the Service and Support processes are all intended to keep customers content. In all considerations on optimizing processes, you must always ask what advantages will be gained for the customer, or how you can improve the competitive advantage.

Enterprise Strategy

The *enterprise strategy* springs from the demands of your existing and would-be customers and studying how your competition tries to meet these demands. The IT strategy then evolves from the enterprise strategy.

Enterprise Culture

The factors mentioned are all specified by the *culture* and *organization* of an enterprise—how it came about and how it has evolved over the years. You must also consider the impact of mergers and takeovers.

Such factors are usually looked at during optimization projects. Throughout the duration of the project, you should ensure that no important points have been overlooked. If processes must be implemented in numerous different locations, or the project team consists of many members or external consultants, you must conduct regular checks to verify that all factors have been addressed in the context of all business locations and all parts of the enterprise.

4.1.4 Health Check

A *health check* should serve as an objective basis to evaluate the efficiency of the current support processes in an organization. The goal of this check should be to identify process flows that work well; to discover where Best Practices have been used, both of which should be maintained; and, to expose problem areas and shortcomings. You can then use the recommendations ascertained as a result of the health check to determine the priorities of the upcoming changes.

Objectives

The objectives of a health check are:

- To assess the effectiveness of the Service and Support processes
- To identify problems and limitations
- To indicate ways in which processes could be improved

You should pay particular attention to areas that limit the performance of the Service and Support processes, but are not directly attributed to IT. These include, for example, personnel and resource management, general administrative processes and specifications, and disputes over competence. These factors can frequently have a considerable influence on the efficiency of the Service and Support processes.

Content

You should ensure that a health check includes the following general aspects:

- A strategic business plan
- A description of how this plan provides for the necessary IT planning
- The extent to which IT supports the requirements of the business
- A comparison of how the IT department should grow in relation to the business

Furthermore, the following process elements should be analyzed in a health check:

- The individual activities and steps of the Service and Support processes
- The tasks and responsibilities of the individual support organizations or groups
- The communicative associations between processes

- The general control of the Service and Support processes
- An exact description of all areas of the IT infrastructure
- Control and responsibility for all changes in the IT infrastructure
- The level of user satisfaction with all Service and Support processes

Quick Wins

When making improvements to processes, the actual implementation often entails massive fundamental changes to current processes or to the organization itself. Therefore, a considerable length of time may be required for the implementation. In collaboration with all those involved in the change process, *quick wins* must first be realized and communicated as such in the organization so that those involved and affected can see that efforts are successful, even before the final objective has been achieved. A health check can contribute greatly to identifying the necessary quick wins.

Maturity of Processes

Health checks and self-evaluations are also useful to determine the *degree of maturity* of a Service and Support organization. This is even more important if the goal of the improvements is to align the objectives of the IT organization with those of the business. If the Service and Support processes have been perfected over the years, fewer changes will be required during an optimization. However, the improved processes should also be aligned with current business requirements.

Depending on the size of the enterprise and the development of the Service and Support processes, the health check can be carried out in different ways. Regardless of how it is expedited, management support is always necessary. Without the explicit support from management, decisive steps cannot be initiated and decisions cannot be made. Furthermore, management support is required so that all parties involved in the Service and Support processes can participate in the planned steps; otherwise, even the best plans can fail due to poor implementation.

4.1.5 Quality

Service and Support processes comprise individual steps and activities. The organization and flow of these activities determine the quality of the processes.

Deming Circle

A simple and useful model for controlling the activities is the Deming quality circle or the *Deming circle*. Based on developments at Bell Laboratories during the 1930s, W. Edwards Deming's quality circle was published and recognized as an important component of quality management during the 1950s.

The Deming quality circle should be used to control and coordinate continuous improvement programs. The circle represents a continuous cycle whereby improvement programs begin with careful planning and continue even after effective implementation. Rather, the results of the implementation, together with the goals defined, must be compared with new challenges. If any discrepancies or holes in the process are found as a result of this comparison, planning begins again and the circle continues.

Phases The quality circle assumes that in order to achieve good output, the following steps must be repeatedly carried out:

1. **Plan**
   Determine what must be done, who must do it, and how the plan must be designed and implemented in order to improve business processes.
2. **Do**
   Carry out the planned activities.
3. **Check**
   Compare results with the plans.
4. **Act**
   Based on insights gleaned from the previous step, the Check phase, decide on changes needed to improve the plan.

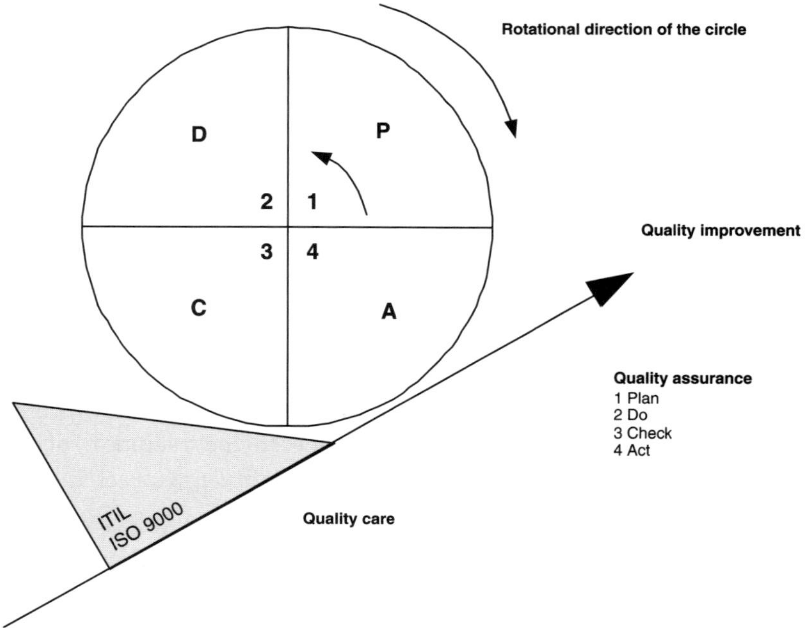

Figure 4.4 The Deming Quality Circle

To be able to permanently check the quality, the individual activities in processes must be organized and documented using separate plans and check points for each. In addition to the activities, these plans must also include the responsible organization with clear roles and responsibilities.

Quality Care

Quality care is the responsibility of all employees in a Service and Support organization. Everyone must be clear of his or her role and contribution to the achievement of the required quality. Quality care also implies that it is the permanent search for improvements within the IT organization and the execution of activities that make it possible to improve quality.

Quality Assurance

Quality assurance is integral to the management of an enterprise. This includes all measures and procedures that help ensure that the services to be provided comply with the expectations and agreements of internal and external customers. Quality assurance must guarantee that suggestions for improvement are implemented and adhered to.

And finally, a quality system (such as ISO 9000, i.e., standard operating procedures or SOPs) includes the organization of responsibilities and the agreed upon procedures.

4.2 Optimization Project

In this section, we'll examine the individual processes and components of a Service and Support optimization project. These include all the relevant factors that are considered as being required for the optimization. The processes to be tackled when optimizing the area of Service and Support for SAP environments are aligned with ITIL Best Practices. The technology required to support these processes is described in Section 4.3.2.

4.2.1 Factors and Components

Processes

In optimization projects, the focus is clearly on the Service and Support processes. The project begins with the analysis, followed by a description of new processes, and continues with the implementation of these processes.

Employees

The Service and Support employees are necessary for the realization and the execution of processes after implementation. Some employees help to define, test, and introduce the new processes. Many others, however, must first be made aware of the need for change so that the introduction and implementation don't fail or suffer unnecessary delays due to resistance. Apart from the actual launch, key employees should be involved in working out the new processes—especially in the test and pilot phases. Intensive instruction and training pave the way for productive implementation.

Technology In addition to planning the new processes, the necessary technology must be defined, selected, assessed, and tested. It is irrelevant whether an existing product is to be enhanced or used in a different way, or whether the plans entail using a new tool to meet the new demands. When selecting tools, you should ensure that potential future demands are also included in the assessment. Interfaces to other systems can also have a strong impact on the selection and evaluation of a tool.

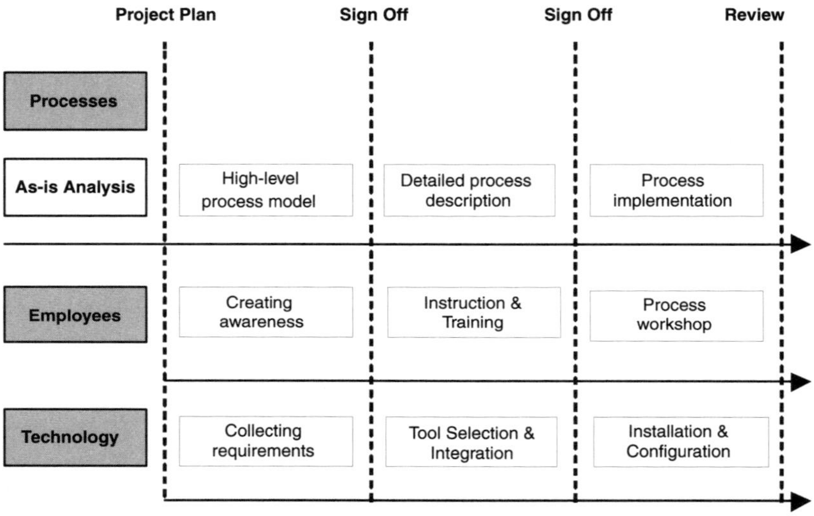

Figure 4.5 Factors and Components of an Optimization Project

Milestones In addition to the procedure described, you should also establish milestones, against which knowledge gained can be tracked and verified.

After the implementation of the new processes and tools, you must compare the results achieved with the guidelines and, if necessary, refine them.

4.2.2 Service and Support Processes

The operation of large and distributed SAP systems for global enterprises with many users, spread over different business locations in numerous countries, places high demands on support and the specification of Service and Support processes. In particular, the ever- expanding system integration and the dovetailing of systems and the business processes that run on them, also require the integration of the support organizations. A support organization must adapt to new requirements and technologies evermore rapidly, although many enterprises are still coming to terms with the necessary organizational and linguistic conversion or consolidation after mergers or takeovers.

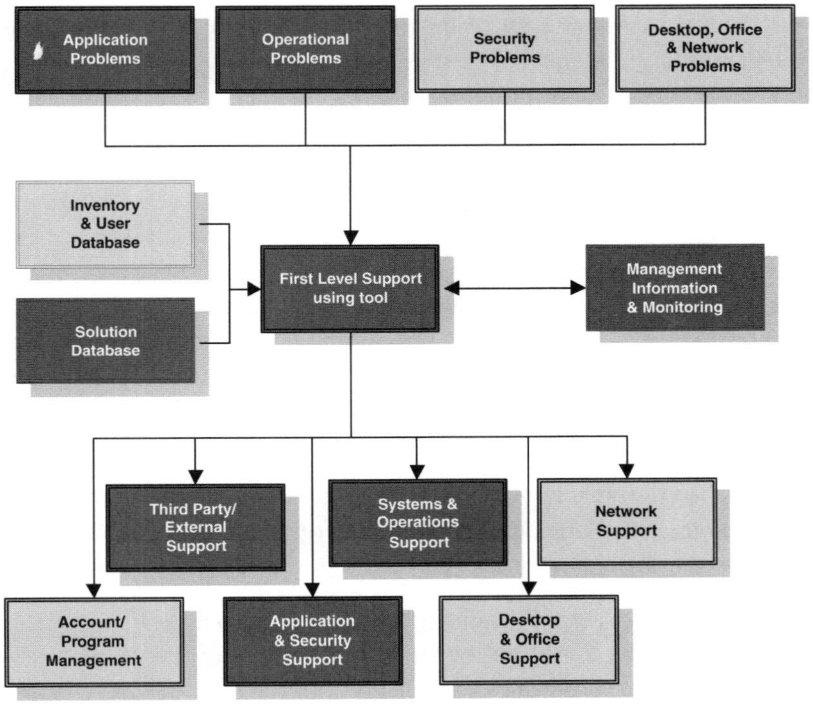

Figure 4.6 Structure and Tasks of a Support Organization

Structure

Figure 4.6 shows a simplified structure, typical for those commonly found in the SAP support environment. In general, however, only the dark areas in the graphic are considered in planning, as they are typical structures in SAP support. The First Level Support logs application or operational problems, tries to resolve them, and forwards them to the appropriate higher support level if required. During the problem resolution, external support from hardware or software suppliers is called in if necessary. Sometimes internal solution databases or third-party solution databases are used in the problem-solving process. It is often difficult to consider users as key to the support organization. In principle, however, they constitute an integral part of support, even if their responsibility is primarily business-oriented and they can provide assistance only based on their availability.

Integrated View Because of the integration of system and business processes, you cannot consider support solely in terms of SAP. Other applications are linked to SAP via interfaces; the SAP GUI as a front-end application must be supported when necessary; and this, in turn, is linked with a network (LAN, or, WAN, if necessary in multiple business locations). When designing and optimizing the support organization and the support processes, you must have an integral view of the system and business processes as a whole, so that problems won't arise later due to incomplete processes, and media failures of insufficient interfaces between the support organizations. When developing support organizations, don't forget to consider the Account or Service Level Management: a team made up of support employees and customers, which plays a vital role in the event of new requirements or changes. The integration of a user and inventory database often poses a great challenge. The data required is usually inconsistent, incomplete, or distributed across different platforms or databases. To collect and clean this data and ensure that it is consistent can be very time-consuming; all too often, support organizations must therefore implement interim solutions.

The Service and Support processes, as used by ITIL and made available as Best Practices, make up the content of the following sections. Our goal is to list and provide a brief introduction to all relevant Service and Support processes. For a detailed description of these sources, see Appendix A.

The ITIL processes are subdivided into the areas *Service Support* and *Service Delivery*. After them, we list the IT infrastructure management processes, which you should also consider in optimization projects.

Service Support

The area of *service support* describes both the processes for the support and operation of IT services and also how they are prepared for users and customers:

- **Service Desk**
  The *Service Desk* is the first point of contact in the IT organization for the user. In addition to the recording, processing, and monitoring of malfunctions, the Service Desk supports the different Service and Support processes. ITIL considers the Service Desk to be an independent organizational unit or function and not a self-contained process as is ITIL.

- **Incident Management**
  ITIL differentiates between malfunctions and problems. The advantage of this distinction is that the quick restoration of the IT service and the search for and removal of the cause of a failure are done independently of one another.

  Incident Management tries to remedy breakdowns immediately and to restore the IT service as quickly as possible. Faults are recorded and the quality of the information recorded is instrumental in the effectiveness of other processes (such as Problem Management).

- **Problem Management**
  Problem Management analyzes the causes of failures and also monitors the structural difficulties in the IT structure.

  If, via the analysis, the root of a problem is uncovered, then a business decision is made as to how the cause should be removed or if measures to improve the IT infrastructure are necessary to avoid further breakdowns. The recommendations are then forwarded to Change Management in a Request for Change (RfC).

- **Configuration Management**
  Configuration Management monitors the current status of a constantly changing IT infrastructure. It is also responsible for defining what are known as *configuration elements* (inventory, mutual relations, verification, and registration), collecting and managing documentation, and plans for the IT infrastructure and providing information for other processes.

- **Change Management**
  Change Management plays a central role in all system environments and especially in the SAP environment with numerous systems and dependencies. Change Management monitors the planning and controlled execution of changes within the IT infrastructure. Change Management experts must determine what changes are necessary and foremost, how these changes should be implemented without causing further disruptions or even breakdowns. A request for changes comes from the customer organization, Problem Management, or various other processes. In collaboration with status monitoring in Configuration Management, the planned and agreed upon changes are then implemented following a set sequence.

- **Release Management**
  A *release* is a combination of different hardware and software elements of a particular version that have been successfully tested together and

should be transferred to the production environment together. The successful implementation of releases, including the necessary integration of tests and the security of changes, is the main objective of *Release Management*. Release Management is therefore also responsible for ensuring that only the correct versions of released programs and systems are made available. Release Management must be very closely dovetailed with Configuration and Change Management.

Service Delivery

The processes that are important to a company for planning and providing IT services are described in the area of *Service Delivery*, along with the prerequisites and measures needed for them.

- **Service Level Management**
  Knowledge of the requirements, how much the customers want to spend, and the capabilities of the IT organization form the basis of Service Level Management. Based on this knowledge, Service Level Management decides on *Service Level Agreements* (SLAs) with the customer and then coordinates the implementation of these agreements.

  Successful Service Level Management is based on a strong orientation to the needs and information requirements of the customer and not on technical possibilities. The principle tasks of Service Level Management are:

  - The continuous coordination of IT services with the customer
  - The recording of business agreements in an SLA
  - The monitoring of the IT services
  - The safeguarding of IT services with appropriate agreements with internal (OLA, Operation Level Agreement) and external (UC, Underpinning Contract) service providers.

- **Financial Management for IT Services**
  Financial Management for IT Services is responsible for the tenable specification of IT services. From a business management viewpoint, by looking at the cost structure of the services, financial management for IT services can specify an optimal price/performance or cost/benefit ratio when new services or changes to existing services are agreed on.

  To discover the root of these costs, financial management for IT services must permanently identify the relevant cost pools, assign the appropriate IT services, monitor costs and prepare them, based on forecasts and financial planning or cost estimates.

Increasingly, financial management for IT services is required to help develop concepts for allocating and passing on service charges in the SAP environment. The objective is to generate greater cost-transparency and to move away from the allocation of overhead costs to a more expense-related allocation of costs. Simple models are based on the apportionment of costs per user, per department, or per business area. More complex models use benchmarking to determine the cost-generating transactions in the SAP system and then use intelligent reporting to allocate the costs according to level of use by these transactions. Other models are based on the accounting model from the mainframe world, with costs allocated according to degree of CPU usage. Unfortunately, for every intelligent accounting model, there are loopholes and alternatives, therefore, usually a combination of fixed and variable costs is selected.

- **Capacity Management**
  The main task of *Capacity Management* is to optimize the use of IT resources on the basis of agreements with the ordering party. This includes the administration of resources, the management and optimization of performance, support for capacity requirements to avoid bottlenecks, and help with the dimensioning of applications and systems. The key task of Capacity Management is—without a doubt—medium- and long-term capacity planning in order to prevent bottlenecks and achieve or maintain service levels.
- **Availability Management**
  The goal of *Availability Management* is to ensure the availability of IT services, as agreed on with customers, using all necessary means, methods, and technologies. Availability Management is critical in the SAP environment because almost all productive systems must meet high-availability demands. Today, availability planning can no longer be limited to individual systems; instead, we must ensure the availability of business processes. As business processes can take place over several systems or even over the Internet, the demands made on design and especially on maintenance can be very high. For this reason, Availability Management is particularly concerned with optimizing maintenance and using measures to minimize the effects of malfunctions. This objective requires a collaboration with Problem Management and Change Management so that the underlying causes of even seemingly minor malfunctions can be detected.

- **Security Management**
  Security Management protects the IT infrastructure from misuse and unauthorized data access. The activities of Security Management are based on the security requirements in the SLAs, on agreements in contracts, on legal requirements, or on the strategic stipulations of the enterprise.
- **Continuity Management for IT Services**
  Continuity Management for IT Services is responsible for planning and ensuring the availability of IT services in the event of catastrophes. Continuity Management for IT Services is based on an enterprise's availability requirements regarding all process flows that are necessary for business and organization in the event of serious malfunctions. Continuity Management for IT Services is responsible for planning and implementing technical, financial, and organizational measures. Therefore, it is a necessary process to ensure the level of continuity of IT services agreed on with the customer after the occurrence of problems.

IT Infrastructure Management

As we mentioned at the beginning of this chapter, you cannot consider Service and Support processes only when looking at SAP applications and SAP systems. Instead, you must consider the entire system and application environment in order to cover all aspects of application support and the operational running of the system.

Now, we shall briefly describe the operative processes of IT infrastructure management. In contrast to the processes inherent in *Service Support* and *Service Delivery*, the operative processes have not yet been documented. The IT Infrastructure Management book is currently being written and will soon be published by the ITIL organization.

- **Network Services Management**
  Network Services Management monitors the planning and control of communication networks, which includes telephone systems, and LAN and WAN networks. This process focuses on the medium- and long-term communication requirements of an enterprise and works in close collaboration with Capacity Management.

  Network Services Management is becoming increasingly important as the internal and external integration of systems and the tighter cooperation among individual enterprise sections place very high demands on the planning and implementation of communication networks. Concurrently, the technology used is also developing rapidly.

- **Operations Management**
  Operations Management specializes in the operation and management of systems (hardware) and base programs (system software). Before, the main focus of Operations Management used to be on production tasks in an environment with large-scale computer systems. Now, however, increasingly more SAP systems are expanding to these dimensions and therefore need similar structures to operate and control process flows. Thus, Operations Management is becoming increasingly important.

  Today, it is common for large corporate groups to outsource system operations. Here, it is advisable to outsource clearly described procedures and standardized processes to external partners while ensuring that the planning and support of business requirements and processes are done in-house. The operation of large and highly-available SAP systems in system groups requires a high degree of specialist knowledge and the availability of the Service and Support processes at all times.
- **Environmental Management**
  Environmental Management is usually linked directly with Operations Management. Per ITIL, Environmental Management refers to the planning of environmental conditions for the IT infrastructure such as buildings and accommodations, power, air-conditioning systems, and so on. The main task of this process is to prepare Best Practices for setting up and maintaining computer and network spaces according to the guidelines in place.
- **Management of Local Processors**
  Management of Local Processors monitors the increasingly important management and planning of IT systems at distributed and decentralized locations. The main focus in this process is the provision and support of IT services on site for customers or users. The coordination and agreement of central and local activities and the assignment of roles and responsibilities determine the availability of IT services and the level of customer satisfaction. In distributed organizations, it is essential that the flow of information between the business locations, the Service and Support teams, and the processes runs smoothly because often it is only during the Problem Management process that the actual responsibilities can be determined.
- **Computer Installation and Acceptance**
  Given the increasing integration and networking of systems and the associated high demands made on the specification and quality of subsystems (also, for example, the user's PC), detailed planning and test-

ing are required for new projects and before modifications are introduced to existing projects. The *Computer Installation and Acceptance* process is specifically designed to meet these requirements. Its main task is to establish the guidelines for planning the acceptance, the installation, and later, the removal of computer systems within the enterprise IT infrastructure. Usually, these guidelines are the result of activities from the Change Management and Release Management processes.

- **Applications Management**
  Applications Management provides Best Practices for the management of the software lifecycle and, in particular, for software lifecycle support and software testing. One of the main tasks of Applications Management is to spot changes, trends, and standards in the sector and to respond to them accordingly. The main focus here is on the clear formulation of requirements, followed by the implementation of a solution for the user, which is customized, as needed, to meet these requirements.

  - **Software Lifecycle Support**
    In an environment of highly integrated systems, *Software Lifecycle Support* is critical. Here, decisions are made as to how programs are designed, created, tested, implemented, maintained, and finally, rejected or replaced. The areas responsible for software development must then, together with Software Lifecycle Support, determine binding specifications for all work done during the entire lifecycle of the program. Agreements are also required between the development and use of the software. The choice of model for Software Lifecycle Support can have a direct influence on the IT service.

  - **Testing an IT Service for Operational Use**
    The operation of integrated and distributed systems places high demands on the testing of new or changed processes before they can be used in production operation. The process of *Testing an IT Service for Operational Use* ensures that system, installation, and acceptance tests are carried out to guarantee functionality, faultless installation, and integration with the appropriate infrastructure. The main focus here is to ensure that the user gets the required and contractually agreed upon functions.

4.2.3 Tools and Technology

The Service Desk as an independent function, as described in the area of *Service Support*, should support the enterprise and its users and support employees with the appropriate tools and technologies.

Investments in tools and technology require strategic and technical planning based on existing and future demands for supporting business processes.

Requirements for Tools

Today, tools and technology for the Service Desk environment have to meet the following demands:

- Support for application and operational support
- CTI (Computer Telephony Integration) functions and support for VoIP (Voice over IP)
- Interactive Voice Response (IVR) systems
- Integration of mail systems
- Support for fax servers for calling up and distributing information
- Integration of Unified Messaging and Mobile Services
- Provision of solution databases and search functions as well as tools for automatic diagnostics
- Integration of network and system-monitoring tools

The support of a Service Desk determines the efficiency, quality, and cost-effectiveness of a support organization. Thanks to easy access to existing solutions, history data, and management information, the processing of malfunctions, problems, and changes with a tool allows for fast and high-quality support.

Today's Service Management systems control, track, and monitor service requirements, contractual obligations, resource management, and decisive workflows. They also safeguard integration with other service components such as equipment and user management, controlling, and tools from the operational and network environments.

Advantages

The use of Service Management Tools can generate the following advantages:

- Access to all current and past malfunctions and requirements for all Service and Support employees
- Higher throughput of malfunctions and demands

- Improved tracing of malfunctions and requirements thanks to automated workflows and, if necessary, escalation mechanisms
- Improved and faster access to internal and external solution databases
- More precise management information and consequently, better planned security and decision-making support
- No duplicate processing or loss of incidents
- Easier assistance for complex support tasks and calculations
- Incidents are no longer linked to key persons
- The electronic storage of all incidents and worksteps, therefore, they can be forwarded to different support units at any time

Requirements and Factors Critical to Success

Even if the tools available today appear to meet many of the requirements listed, additional prerequisites still need to be checked before enabling the use of these tools, especially in large and distributed environments:

- To what extent does the tool support the high demands placed on the Service and Support process?
- Is the quality of the tool and its manufacturer supported with suitable references?
- Will the basic requirements be supported by the tool without major adjustments?
- In view of future enhancements, is the tool flexible enough, i.e., by providing (standardized) interfaces, for example:
    - Email and other communication systems?
    - Web interfaces?
    - Integration of monitoring and automation tools?
- Does it support different platforms, databases, multiple languages, and character sets at the same time?
- Are resources (in-house or external) available for planning, implementing, and operating the solution?
- Are the costs of buying and running the solution proportionate to the requirements and the usefulness of the solution?
- Can existing operating models be used, conditional upon the use of the same technology (for example, databases)?
- Does the tool support distribution to different frontends in different business locations via WAN/LAN lines? Can the existing infrastructure

be used for this? Does it support all technologies and network protocols used in the enterprise in all business locations?

- Can the tool exchange incidents with other tools or multiple instances? Unidirectional and bidirectional?
- Are the company's security specifications supported (especially regarding systems containing personal data)?
- Is the tool sufficiently scalable to meet potential future demands?
- Are external employees or parties integrated or supported by the interfaces in question, today and in the future?

Checking the currently used or planned Service Management Tools for compliance with the criteria listed and in consideration of current, and especially future demands, is an important pillar of any optimization project.

Large SAP applications over distributed locations can no longer be managed without the support of one tool or a combination of tools. This is true for the processing of malfunctions and problems, but it is especially accurate for the increasingly complex and critical changes to systems.

4.3 Examples and Scenarios

This section contains examples and scenarios for optimizing Service and Support concepts.

4.3.1 Optimization Project

Given the various technical possibilities of the SAP Solution Manager, the question of how to approach an optimization project arises time and again. The SAP Customer Competence Center (CCC) originated in an effort to meet the key challenge of saving costs while providing better support for more users 24/7, in addition to monitoring the current system landscape and analyzing new tools and systems regarding their usability.

Despite this added pressure, don't be tempted to tackle everything at once. On the one hand, each change creates a lot of work for the Support Organization by tying up resources and because of the time involved. Furthermore, optimizing a single support process, for example—or even introducing a new tool—has so many implications for other processes and the support organization, that most project organizations are overtaxed and projects fail or don't produce the desired results.

Analysis Before the actual optimization project, an analysis should therefore be carried out to determine where most of the effort is needed. The basis for this analysis can be the individual processes in ITIL, as described above. The support organization often knows, without a detailed analysis, where the problems and weaknesses lie. When performing an analysis, having external consultants involved can be advantageous because it may be easier for them to articulate problems and weaknesses, notwithstanding political aspects and power struggles.

Many Service and Support organizations for SAP systems have evolved over time, emerged from the project organization of an SAP implementation project, worked closely with users for a long duration, and then moved on to form a separate support organization. Throughout, however, the close relationship between users and support employees that was already in place has been maintained. Consequently, the support organization is often not divided into different support levels to address specific issues of incident or problem management. Typically, users want to have dedicated support employees assigned to their specific problems, out of concern that they might not get the personal attention they need and, consequently, their call for help might go unaddressed. However, only if this division (user/support employee) is made, can longer support times be achieved and virtual support organizations be established to monitor a distributed system landscape. To support this approach, an appropriate tool is needed, which all support employees can use to help with problem management.

Implementation Project Based on experience from optimization projects, many SAP CCCs have begun to introduce a support tool that specializes in supporting SAP systems to optimize the incident and problem management process. After it has been successfully designed, implemented, and rolled-out in other organization divisions or locations, the optimization of the change management process must then occur. Optimizing other processes then follows in several partial stages, depending on the degree of maturity of the service and support organization.

From past experience, we know that the implementation of an SAP Solution Manager and the mapping of the problem management process takes three to six months. Most of this time is needed to carry out a comprehensive as-is analysis and to define the target processes and requirements. The actual implementation of the tool and the technical reproduction of the problem management process often takes only a few weeks. Then, a lot of time is required for comprehensive tests, the orientation and training of key personnel and support employees, and selling the solution within the enterprise—something which should not be underestimated.

In the following sections, the optimization focal points mentioned are listed together with their most important elements and key performance indicators.

4.3.2 Service Desk

The implementation of a *Service Desk* in the SAP support environment is critical to the success of an optimization project, since the support of large, distributed SAP landscapes makes particular demands on the Service and Support process.

Maximizing the use of tools, such as those used in the Office support environment, for example, quickly reaches its limit in the area of SAP support. Many companies and support organizations have already realized that the extensive use of mail systems and user-developed databases is no longer sufficient to meet today's high support requirements.

SAP Solution Manager

The *SAP Solution Manager* is designed, among other things, to help with the Service and Support of SAP systems. It has many functions and options that cater explicitly to the needs of SAP systems and their operation and support. In addition, the Support Desk, which is an important component of the SAP Solution Manager, can be adjusted to meet the individual requirements of a support organization. The integrated Solution Database can also support the information requirements of a distributed and multifaceted support organization. Because the SAP Solution Manager can be seamlessly integrated into the SAP environment—thanks to the use of standard SAP technologies—you can align the Service and Support process with ITIL Best Practices. In fact, in a large decentralized SAP environment, the SAP Solution Manager is indispensable when it comes to providing fast and high-quality support.

A Service Desk should fulfil the following requirements to ensure that the support organization can be guaranteed optimal technical support.

Functional Requirements

The functional requirements are:

- An easy-to-use tool for both the user and the support employee
- Multi-level support structures (for example, key user, multiple support levels, external support, and so on)
- Workflows that help to facilitate the automatization of standardized process flows

- Integration in the SAP environment that enables the easy access of information stored elsewhere (for example, user data, asset management)
- Flexible mapping of the support organization that allows for the easy implementation of changes and substitutions
- Structuring escalation management to support both functional (forwarding to the next support level) and hierarchical (management information) escalation
- A compilation of evaluations and reports with access to information stored in problem tickets
- Integration of a solution database with interfaces to maintain and transfer information from external sources
- Integration of processes with external support organizations such as SAPNet R/3 Frontend or suppliers' support departments
- The automatic recording of all activities for processing malfunctions and problems
- Extensive search functions with previously solved problems to help resolve problems faster
- The possibility of defining an authorization concept to delimit support organizations from each other (this is particularly important for the support of personnel systems)
- Interfaces to the Internet so that, for example, information can also be displayed using a browser, and status information for distributed or approval workflows can be reproduced over the Internet

Technical Requirements

The technical requirements are:

- The simple integration of the Service Desk into the standardized operation of SAP systems (monitoring, maintenance, backup, and so on)
- High-system scalability regarding disk space and system performance
- Support of several platforms (hardware, operating system, and database) to maintain own standards
- Optional system enhancements with high availability
- Complete integration in the SAP environment and support for all SAP releases and components
- Extensive interfaces to other systems for exchanging problem tickets and status information

- Interfaces to systems involved in system operation, so that, for example, in the event of problems, or if threshold values are exceeded, information can be sent quickly and automatically to the Service Desk and to incident management
- A frontend that is easy to install and maintain via a user-specific GUI, or a browser to also support access to the system via WAN connections (between business locations or home office)
- Support of numerous languages and code pages at the same time (this is vital for global support organizations)

Other Requirements

The other requirements to keep in mind are:

- High-investment protection due to the use of a standardized tool that can also be extended and maintained in the future
- Possibilities for the simple maintenance and, if necessary, individual customizing of the tool by company employees
- The Service Desk should be easy to extend so that it can be adjusted to meet the requirements of the company
- The tool should offer an optimal cost-benefit ratio for the implementation and operation of the solution

The SAP Solution Manager with the SAP Support Desk fulfils the requirements listed above to a large extent and currently offers most advantages for supporting SAP environments.

4.3.3 Incident and Problem Management

An optimized incident and problem management process should fulfil the following requirements:

- Proactive monitoring of all important IT components such as the availability of systems and sub-systems, interfaces, batch jobs, and so on.
- The automatic generation of problem tickets when problems are identified or threshold values are exceeded
- Assistance for support employees via the creation of an incident or problem ticket with automatic completion of information (for example, integration of telephone switches, automatic context information with support messages from an SAP system)
- Automation of processes, such as feedback or questions for users, sending status mails, changing message status, forwarding to other support teams, employees, or external support organizations

- Automatic recording of all activities when analyzing or processing a message
- The flexible development of escalation management: Escalation in clearly defined cases only and for defined processes, avoiding "information mails"
- Unambiguous assignment of incidents, problems, and solutions
- Integration of problem solving in message processing, for example, access to the SAP Service Marketplace from the Support Desk and transfer of solution suggestions from SAP directly to the problem ticket
- The simple classification of an incident (implication and priority), supported by the corresponding specifications and agreed on procedures, and by the Service Desk Tool
- The complete integration of message processing in one environment: The support employee should not have to leave message processing in the Service Desk environment at any time, for example, to write an email to a user
- The Service Desk Tool should support the clear classification of an incident or problem to the greatest possible extent (for example hardware, Office or SAP and other sub-categories such as system name or client and SAP module), so that, for example, it can be automatically forwarded to the support group responsible, based on existing information and classification
- Automatic acceptance or standardized transfer of problems and solutions to a solution database
- From problem processing, you should be able to generate a *Request for Change* (RfC) without recreating the ticket again. Then, you should be able to implement the RfC as appropriate, after acceptance by the responsible people for Change Management. For this, you must be able to clearly distinguish the relationship between problem and change management.
- When solving a problem, communication with the user should be integrated directly into problem processing. For example, after an email is sent directly to the user from message processing, the user must then be able to send the reply to a specific address so that it can be assigned directly to the message and the support employee can be informed of the feedback.

- Automatic monitoring of message processing in terms of adherence to agreed time limits or specific problems (system downtime, certain interfaces, and so on)
- Constant reports and reviews on the number and type of messages to identify trends from early on and to allow for the introduction of measures if necessary

The incident and problem management processes should not be analyzed during the introduction and optimization only; they should also be revised regularly (once a month) and inspected for problem areas. If changes are made to the business processes or the system landscape, or if new organization structures or employees are introduced, you may have to adjust the processes.

Fixed Targets

It might be helpful to set fixed targets against which the efficiency of processes can be measured and compared at any time. These targets may be different during implementation and optimization than during operation. If the actual performance levels don't meet the fixed targets, you must verify whether this is due to poor performance, or whether the targets need to be adjusted to reflect the new requirements.

Key Performance Indicators

The following *Key Performance Indicators* (KPIs) are intended to serve as an example:

- The number of problem tickets in relation to the following criteria:
    - Absolute number
    - Priority of the message
    - The system affected or problem category
    - SAP module
    - User's location
    - The problem ticket or user's language
    - Open and closed tickets over a particular period of time
    - Escalated tickets
    - Ratio of solutions per support level
- Time taken to process problem
    - Average processing time per priority class
    - Time taken per problem ticket and per SAP system (R/3, BW, APO, Portal, and so on)

- Time taken to process problem tickets per SAP system and per module
- Time taken to process problems related to individual developments or specific transactions

It is important to note that the KPIs mentioned can easily be misinterpreted. By no means, should they be used to gauge the competence of employees or to compare employees. Such practice could have a negative impact and lead to workarounds, resulting in further false evaluations.

5 Optimizing Business Processes

The pressure of competition means that all companies are constantly thinking about how they can optimize their goods and services. This chapter shows how you can optimize your business processes and which processes can be compared and integrated.

5.1 Methods and Approaches

In the early 1990s, the term *business process* was an integral point of discussion in business management literature. The radical concept of *business process reengineering*[1] generated many myths that repeatedly focused on downsizing, client-server computing, Total Quality Management (TQM), and so on. Today, the fever seems to have abated and there is a growing acceptance that business processes are an issue for management and as such, suitable process management must be adopted and implemented. Despite the radical BPR approach, companies have a wide range of different optimization approaches that can be characterized as irregular, incremental, or steady.

There is no question that IT is a driving force behind many methods for redesigning business processes. It would therefore seem logical to consider the subject of business process optimization against a background of IT use.

Business processes basically form part of strategy implementation in an enterprise. The strategy determines which services must be affected for which strategic business unit and certain business processes are instrumental in ensuring the implementation, with the support of information systems. These three levels influence each other in turn (see Figure 5.1). Not only does information technology allow you to automate business process flows; it also changes how people do business; for example, the technical process in which business takes place between companies changes (e.g., electronic invoicing), as does the relationship between companies and people when they are conducting business transactions (e.g., a company presents its products to a wider range of customers via the Internet). The redesign of business processes is then reflected in new strategies.

1 Hammer, Michael; Champy, James: *Reengineering the Corporation. A Manifesto for Business Revolution*. 4th Ed., Harper Business 1993

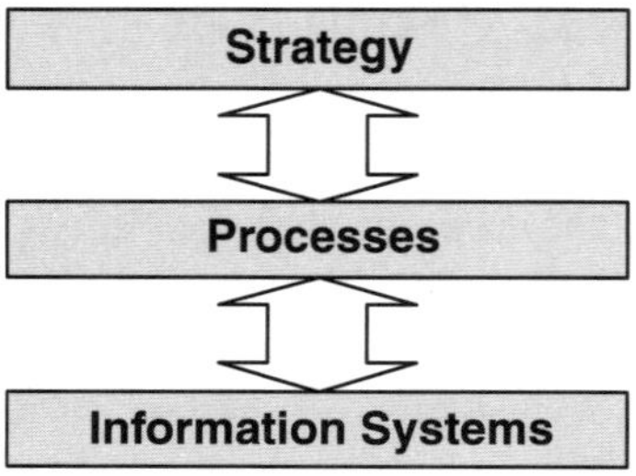

Figure 5.1 Strategy, Processes, and Information Systems

Optimization Strategies

The different strategies for optimizing business processes occur at different places within the hierarchy shown (see Figure 5.2).

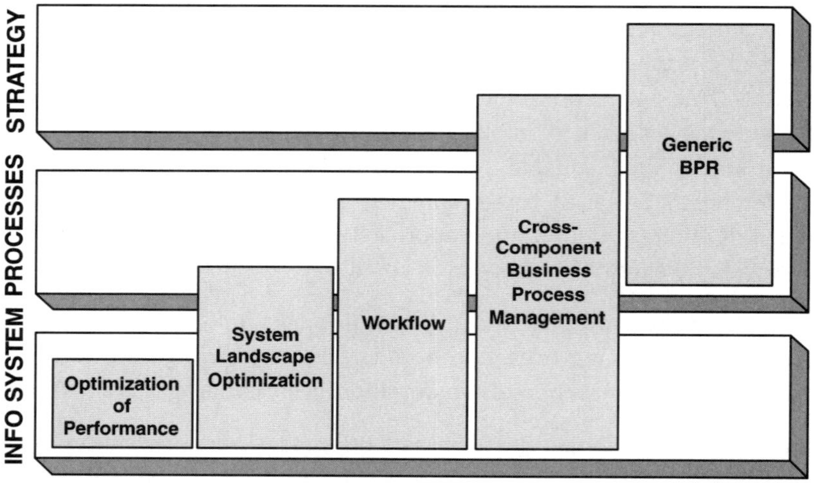

Figure 5.2 Strategies for Optimizing Business Processes

- **Performance Optimization**
  The quality of business process handling is greatly influenced by the performance of mySAP system support. The SAP Solution Manager is the instrument used to monitor system and process performance (System Monitoring, Interface Monitoring, Business Process Monitoring, and Service Level Reporting) and it prepares the necessary system and application tuning measures (see Section 5.2).
- **System Landscape Optimization (SLO)**
  Significant structural changes in the enterprise and efforts to consolidate the IT organization of an enterprise can result in the need to adjust the mySAP system landscape. To do this, you can use special procedures and software tools (see Section 5.3).

- **Business Workflow/WebFlow**
  The automation of business processes using business Workflow/Web-Flow holds great optimization potential. Workflows are automated, electronic representations of business processes. They improve the speed, consistency, and quality of process handling (see Section 5.4).

- **Reverse Business Engineering**
  The *Reverse Business Engineer* (RBE) supports the analysis of SAP production systems. The RBE extracts data from SAP R/3 production systems, which describe the usage patterns of business processes and provide information on functions that have not yet been used. You can use the RBE analysis as a starting point for an optimization project (see Section 5.5).

- **SAP Exchange Infrastructure**
  The SAP Exchange Infrastructure (XI) enables the integration of business processes outside application and enterprise boundaries (see Section 5.6).

- **Generic Process Redesign**
  Because business process redesign isn't linked to the availability of a particular technology, we will look at generic process redesign techniques as well (see Section 5.7).

5.2 Performance Optimization

The performance of a data-processing system is defined by data throughput and response time. Optimizing the performance of existing systems is the first step in optimizing business processes. This doesn't change the structure of the business process, but it does enhance performance, which is imperative if you are to optimize your business processes.

Performance optimization can be divided into two categories:

- **Technical Tuning**
  Technical tuning enables you to adjust the operating system, the database, the application server, and the network so that the load created by users is distributed optimally over the system and performance bottlenecks are avoided.

- **Application Tuning**
  Application tuning examines how resources are used by applications (main memory consumption, CPU usage, I/O activity). Performance problems can sometimes occur as a result of customizing the SAP standard functions; however, they are most often due to customer-defined

ABAP developments and modifications, which are usually done hurriedly and are tested for functionality only and not for performance.

Figure 5.3 shows an example of the relative optimization potential that can be achieved.

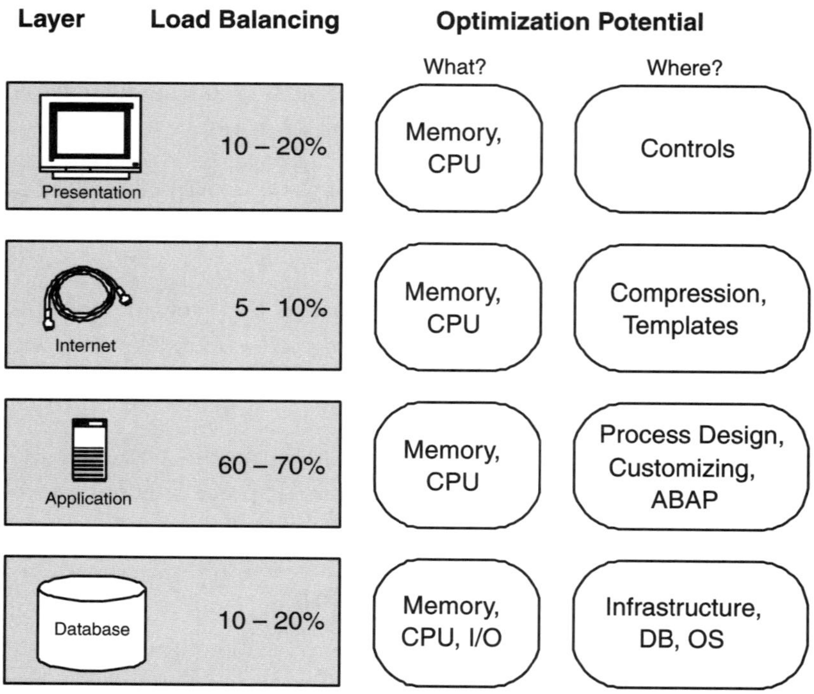

Figure 5.3 Performance Optimization Potential

There are always three steps involved in implementing performance-tuning measures:

- Analysis and identification of the problem
- Implementation of tuning measures
- New analysis and confirmation that the problem has been resolved

You can use the Computer Center Management System (CCMS), which is a part of SAP Basis or the SAP Web Application Server (SAP Web AS), to monitor, control, and configure the SAP system. The CCMS provides an entire range of powerful monitoring programs to oversee the system.

Monitors for Technical Analysis	
Global work process overview (SM50)	Capacity load of work processes for all instances active in the system; identification of locks in the database
System load monitor (ST03N or ST03)	Analyzes the statistical data of the SAP kernel; overview of load distribution in the SAP R/3 system
Global system load monitor (ST03G)	Analyzes statistical data from SAP and non-SAP systems
Operating-system monitor (OS07 or ST06)	Utilization of the CPU and the physical main memory based on data from the background collector SAPOSCOL
SAP buffer (ST02)	Fine-tuning the settings of the buffer (client cache)
Monitors for Application Analysis	
System load monitor (ST03N or ST03)	Identifies transactions and programs that—and users who—create high-system load
Application monitor (ST07)	Analysis of resource usage per R/3 module
SQL trace (ST05); ABAP trace (SE30)	Detailed analysis of database accesses and ABAP programs

Table 5.1 SAP R/3 Performance Monitors

When optimizing, you should note that runtimes can differ greatly within the runtime environment. Runtimes in the application server are about 10 times faster than they are between the application server and the database server; runtimes between the database server and the database are 10 times slower. From these varying runtimes, we can deduce that the number of database accesses is critical to performance. However, programming can also improve performance, for example, data selection with a correctly formulated `WHERE`-statement and the use of database indices. You will find a detailed description of the possibilities of performance optimization in Schneider 2003.[2]

Classical system monitoring is increasingly reaching its limits. The mySAP system landscape is made up of a growing number of components (SAP R/3, mySAP CRM, SAP APO, ITS, and so on), some of which are based on SAP Basis (R/3, CRM, APO), some without SAP Basis (ITS, BC), and a third group are made up of software products from third-party suppliers. Each

2 Schneider, Thomas: *SAP Performance Optimization Guide. Analyzing and Tuning SAP Systems*. 3rd Ed., SAP PRESS 2003

component uses its own administration and monitoring tools. The tasks in business processes are increasingly spread over several systems and therefore, the separate monitoring of systems can no longer ensure the accurate execution of business processes. IT departments are faced with increasing fragmentation—additional and more intricate components need to be monitored, the know-how for developing and operating these components is more complex—all of this and a diminishing IT budget.

Consequently, SAP no longer speaks of System Monitoring, but of *Solution Monitoring*. This concept includes the following key points:

- It is no longer sufficient to monitor only individual hardware and software components; the flow of information all along an entire business process, via several software components, is integral to monitoring and optimization.
- Availability, performance, correct execution, and security must be monitored.
- It is necessary to differentiate between real-time monitoring (spotting problems as they occur (alerts), getting to the source of the error and eliminating the problem) and long-term monitoring (service level reporting, monitoring performance indicators, and so forth).

The central instruments for solution monitoring are the CCMS and the *SAP Solution Manager*. These instruments can be used to centrally monitor SAP systems and non-SAP systems (System Monitoring), business processes and interfaces (Business Process Monitoring), and measure them against predefined performance indicators (Service Level Reporting).

All monitoring data is recorded by the CCMS and can then be assigned to a system, an interface, or a process step. Therefore, in the SAP Solution Manager GUI, you can easily detect where a problem has arisen in the system landscape or in the process chain. Monitoring data can also be imported from or exported to system management products from other suppliers, provided that the third-party supplier supports the interface to the CCMS. This does not mean, however, that system management tools from third-party suppliers can be completely replaced by the SAP Solution Manager. Instead, it means that these tools from outside vendors should be integrated.

SAP offers services to support performance analysis and improvement, for example, the Early Watch Service or the GoingLive Check.

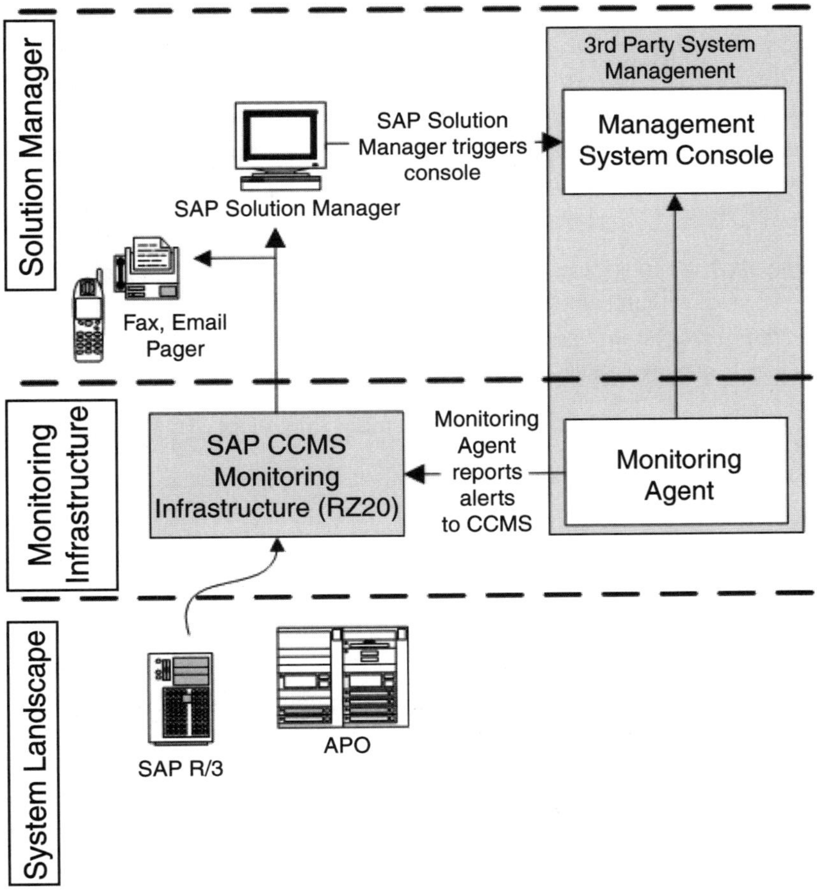

Figure 5.4 Interaction of the SAP Solution Manager with a Third-Party System

5.3 System Landscape Optimization (SLO)

mySAP production system landscapes frequently need to be restructured into a larger environment because of changes in the enterprise. This requires new approaches and services.

5.3.1 Reasons for SLO

Many companies have built up complex mySAP system landscapes over time, which must ensure information processing to support their business processes. The availability and performance of these solutions is an absolute prerequisite for meeting the daily business requirements and therefore, forms the basis for strategic and operative decision-making.

Market Requirements as a Trigger

Global competitive pressure means that enterprise services are increasingly offered world-wide, service efficiency must be constantly improved, and enterprises must often be restructured in a very short time. Enterprises are bought and sold, divisions are spun off, function areas are restructured, business processes are fundamentally changed. Coupled with these external factors is the growing internal concern of rising IT costs.

Effects on the System Landscape

Changes in the enterprise will, of course, mean that adjustments must be made to the system too. SLO defines the procedures and tools for making these adjustments within the mySAP landscape. SLO is also based on converting the system landscape, not reactively in response to a trigger event, but methodically via an architectural restructuring.

SLO Scenarios

The following scenarios represent the main triggers of SLO projects:

- Integrating enterprises
- Spinning off enterprises
- Restructuring enterprises
- Optimizing business processes
- Consolidating IT system landscapes

We will address these scenarios in greater detail in the next section.

5.3.2 Key Aspects of SLO

Now, we'll look at the main triggers of SLO and analyze the strategies for each:

- **Integrating Enterprises**
  When an enterprise is bought, a decision must be made as to whether the enterprise data of the newly acquired company should be integrated into the existing information systems. Frequently, the existing solution in the newly acquired company is left in place; however, the disadvantages of this decision soon become apparent. Internal communication is more difficult; it is very laborious to try to compare data; and, the administration of the corporate group suffers. In order to integrate data, you must convert the data in the newly acquired enterprise. For example, the new company often uses a different material numbering system than does the buyer, which ultimately must be changed.
- **Spinning off Enterprises**
  When an enterprise is sold, the data that belongs to this enterprise will have to be deleted from the SAP system of the corporate group. There are two ways to do this: You can export the data of the company sold

to a new client via data transfer, or, you can copy the entire client to a new system. The data that is no longer needed is deleted.

- **Restructuring Enterprises**
  An enterprise realizes that the currently used definition of controlling areas according to sales region is not constructive and wants to present cost accounting at the group level. To do so, the controlling areas must be brought together.
- **Optimizing Business Processes**
  An enterprise wants to abandon its practice of using different charts of accounts in favor of using a single chart of accounts. To do this, the accounts and the cost elements must be renamed or combined.
- **Consolidating IT System Landscapes**
  In large corporate groups, different SAP systems have been implemented in different business locations over time. To reduce IT costs, SAP systems are often consolidated. Thanks to the marked improvements in hardware and network solutions in recent years, this procedure is advisable. One way of consolidating IT SAP systems is to copy several clients to the same system, however, this dependency among the clients has certain disadvantages. It is preferable to integrate systems via migrating clients to a common target client. In order to do this, the data and processes must first be aligned. This unquestionably more complex scenario will be more useful for the company: Interfaces are no longer necessary, cross-company processing is made easier; additional systems—such as a fax-server—can be introduced consistently and the basis for future projects is the same throughout the corporate group.

5.3.3 Support Services and Software Tools

SAP offers services with the following focal points to support customer projects:

- **System Landscape Change Consulting**
  All change requirements in the system landscape—such as centralizing systems or spinning off companies from the system—are covered by this service. Examples include system or client consolidation or division.
- **Organizational Structure Change Consulting**
  Changes that affect the SAP organizational units—such as company codes in the controlling areas—are supported by this service. This would include, for example, merging company codes, deleting company codes, and merging, separating, or deleting controlling areas.

- **SAP Conversion Service**
  This service offers solutions for problems in the area of data changes. Examples include conversion of cost planning, business year conversions, converting material numbers, or customer numbers.

SAP provides two software tools for the technical conversion of SLO projects:

- Conversion Workbench (CWB)
- Migration Workbench (MWB)

Technical Conversion with Data Conversion

Conversion Workbench

The *Conversion Workbench* (CWB) prepares all the necessary conversion programs for all tables identified by the where-used list in the Data Dictionary (DDIC) that undertake data changes, for example, converting the number system of the material master. Data conversion is always done per table, directly on the database. After the conversion, only the changed values are available on the system and the system behaves as if the values have always appeared in this way. The conversion affects master data as well as transaction data and customizing data. With the CWB's help, you can convert standard tables and customer-defined tables automatically if the customer-defined tables reference SAP standard domains. A special solution must be developed for non-standard domains.

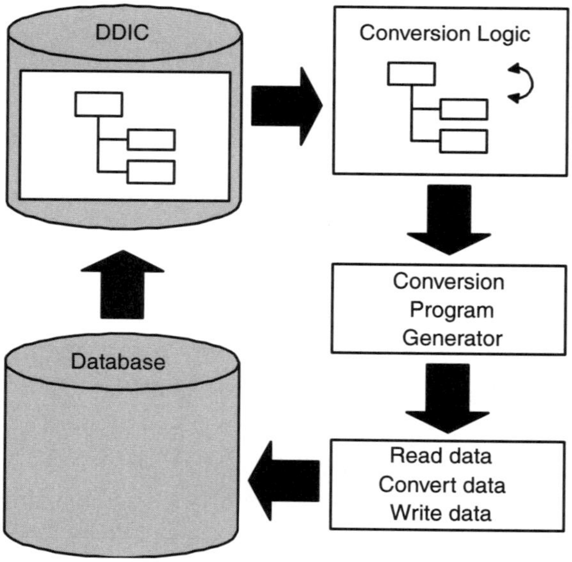

Figure 5.5 How the SAP Conversion Workbench Works

Impact and Limitations

If an SLO project uses the CWB to convert data, you should consider the following effects and limitations inherent with this method:

- A data conversion always applies to the entire data set. You cannot set restrictions such as "for specific business years," "from a certain date," or "for individual applications."
- The data conversion takes immediate effect on systems and applications that communicate with the system to be converted via interfaces (such as ALE).
- Archived data cannot be reloaded into the SAP system after the conversion.
- Authorizations and authorization objects are not converted and must be adjusted to the new conditions manually.
- Data from the HR (Human Resources) module is not converted.
- Data from sector solutions and from mySAP products is not converted.
- The size of the database to be converted will influence the runtime of the conversion. This can be an important limitation to converting the SAP production system.

You should also note that in addition to the database, you will have to customize the ABAP code that works with the data to be converted. Report variants and authorizations must also be adjusted.

Prerequisites for Executing the Project

To successfully execute the project, certain technical prerequisites must be met by users:

- The external auditor should be involved in the project from early on. The auditor defines the requirements for the documents in the data conversion. Generally, the system status before and after the conversion must be recorded, as DS: well as the exact conditions during the actual conversion (What is changed? Where and how?).
- User departments play an important role in what is otherwise a very technical project. The user departments define the data conversion rules, analyze the effects on the day-to-day activities, and are primarily responsible for specifying and running tests. You can confirm that the conversion has been executed correctly only by running tests.
- Conversion is first done on a test system. This should contain a recent copy of the data in the production system and the hardware dimensioning should mirror the productive environment. The test system is available only for the purposes of the conversion project. Parallel projects should not make any more changes to this system or to the production system.

- The production system will not be available during the productive conversion.
- You will have to do a data backup before the productive conversion.

New Areas of Application The tools provided by the conversion technology pave the way for new areas of application, for example, process template rollouts in productive systems can be simplified. A delta analysis shows what adjustments need to be made to the templates at the data level for productive use. The adjustments are then carried out by converting data.

Technical Conversion with Data Transfer

The *Migration Workbench* (MWB) allows you to transfer objects between different SAP systems. Such objects include business objects (sales orders and so on), organizational units, and clients. You can also use the MWB between different levels of the participating SAP systems.

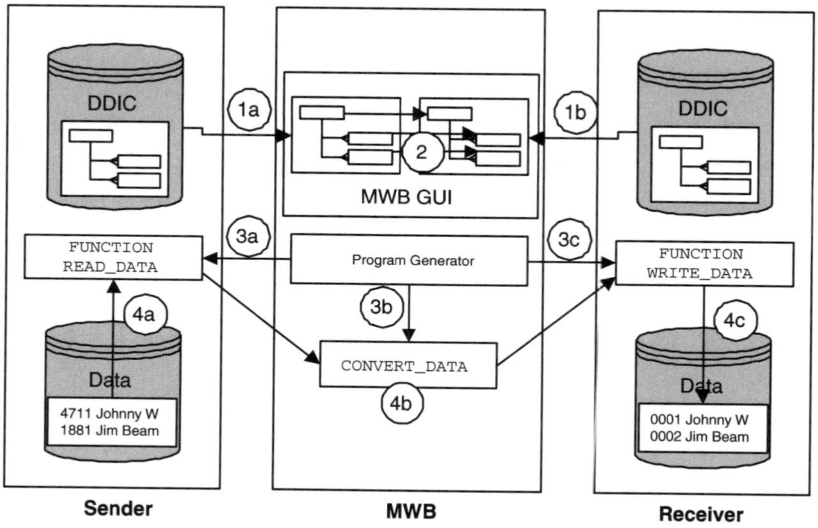

Figure 5.6 How the Migration Workbench Works

5.4 Business Workflow/WebFlow

5.4.1 What Is Business Workflow/WebFlow?

Workflow is the electronic presentation of a business process. The SAP workflow engine has been a component of the SAP Basis system since Release 3.0 and is available for most SAP components (R/3, CRM, EBP, and so on). It uses the existing transactions and functions in the SAP system without changing them. Workflows can be used to bring together existing SAP functions. The workflow forms an integration layer "on top of" the SAP standard functions.

How It Works

A workflow functions in approximately the following way:

- Workflows can be started by a user in dialog or by the SAP system automatically (by a trigger event). As soon as a task is queued for processing, it is aligned with (i.e., assigned) to the employee responsible.
- Tasks that don't require user interaction run in the background.
- The workflow contains the instructions and documents that are required to execute the task.
- The workflow shows what has to be done next, the exact status of the flow, and who did what and when.
- The workflow contains information on the times allowed for processing individual tasks and monitors the deadlines.
- The workflow provides all statistical data on the business process. This data can be analyzed, bottlenecks identified, and the process improved.

Since the introduction of the SAP Web Application Server (SAP Web AS), SAP uses the term *WebFlow* instead of Business Workflow, because workflows increasingly cross enterprise boundaries and integrate external partners into the process flow via the Internet. This includes the processing of the steps in a workflow with the help of a Web browser via XML integration of non-SAP systems.

5.4.2 Applications and Potential Use of Workflows

Examples for Using Workflows

The functions of the SAP system can be enhanced via the use of workflows. They can be used for various purposes. Examples include:

- **Distributing Information**
  - Information about a received sales order to a specific product group
  - Information about a goods receipt
  - Information about an exceptional situation, such as missed deadlines

  Potential Benefits:

  - Relevant information is immediately available
  - Quick reaction to results

- Processing time reduced
- Information flows secured

- **Authorization Procedure**
  - Approval of leave requests
  - Release of purchase requisitions
  - Release of incoming invoices with the help of scanned original invoices in the document management system

  Potential Benefits:

  - Reduction of processing time
  - Adherence to release guidelines
  - Secures the necessary release procedure

- **Data maintenance**
  - When creating material master data in the SAP system, data maintenance by the different departments can be supported in a workflow

  Potential Benefits:

  - Data consistency and the timely execution of data maintenance are ensured

Potential Benefit

The most important potential benefits of using workflows can be arranged in three categories:

- **Speed**
  The workflow sets who has to do what and in what order; this reduces the need to coordinate and control the people involved as well as the wait times, which determine the overall turnaround time of the process. Time is money and faster business processes are more cost-effective.

- **Consistency**
  The business process always runs according to the same plan. Steps cannot be bypassed or omitted.

- **Quality**
  The workflow can stipulate and monitor processing times so that tasks will not be left undone. The workflow provides the necessary instructions and documents for processing the task.

Workflow support is available for processes that are always executed in the same way and that involve many employees.

5.4.3 Technical Foundations

Definition

Before a workflow can be used, it must be defined in the Workflow Builder. The *Workflow Builder* is the central tool for creating, processing, and displaying a workflow definition. The workflow consists of different steps that are executed during runtime. The steps either control the workflow directly (loop, condition, and so on) or reference a task. The *task* is a basic business activity. Tasks always apply methods of an object type from the *Business Object Repository* (BOR). The object type describes the data with which the workflow is working (for example, material). It is made up of attributes that present data on the object type (such as material number), methods that determine the possible data processing (for example, create material), and events that define changes in the status of an object (for example, material changed). Tasks can be executed by a user in dialog mode or automatically by the SAP system in the background. Possible agents are assigned to the tasks. These agents are maintained in the *Organizational Management* component. The organizational plan in Organizational Management monitors task routing.

Execution

At runtime, the user receives information on the tasks (work items) to be carried out in the Business Workplace or in the iView *Universal Worklist* in the SAP Enterprise Portal. The *Business Workplace* is the interface between the user and the workflow system. The tasks assigned to the user—as recipient—generate work items in the user's workflow inbox. The work item shows the user that he or she has to do something; it also has direct access to and the necessary instructions for the planned way in which to carry out the work.

Let us take a closer look at the individual elements. The business process can be structured with the help of the following questions:

- In What Sequence?
- What?
- How?
- When?
- Who?

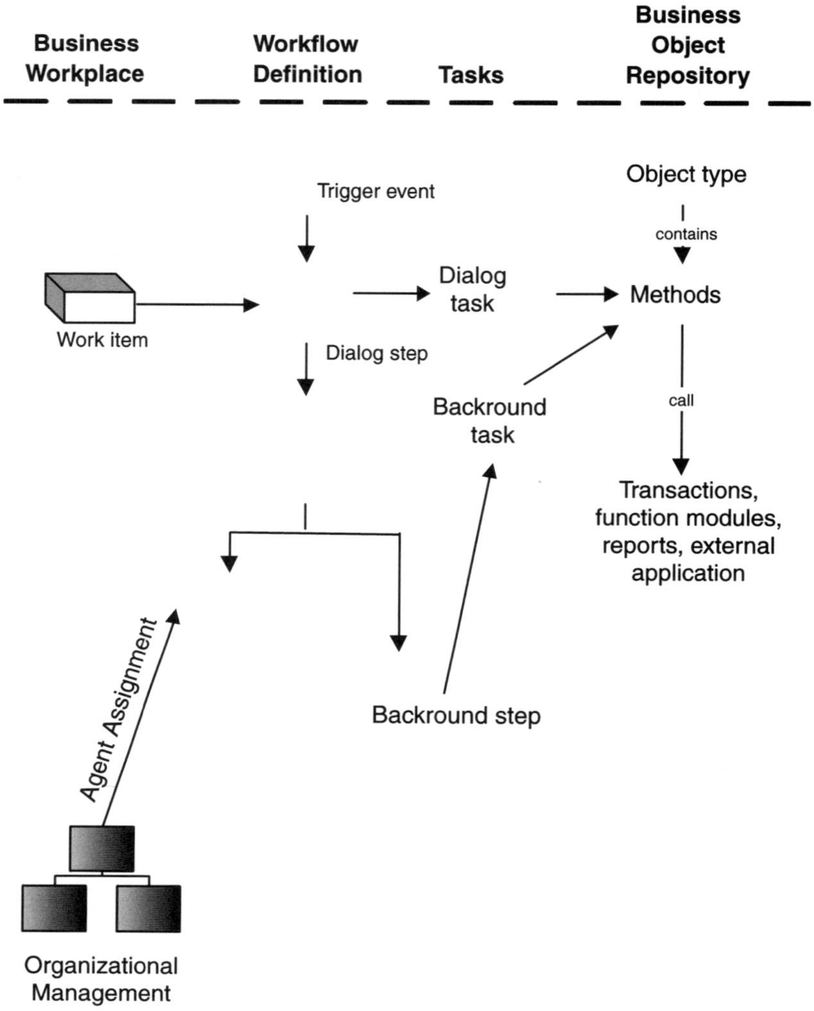

Figure 5.7 Technical Structure of the Workflow System

In What Sequence? The workflow definition controls the business process. The Workflow Builder is the central tool for defining, displaying, or changing a workflow. The workflow definition consists of a flow diagram that sets the sequence for the steps and the temporary data that is required to execute the workflow. The workflow container holds the temporary data (container elements). *Container elements* correspond to data that controls the workflow and data that should be forwarded from one step execution to another. The interface of the workflow is structured by container elements for which the import/export indicator is set. The individual steps in the workflow are either activities that refer to tasks or present control logic, for example, a user decision, or a loop condition, if a series of steps has to be executed several times. There can be single-step tasks that refer to an object method or multi-step tasks that refer to a workflow definition.

What? How?

The workflow consists of steps of different types. One group of step types sets the logical control of the workflow while the other groups monitor the actual business activity. The step types *Activity* and *Web activity* belong to the latter group. They reference tasks. The task may consist of calling a report, or executing a transaction, a function module, a routine in an external system, and a PC application. The task always refers to the methods of a business object in the Business Object Repository (BOR) and therefore uses SAP functions. The business analysis of tasks within the business process must therefore always be aligned with the available methods in the BOR. In most cases, you'll find a method that fits. If not, you must develop a new method for an existing object, or create a new object with its own methods. We should add that this type of workflow programming will greatly increase the work involved in the project. If you prefer quick and simple projects, you should use the SAP-predefined workflow templates.

When?

Workflows and tasks can react to events. An *event* can be generated by any application program and have a rippling effect throughout the system. Examples of event generation that can be read by the workflow include writing change documents, status changes, or triggering messages using message control; actual examples include canceling an order, changing a customer master data record, or authorizing a request. Any number of users can respond to these events. Events are used to start a workflow or a task, or to end a task. Data from an event is stored in the event container. If you have to define triggering or terminating events in a task, you must establish the data flow from the event container to the task container. The outbox of a step displays the different results for the methods used in the task, including exception situations.

Who?

Tasks are assigned to one or more possible agents, and each part of the organization plan relevant to task assignment must be stored in the system. For this, data must be maintained in the *Organizational Management* component. It is not absolutely necessary to use SAP HR, however, if Personnel Administration is already integrated with Organization Management, this structure can also be used for the workflow system. In this case, you would have to define both components in the same client because the Organizational Management settings are client-dependent. Maintenance in Organizational Management includes the following steps:

1. Create the organizational units, which can be departments, groups, or project teams. The top node in the tree structure is the root organizational unit.
2. Maintain the staff assignments of the organizational unit, that is, assign positions to the organizational units. A *position* refers to an actual post in the staffing assignment of an organizational unit that is to be occupied by a person. Each position is also linked with a job. The *job* is a general job description, containing general tasks that it passes on to positions. The position is then linked with the actual user—the position holder.
3. Lastly, link the workflows or tasks with the jobs, positions, or users.

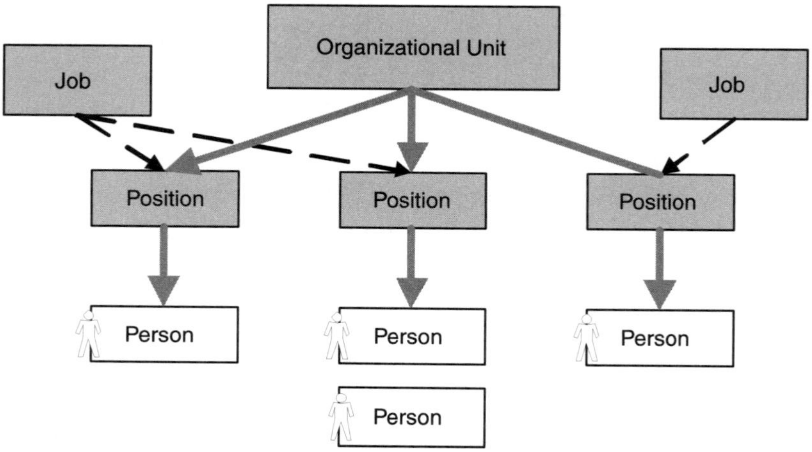

Figure 5.8 Organizational Management

Another control possibility for finding the agent responsible is to define rules that must be evaluated at runtime. For example, a rule can be used to determine the person responsible based on sales order data.

The SAP system already contains a lot of preconfigured workflows that can be used as-is or with just some minor adjustments. You can cover special requirements that aren't available in the standard by developing your own object types and object methods in the BOR.

5.4.4 Integration of Non-SAP Systems

The WebFlow function allows you to extend the workflow to inter-company processes via the Internet or intranet. The WebFlow function can generate an XML document for the data to be transferred and send it to another system. In this way, you can communicate and synchronize between workflow systems.

The transfer formats supported are:

- Wf-XML by Workflow Management Coalition (*www.wfmc.org*)
- SOAP Standard 1.1 from W3C (*www.w3c.org*)

The transfer protocols HTTP or HTTPS are used. Confirmation of the SEND operation is synchronous, but the answer is asynchronous so that the master workflow can continue working while it waits for the reply from the remote workflow.

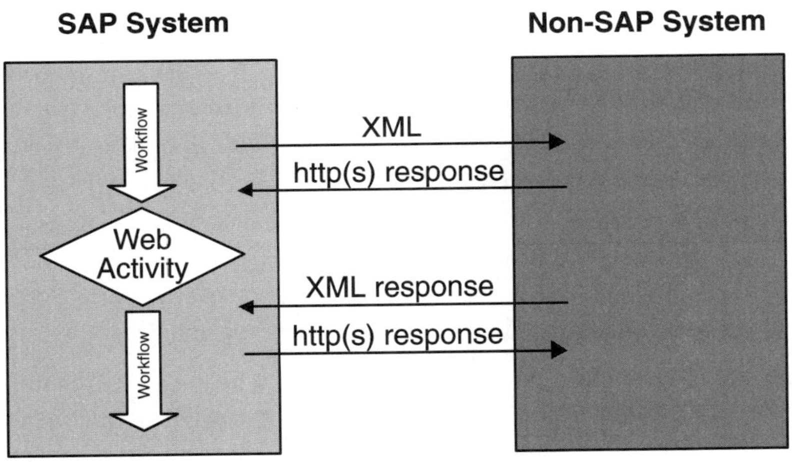

Figure 5.9 Inter-Workflow Communication

To use the Wf-XML interface, you must configure a Web server for the sending system.

Another interesting possibility is the use of forms in the SAP workflow. By using online forms, users can communicate directly with a Web browser via the Internet and start workflows or process work items. In order to do this, an ITS server must be set up. Alternatively, you can use SAPforms. With SAPforms, you can have both a synchronous online RFC connection to the SAP system and also an asynchronous offline mail variant. SAP-forms are drawn up in Microsoft Outlook or Microsoft Visual Basic.

A Web service can also be called from a Business Workflow. It can be called in dialog mode or in the background. With synchronous processing, the workflow waits until the Web service sends back a result. In asynchronous processing, the calling workflow gives the Web service an address to which the Web service can return the result. Web services that should be linked in a workflow must be registered in the SAP system. In this way, the access information is revealed.

Email integration is available for users who don't, or only occasionally, work with the SAP system. Therefore, work items can be sent directly to Lotus Notes or to the Microsoft Outlook email account using SAPconnect.

5.4.5 Project Procedure

So, what is the general project procedure for a workflow implementation?

Organizational Plan

Because the organizational plan in the Organizational Management component is mapped, it can be copied without any changes, even if the component is already being used for Personnel Management. Note that in order to assign tasks to positions, you must first clarify responsibilities for individual posts within the project-relevant part of the organizational plan.

Objects

Then, you must identify those objects in the Business Object Repository that are relevant to the business process, along with the methods, attributes, and events. Any requirements that aren't covered by the available objects can be added to a list for additional programming.

Process Flow, Tasks

From the first definition of the business process to be mapped—the task chain—you can derive the tasks and the possible agents. Many enterprises have a somewhat accurately defined and documented process organization. Keep in mind that translating this document into a workflow-compatible specification can be difficult. In any case, it isn't helpful to adhere to the written specifications too literally, which can be very laborious and time-consuming. Instead, you should develop a prototype in the system as soon as possible and, together with the users, define the additional requirements directly in the system. We also recommend that you divide up the entire workflow to get a serviceable definition for the components. The tasks identified are assigned to the object type and the method. In addition to the tasks, you should also define the planned processing times for individual process steps. The tasks that cannot be executed within the workflow and the SAP system must be integrated into the process.

Within the task chain, you must identify the triggering and controlling events and assign them to the object type events. If the event is not defined in the object type, the object type definition must be extended and you must ensure that the event can be triggered in the workflow.

Events

5.5 Reverse Business Engineering

5.5.1 Use and Benefit

The *Reverse Business Engineer* (RBE) is a PC-based software tool used for the process-oriented analysis of SAP production systems. The RBE is a standalone system and is based on Visual Basic and a Microsoft Access database (VI) or MS SQL server (V2). The main application of the analysis is to identify gaps and optimization potential in the business process handling supported by the system.

Analysis Possibilities

The RBE is a bottom-up approach. The use of SAP functions is presented in a process-oriented way, based on data extracted from the production systems. The analysis possibilities offered by the RBE include:

- Comparing different SAP R/3 installations, SAP R/3 clients, and organizational units
- Determining thread information on the usage of the business processes relevant to the enterprise
- Planning a release upgrade by presenting the SAP R/3 functions used in the Q&A database of the target release
- Preparing for system consolidation
- Starting point for re-documenting an already productive SAP R/3 installation
- Support for determining how often reports are used

Note that users—with the aid of experienced consultants—must draw their own conclusions from an analysis conducted with RBE's help, because the RBE doesn't provide any tips on how to implement and improve new and existing processes.

Use

Use of the RBE can be divided into the following steps:

- Data extraction
- Data analysis and report preparation
- Data transfer (optional)

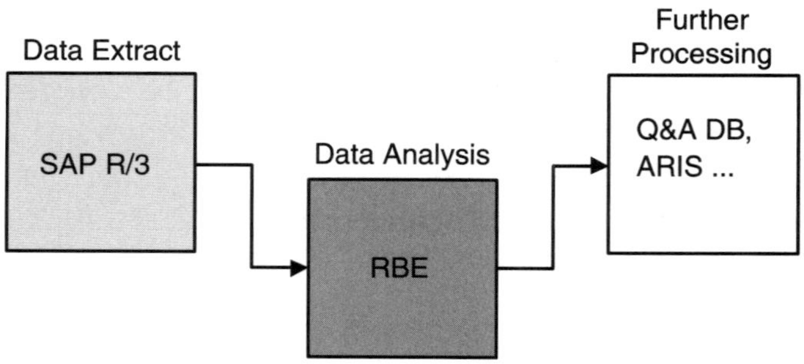

Figure 5.10 Procedure for an RBE Project

First, the data is extracted from the SAP R/3 system and imported into the RBE. The application components in SAP are arranged in a hierarchical order and can be evaluated in different ways and presented in reports. Optionally, data on the range of functions used in the Q&A database can be forwarded.

Main Functions

The main functions of the RBE include:

- **SAP RBE Explorer**
  The *SAP RBE Explorer* generates the ABAP code required to extract data from the SAP production system. The extract dataset is written to a text file and imported into the RBE. The RBE Explorer then analyzes the imported data and displays it in graphical form.
- **Reverse Modeling Engineer**
  The *Reverse Modeling Engineer* administers and maintains check rules for evaluating transaction and configuration data, and generates customer-specific check rules. The assignment of these rules to process structures allows you to determine how often software elements are used in SAP R/3 for processing.
- **Analysis Reports**
  Analysis Reports are evaluations based on the analysis results, that is, single analysis or comparisons between multiple analyses.

5.5.2 Procedure

An RBE project progresses through the following steps:

1. Check the transaction monitor (in the system load monitor, Transaction ST03 or ST03N). Because the RBE evaluates statistical data from the transaction monitor, you must ensure that the retention time for these

records is at least two months. Note that full (complete) months only can be considered.

2. The RBE contains a text file with the ABAP source code for data extraction. Load this text file into the relevant SAP systems for each upload. If necessary, you can restrict the data extraction. ABAP writes the extracted data (i.e., transaction data, configuration data, master data, or organizational data) to a text file. Note that this text file can exceed 100 MB.
3. Import the extract file into the RBE.
4. Before carrying out the analysis, you must set the scope and details of the analysis. The scope can be limited, for example, to *Sales & Distribution* and *Materials Management.* Details are generated through a combination of check steps, check cases, and an analysis structure. You carry out the analysis via an analysis structure, for example, the application component hierarchy for Release 4.6C or the reference structure for business processes. Check cases are assigned to the elements in the analysis structure. One check case bundles together several *check steps* (rules). The check cases examine the use of transactions, customizing settings, and master data. For example, one check step can verify whether Transaction VA01 (create sales order) is used and if so, how often. You can use threshold values to categorize usage (active, probably active, probably inactive, inactive). In addition to these transaction-related check steps, there are SQL check steps that you can use to evaluate master data, for example, to analyze the number of sales orders for a particular sales document type. The standard already contains the most important check cases and steps for these objects. If you want to check user-defined transactions and reports, you must add the relevant check cases and steps. You can enhance the analysis structure, the check cases, and the check steps on an as-needed basis. For information on the use of transactions by particular organizational units, you must be assigned to these specific organizational units.
5. Data from the analysis is available for various different reports.
6. A transfer file is created for processing the analysis results in other applications.
7. The results of the analysis can be transferred to other applications such as the ASAP Q&A database.

5.5.3 RBE Scenarios

Overview of SAP Processes Used

A first analysis usually requires that you have an overview of the SAP functions used. To get an overview, you must extract transaction data from the SAP production system. You can use this overview to examine the use of transactions and reports. Customer-specific transactions must be assigned to the analysis structure. An analysis of user-defined reports and transactions provides information on how often they are used and therefore, which user-developments are no longer used and need not be considered from this point on. An analysis of the use of transactions by different organizational units can be useful as a basis to justify IT costs.

Comparing Different R/3 Installations, Clients, and Organizational Units

The RBE allows you to compare different analyses. In this way, you can learn how the SAP functions are used differently in different SAP systems, clients, and organizational units. If there are different values for the various SAP systems, you can see what effect these values have on system usage. You can also determine if the SAP system is used as intended in the design. This type of conclusion can be the starting point for possible improvements. A comparative analysis is very appropriate when preparing to consolidate SAP R/3 systems. This analysis allows you to quickly and comprehensively determine the functions used and the deltas that should be considered in a target system. To do this, you must ensure that you have a uniform check rule base.

Optimizing Business Processes

An RBE analysis can contribute greatly to the optimization of business processes. The analysis reveals unused SAP functions, or gaps in system support for process development. The analysis can also produce key figures, from which objectives can be derived. If you run another RBE analysis after optimization, you can check the effect of the measures introduced.

System Documentation

You can use the RBE analysis to provide a framework for system documentation that is based on the functions used.

Upgrade

You can use the RBE analysis to determine the functions used, in preparation for an upgrade. In this way, you can determine whether these functions can be transferred to the new release unchanged; whether functions that have been used up to this point should be used in the upgrade; and, whether customer-developments should now be replaced by standard functions, and so on.

Test Plans

In the event of a system installation, upgrade, or system enhancement, you must run tests to ensure that the system functions flawlessly, particularly with regard to business process development. The RBE provides a comprehensive framework for test planning.

5.6 SAP Exchange Infrastructure

The *SAP Exchange Infrastructure* (XI) enables you to integrate processes in heterogeneous system landscapes, across SAP and non-SAP components, via the exchange of XML messages. With this tool, SAP goes far beyond existing Enterprise Application Integration (EAI) approaches and provides a component that can integrate systems from different manufacturers in different versions and on different platforms. Therefore, you can also integrate business processes across enterprise boundaries (collaborative processes). As a subcomponent of SAP NetWeaver, the XI is set to become the single component for integrating processes from SAP and non-SAP solutions. The Release 2.0 SR 1, which is the release described here, is based on the SAP Web Application Server (SAP Web AS) 6.20.

The problem of integrating applications is not a new one. Different approaches can be used, such as standardization to just one business application or as few as possible, the point-to-point linking of individual applications, or the implementation of a central instance to allow for the exchange of messages between applications (see Figure 5.11).

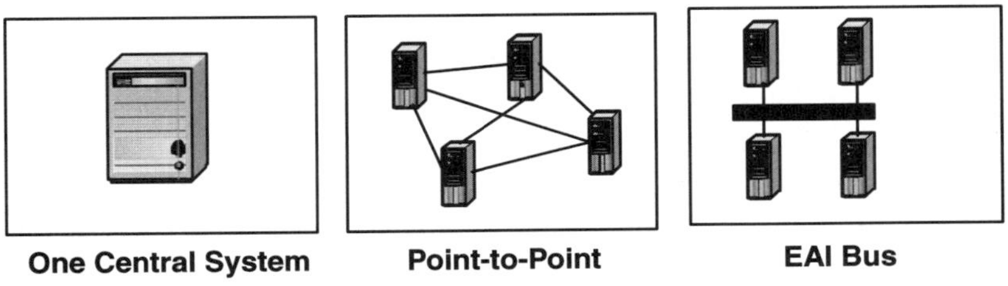

Figure 5.11 Different Integration Scenarios

SAP XI uses open standards; HTTP is used for communication; the application-specific content of the message is transferred from the sender to the recipient in a freely definable XML schema via the Integration Engine, which is the central component of the Integration Server. All systems that communicate with each other via the Exchange Infrastructure send messages to or receive messages from the integration server.

SAP XI architecture is made up of three parts, which reflect the three phases in an integration project:

Design Phase

1. The first of these parts—the design phase—involves the design of an integrated business process or a business scenario (several business processes) from a departmental and a technical point of view. The integration builder provides a development environment with which busi-

ness scenarios, interfaces, and mappings can be described, independent of a particular system landscape. A business scenario forms a complete collaborative process with all of the objects involved. The objects are stored in the Integration Repository. SAP already provides a number of ready-made business scenarios with the Information Repository. The system landscape is managed in the System Landscape Directory (SLD). It contains a directory on all available software components with details on release, support packages, platforms supported, and so on. In the system landscape description, you can select the components that will be installed. The necessary software components must be imported from the SLD for the design phase. The SLD is also endowed with content.

Configuration Phase

2. The second phase—the configuration phase—reproduces the template created in the design phase on the actual system landscape with all technical parameters such as routing rules and mappings. All information required for the message exchange at runtime is stored in the Information Directory. In this way, all of the integration information on a collaborative process is stored centrally in the Integration Repository and the Integration Directory (Shared Collaboration Knowledge).

Runtime Phase

3. The third phase—the runtime phase—puts into practice the integration logic created in the design and configuration phases and monitors and maintains it. Messages are exchanged centrally via the Integration Server, which is the runtime environment of the Exchange Infrastructure. The integration server also provides services such as recipient identification (routing) and the transformation of message content between sender and recipient (mapping). To provide these services, it accesses the parameters in the Integration Repository and the Integration Directory. Each individual message is logged in what are known as *container tables* using the Integration Monitor.

Integrating Systems

There are two basic options for integrating systems:

- The concept of *proxy generation* facilitates the development of new interfaces to and from the mySAP system world. First, a platform-independent description of the interface is created in WSDL format in the Integration Repository from which a source code prototype is generated. The object-oriented code is made up of classes and interfaces. Source codes can be generated in various different programming languages, therefore, you can integrate diverse platforms, for example, .NET. The ABAP and Java variants are available as standard in the SAP

Web AS 6.20. These proxies are installed on the source and target systems; they monitor communication with XI.

▶ Adapters enable the integration engine to communicate with older SAP systems (earlier than Release 6.20) or with non-SAP systems. SAP systems since Web AS 6.20 can communicate with other applications via proxies. SAP adapters convert XML documents and HTTP into IDocs and RFCs and vice versa. Other adapters facilitate communication with non-SAP systems (Plain HTTP Adapter, Adapter Engine).

Figure 5.12 shows an example of the Exchange Infrastructure.

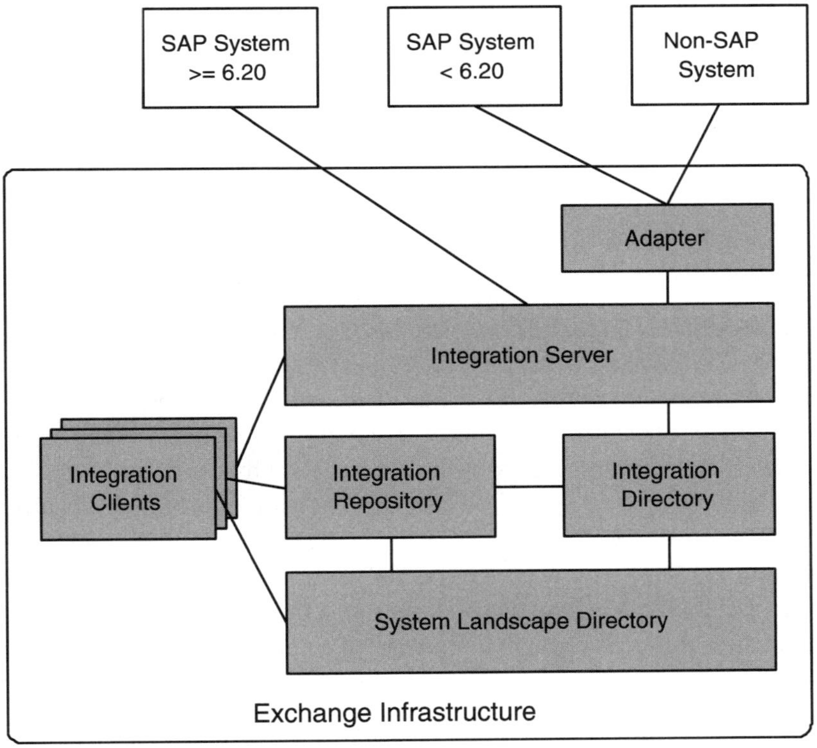

Figure 5.12 Architecture of the Exchange Infrastructure (XI)

SAP XI is a fully-fledged EAI solution. The proxy framework with Web AS 6.20 can also be used without XI for simple integration scenarios. We do not recommend that you use the SAP Business Connector in new projects because it has reached the end of its lifecycle. The SAP Business Connector is still delivered with Web AS, up to and including Release 6.40.

5.7 Generic Business Process Redesign

The design and optimization of business processes is not inherently linked to the availability of a certain technology, although technological innovations increasingly prompt a rethinking and the subsequent adjustment of business process design to meet new requirements. In this section, we shall introduce some basic aspects of business process optimization—from a business perspective—that play a role in many optimization projects. By *redesign*, we refer to a reorganization that originates in the business strategy, that is, a comprehensive restructuring. This restructuring by redesign basically works from the top down, and therefore, assumes a high degree of abstraction.

5.7.1 Business Process Design as a Part of Strategy Implementation

The design of business processes forms an important part of implementing the chosen strategy in an enterprise. The strategy defines which services the enterprise will provide for which product/market segments; the business processes specify how these services should be performed.

The availability of integrated information systems allows for fundamental changes to be made to the process organization in an enterprise. At first, the focus was on internal processes; later, with the explosive development of Internet applications, inter-enterprise processes were also included. Information technology plays a pivotal role in the redesign of how services are performed. However, the full potential of business process optimization cannot be realized with the implementation of information systems alone; rather, the organizational aspects of the restructuring must be clarified before the technical implementation. The processes then illustrate the connection between the enterprise strategy and the IT systems. In order for an enterprise to be successful, the processes, the strategy, and the IT systems must be aligned. Thus, business process design also plays a vital role because it can help to bring together very different organizational cultures in an enterprise:

- The enterprise strategy is developed by experts in the company who know and understand the overall business context. Frequently, these people don't have an in-depth understanding of the potential of IT solutions and consequently, strategic guidelines remain tucked away in presentation documents and are not effectively implemented.

- Information systems are specified by IT specialists based on business and technical requirements. The necessary formulation does not always meet the approval of the departments—something that is often interpreted by IT specialists as an inability to think technically.

5.7.2 Properties of Business Processes

Business processes define the skeletal structure of the operative working of an enterprise. Various publications offer various definitions of what a business process is or should be. The definition and design of business processes is therefore not an exact science; instead, it relies mainly on wisdom and experience gained from similar recorded situations. What properties constitute the essence of a business process?

Properties of Business Processes

- Business processes perform services for process customers.
- Business processes obtain services from other processes. From a process point of view, therefore, services are exchanged between processes and not between organizational units.
- Business processes are made up of a task chain.
- The individual tasks in the chain are usually distributed over several organizational units.
- Tasks change the status of virtual or real objects.

Using this approach, services are primarily exchanged between processes and not between organizational units. Enterprise boundaries are not important for the definition of processes, therefore, the organizational units addressed can belong to different companies. Processes must be controlled (process management). Attributes (performance indicators) are defined for this purpose, which plan and measure process performance. Attributes are directly derived from enterprise strategy and are usually assigned to one of the categories of time, quality, cost, and flexibility.

Description Methods

The properties of a business process can also, of course, be used to describe it. There are now many approaches for describing business processes, originating either from IT application development or from business administration. The IT-based methods are often not used until an advanced phase of process specification, and they usually require a certain formal knowledge of methods. The business-oriented methods, on the other hand, often seem to terminate just where it starts to get interesting for the application developer. Here, we have selected the business view.

5.7.3 Procedure for Redesigning Business Processes

Obviously, a few pages is not sufficient to present a complete procedure model for a process redesign project. Therefore, we will limit ourselves to a few points and demonstrate why these points are significant. We think it is particularly important not to lose sight of the red thread that runs from enterprise strategy to the processes and then through the information system. These levels must work together and support one another. Unfortunately, so-called redesign projects are frequently restricted to redistributing the tasks in a process within the organizational plan. When looking at the process flow, however, this has not changed; just like a river, the process finds a new channel, but it flows unhurriedly on and achieves more or less the same as before.

Defining Scope and Objectives

In a sense, it may seem almost unnecessary to mention that a redesign project (like any other project) first needs a defined scope and objectives. At the start of a project, the chances of actually realizing the redesign project are also assessed. Inconsistent objectives must be identified as such and corrected. The reasons why redesign projects fail are often due to insufficient support from management and general resistance to change, especially if the objectives set are unrealistic.

Strategy Analysis

As mentioned above, business processes form part of strategy implementation. Thus, initially, you must check how the strategy statements can be practically applied in the process design. The items under consideration are the *strategic business units* (SBUs). The enterprise performs different services for the SBUs. The strategic analysis must demonstrate the *SWOTs* (Strengths, Weaknesses, Opportunities, Threats) and factors critical to success that are characteristic of the SBU and what conclusions can be drawn for the general orientation of the SBU. The factors critical to success can convert inroads into process management.

Process Architecture

The next step is to derive process architecture. Usually, just sub-areas are taken into account and in rare cases only is the entire enterprise considered. In a situation in which the performance of services is to be organized from scratch, an analysis of business objects can be used to determine all of the services and tasks to be performed by the enterprise or the enterprise unit in question. You should think of the business objects as abstract representations of SAP Business Objects.

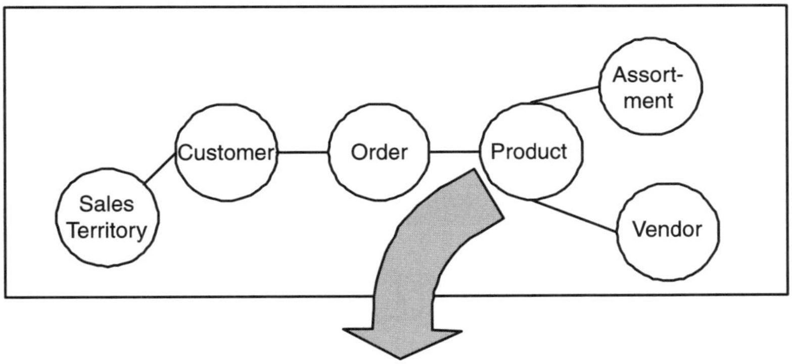

Business Object Product			
Lifecycle	Task	Input	Result

Figure 5.13 Analysis of Business Objects: The Effect of Processes on the Objects, Via Tasks, Generates Results, and Requires Input

Business objects are real or virtual objects that form part of the performance of services such as customer, order, employee, article, assortment. Each business object runs through a lifecycle—from emergence to removal. Business processes have an impact on these objects and, via tasks, they produce a certain result, at which point they require inputs (see Figure 5.13). Each task belongs to a certain phase in the lifecycle of an object. From this phase, emerges a list of tasks, results, and so on. The processes are defined in such a way that the results—the process performance—are grouped together logically. By *logically*, we mean that results are bundled and sorted so that they follow the lifecycle of the process customer interaction. The process customer must be supported as effectively as possible through each phase, from the acquisition of information, to service selection, through aftercare. The process must execute its services in complete synchronization with the customer process. The result packages defined in this way can be related to the process customer, in this case, the SBU. This is a decisive step for defining process architecture. Which result package will be tied to a process? Are these packages different for different customers?

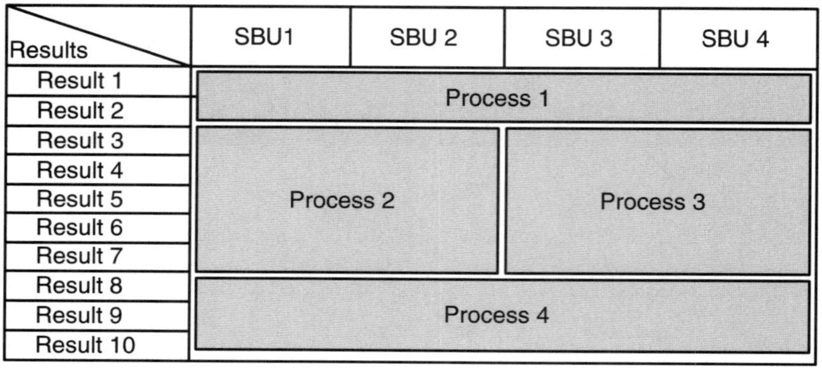

Figure 5.14 Creating Processes by Comparing Performance Results and Their Users

Strong differentiation results in clearly defined processes with few variants. With a more general definition, synergies can be used at the expense of a larger number of process variants that are harder to manage.

The process definition is therefore based entirely on the definition of the process performance and the assignment to users. At this high level of abstraction, we no longer speak of procedure flows or organizational assignments. The processes defined in this way have to be analyzed using various validation steps. Do the services really meet customer requirements? Do we know enough about the relationship between the service performed and the customer process? Are the same or similar results produced by several processes? The defined and validated processes can now be assigned to a network. By doing this, you can determine if the interfaces between the processes might cause problems (see Figure 5.15).

Task or procedure chain diagrams have proven useful for describing the actual process development (see Figure 5.16), because they relate the two fundamental structural axes—organizational plan and process flow—to each other. They are also easy to read, even for non-experts.

The presentation of business processes as task chain diagrams should help to clarify the correlations in the process flow and it should be limited to the important components of the processes being studied. Between 1990 and 1992, SAP developed its own semiformal modeling technique for business processes using the method of the *event-driven process chains* (EDPC). Thanks mainly to support by software tools (and, in particular, the ARIS tool), the EDPC presentation has become widely used.

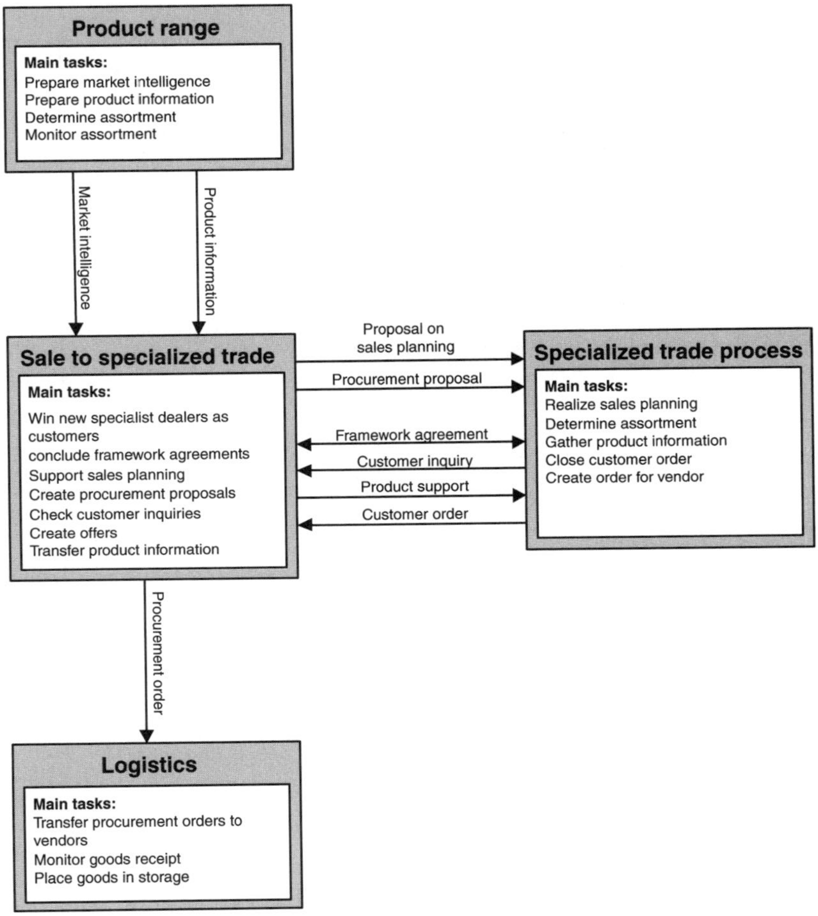

Figure 5.15 Process Architecture for a Retail Company

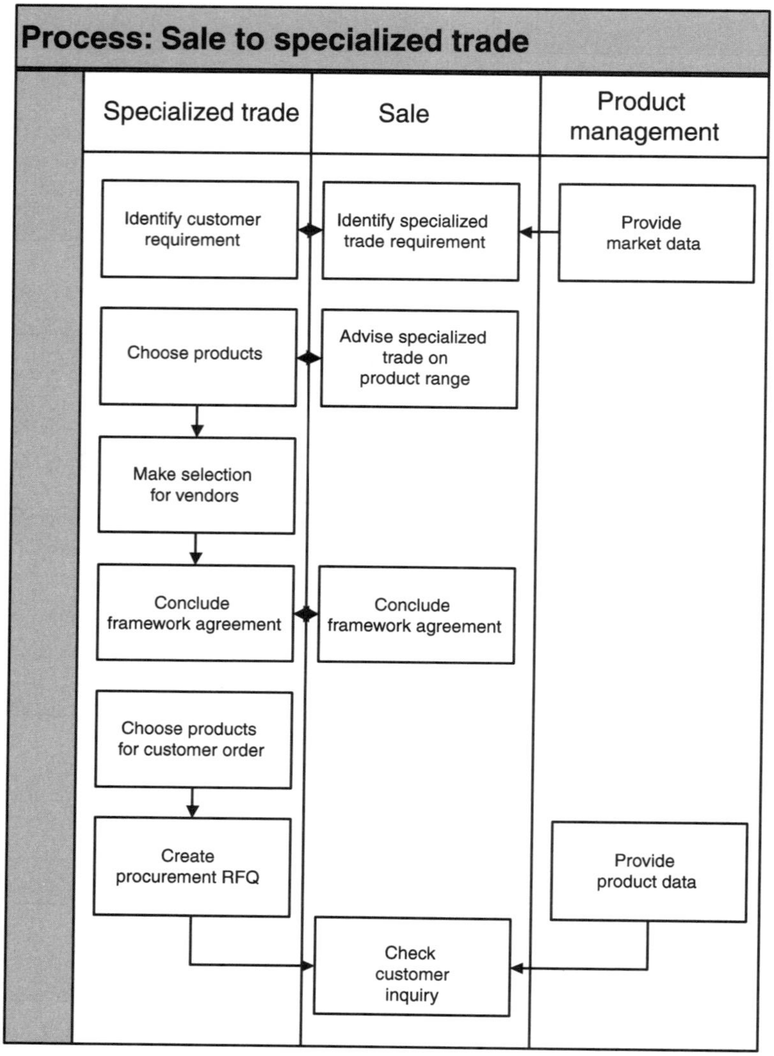

Figure 5.16 Task Chain Diagram

5.7.4 SAP Business Maps

With the SAP Solution Maps and Collaborative Business Maps, SAP provides an extensive collection of templates for analyzing and structuring new business processes, which helps to reduce design time. The Business Maps cover sector-specific and comprehensive requirements. A PC tool called the *Solution Composer* is available for processing the Business Maps.

6 The Way to Real-Time Enterprise

Legal and business requirements compel enterprises to implement effective controls and risk management. In this chapter, we discuss the real-time monitoring of operational processes and how this approach differs from the more common business intelligence methods.

6.1 Motivation

Information technology has become a key factor for the successful implementation of enterprise strategy. Enterprises are continually striving to introduce applications that will optimally map existing business processes. In an age of worldwide market consolidation, this implementation of enterprise strategy has become even more critical as enterprises are forced to constantly reduce costs.

The success of enterprise strategy implementation can be measured—with a certain time delay—using financial key figures to analyze economic success. However, experience shows that this procedure is not satisfactory for corporate management as the time delay is often too long, which, in turn, prevents an enterprise from tackling problems efficiently and effectively.

Offline Calculation of Key Figures

Business Intelligence (BI) systems promised to correct this problem by collecting data offline from applications and using it to calculate various key figures. Usually, however, this is just highly-aggregated, statistical information that shows the intermediate or final status of the value processes of an enterprise. The individual activities of organizational units, displaying all of the business processes, are not the focus of BI systems. In addition, legal requirements (for example, the *Sarbanes-Oxley Act*) and other rules (such as Basel II) impose effective controls of business processes and risk management on enterprises.

A large gap can be seen in enterprise controlling here because the actual performance of an enterprise depends on the efficiency of the business processes mapped, and these must be determined online and in real time.

6.2 Business Process Monitoring Using Reporting

The business process level mapped in SAP and other ERP systems is combined with an information process level that forwards information to management. As before, this is mainly done using reports and evaluations in data warehouses, with the focus on business data that should be of assistance to management for decision-making (see Figure 6.1).

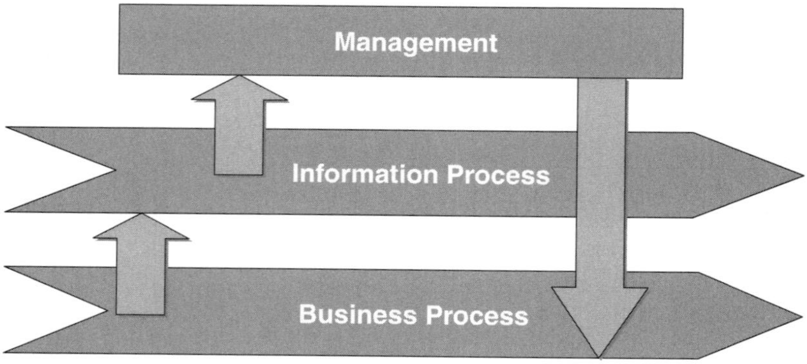

Figure 6.1 Information Flow from Business Processes to Management

Weak Points This procedure of reporting purely business data has some inherent weak points, however:

- Reports show only the past—from yesterday, last week, or last month—instead of providing a forecast of current business conditions. Every problem discovered has been in existence for hours, days, or weeks. The possibility of intervening immediately to limit or avoid rejections and delays has already been missed. Speed, responsibility, and flexibility must be increased to improve performance or to make savings. If problems that require immediate attention arise, you need proactive reporting that reflects the current situation and allows for fast and targeted management intervention.
- Reports are not restricted to relevant data. Most reports present the user with all data—regardless of whether it's relevant. The user is left with the task of combing through each page of the report to find the spot that requires the most immediate attention. This report is then promptly replaced by a new one and the whole process begins again. With insufficient time to dedicate to the task, many users no longer read reports carefully and control is done for only 20% of report analyses. What is needed is the appropriate logic that will make it easier for

the user to find the key points, that is, the points in the report that are critical or show-stoppers. Users want precise information with optimally prepared data. They need it at a particular point in time to work out the problem at hand.

- The information they need is somewhere in the report, however, no one can start working on a solution until the report has been read and the information has been located. An unread report may as well not exist. Problems that aren't found immediately smolder until somebody reads the report, or worse, until the boss or a customer complains. We must change to "active" reporting systems that not only report problems immediately and automatically to all relevant persons, but also offer support in examining and resolving problems.
- Problem forgotten or followed up and resolved? Every time users encounter problems, they have to note them offline and then, follow up outside of the reporting system (i.e., call, email, or fax). There is no recording or linking to automatically track the steps initiated, the current status, and the final outcome. Instead, all of these steps must be managed outside of the reporting system.

6.3 Business Process Monitoring with Real-Time Business Monitoring

In order to resolve the problems identified in the previous section, we established the following requirements for effective business process monitoring:

1. Permanent and automatic monitoring of critical processes and key figures
2. Identification of erroneous transactions, commensurate with priority and beyond system boundaries
3. Automatic reporting of defined exceptions and incidents that require immediate action
4. Simultaneous messages to all relevant participants informing them of the problem that has arisen
5. Follow up the incident right through to the final outcome and the central documentation of the method of solution used

We refer to this method as *Real-Time Business Monitoring* (RBM). The technical implementation of RBM is done with two linked control loops (see Figure 6.2).

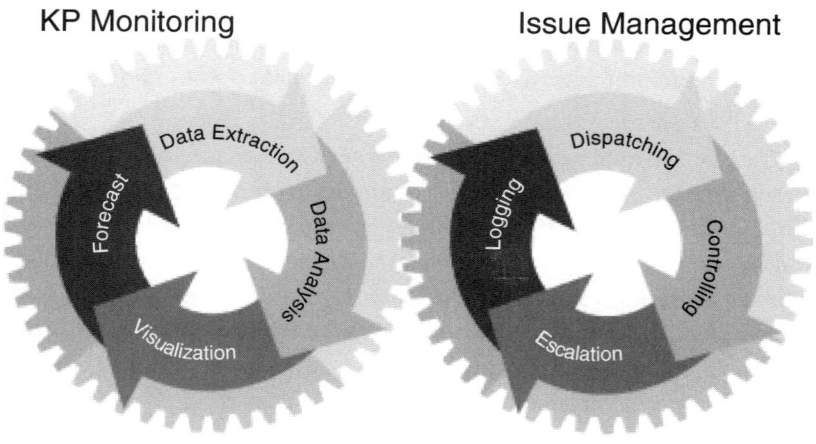

Figure 6.2 Linking the Control Loops KPI Monitoring and Issue Management

KPI Monitoring In the *Key Performance Indicators* (KPIs) monitoring control loop, the RBM system monitors the business processes and determines KPIs across any business systems.

Issue Management In the Issue Management control loop, any weakness and issues that emerge are identified and, depending on their importance, they are reported to the appropriate participants. The issue is followed until the final resolution and the entire issue management is documented.

Avoiding Media Breaks It is essential that Issue Management and documentation, and the building up of a knowledge base, are inherently done in the system. Today, prevalent media breaks—caused by external management of the communication elements of the risk management process, such as communication and escalation via email and the storage of process-related documentation in non-integrated systems—lead to poor acceptance among system users and to a clearly increased occurrence of errors when transferring data. Preference should be given to an automated cycle that can optimize the classical reporting problem mentioned above.

The central interaction between the two control loops is essential for the efficient operation of the entire system; it even allows for the necessary reaction speed. With key figures in the operational area, which in some cases may be subject to high fluctuations over short periods of time, this presents the measure for efficiency.

Data Extraction In RBM, data extraction is typically done at periodic intervals, which should be made as short as possible, depending on the risk factor of the individual key figure. Commensurate with the existing key figure hierarchy, the extraction can either refer to single values on the most detailed level from the source system, which, after all are what make up the key figure, or it can reflect an appropriate aggregation of existing key figures.

The logic to be applied for data extraction is based primarily on the reading of direct system parameters. Technically, a certain abstraction should be undertaken now on the systems addressed. A uniform interface for extracting data with a reusable yet flexible data structure must serve as a starting point for calculating the key figures, so that the integrative and cross-system aspect of RBM will not be negatively influenced. A suitable abstraction at this point contributes greatly to the reusability of the logic for calculating the actual key figures.

Data Analysis

The manual work required with the classical methods of data analysis and evaluation according to risk factor in no way corresponds to requirements on a key figure system that must deal with operational, and thus frequently collected key figures. With RBM, the analysis is done with a flexible set of rules that, in addition to calculating individual key figures, also enables the abovementioned aggregation of key figures over many different levels in accordance with the key figure hierarchy. To allow for the flexible hierarchy of the key figure system, you must also be able to formulate this system dynamically. Only in this way, can you adequately accommodate the constantly changing requirements and shifting of risk factors or KPIs.

Visualization

Huge demands are made on the efficient visualization of linked key figures within a potentially complex system. Once again, the key figure hierarchy is the main approach used. The implementation of a visual drill-down procedure enables you to get an overview of the system's shortcomings, and to quickly locate the cause on the individual key figure level.

This is based on the status of the individual key figures, which is either added or superimposed to be passed on further in the visualized key figure hierarchy. Values that deviate greatly from planned values should be given priority over lesser deviations. Setting an appropriate weighting for deviations for each key figure is therefore a key element of the key figure hierarchy in itself and is usually derived directly or indirectly from the risk factor of each key figure.

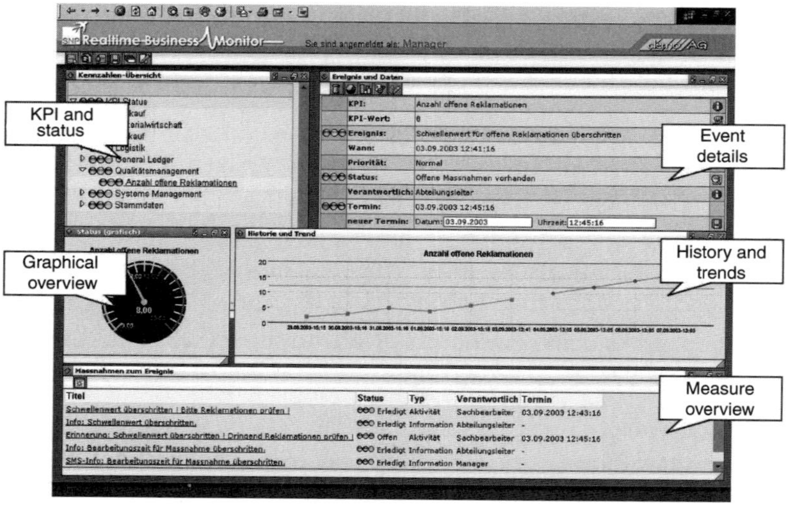

Figure 6.3 Proposal for the Visualization of KPIs

On the individual key figure level, a range of additional information should also be available for special analysis of the cause. This information can be derived from the control loop phases explained in the following paragraphs. Because the visualization of information should also be designed efficiently, the information presented should always be based on the actual questions and preferences of the person who is currently working with the system; for example, the preferences of top management would focus mainly on clarifying the following questions:

- What happened?
- Where did it happen?
- How great is the effect? How high is the risk?
- How did it happen?
- What measures have been taken and who is responsible?

In contrast, RBM users on the functional level—prompted by the dispatching for action (still to be explained)—are interested in other questions that refer less to the contexts within the key figure system and more on specific information relating to cause and if they can be removed.

Forecast

Depending on the risk factor and timeframe for action, the consideration of key figures from the past is not sufficient in many cases because decisions have already been made without knowledge of past errors and therefore, cannot be made again. Effective forecasting procedures must therefore be developed. These procedures draw on both the data available from key figure history and on expert knowledge. In order for these two knowledge bases to work together, it is necessary to analyze and process the existing statistics with the result of a realistic extrapolation of historical values.

Selecting a procedure to calculate future developments based on historical values has proven insufficient, however. To evaluate future developments and trends, the relevant expert knowledge must also be included in the forecast. Currently, the effective formulation of this knowledge represents the most difficult problem.

Dispatching

The use of forecasts far exceeds presentations in graphs of various kinds if the calculation of absolute future values for a key figure is linked with a dispatching mechanism, for example, if predefined threshold values are exceeded. These events can be triggered by changes to individual key figures or aggregated key figures that are determined periodically, manually, or via prognostication.

Once an event occurs, dispatching triggers the appropriate measures. This may be an automated communication mechanism—such as the sending of an email to those responsible for the key figure—or the triggering of an entire event chain, such as initiating measures to remove the problem if a threshold value for a key figure in a critical area is exceeded. Depending on how precisely dispatching management is defined, it is even possible—assuming the appropriate knowledge and representation of internal business processes in dispatching—to identify the individual documents, transactions, and system interactions responsible for the event and to offer direct access to the system in question, as appropriate. The result is that the notification agent is relieved of the task of manually finding the source of the error and the abovementioned media breaks can be avoided.

Distribution Channel

There are numerous distribution channels that you can select from for dispatching purposes. If we return to the issue of avoiding media breaks, we suggest that preference should be given to procedures that avoid such breaks, namely, those procedures that work inherently with the system or that return to the system as quickly and as easily as possible. In the SAP environment, Workflow and WebFlow distribution channels are the first choice, because they use existing infrastructures (and therefore existing investments) and because they are seamlessly integrated into the overall SAP working environment. When dispatching tasks, in particular, preference should be given to the use of these technologies over others. In those cases where information is related to an event that occurred without the urgent need for action, other distribution channels are recommended if notification agents work locally, or if they are temporarily unable to interact with the system, or if it would be more time-effective.

Controlling You can use the dispatching control mechanisms to trace if the measures triggered produced the desired reaction and if they adhered to time limits. In addition to determining the responsibility for each measure per notification agent, at this stage, you should be able to make manual modifications to the otherwise automatic dispatching and escalation process. The need to make manual modifications is greater because each cause contains individual and unclear problem parts for which provision cannot be made in the automated control loop. This situation is compounded if general conditions are changed quickly or temporarily and they are not reflected in the system in the interim. Manual access is then necessary, which usually consists of either intervening to reduce the work load, such as canceling a measure that has already been started and at the same time informing those responsible of this procedure, or intervening to intensify measures initiated, such as reducing deadlines or manual measure control. You must also be able to measure progress in coping with delegated tasks.

Escalation In addition to the active control of the status of attached measures, after events in the system, escalation arranges automated information about conditions within the organization structures, usually in relation to exceeded deadlines. In principle, the same mechanisms should be used here as in dispatching. You must also be able to configure escalation levels flexibly, like the others, so that changing requirements can be met flexibly.

Logging Logging the measures completed after an event plays an important role in the continuous improvement of the ability to analyze errors. Based on a structured and categorized documentation of measure processing, you can make statistical statements on the sources of errors in key figure areas. The possibility of isolating certain problems in this way and then eliminating them marks great progress, in particular with regard to the requirements for an internal or external audit.

To meet the requirements for a consistent and constant documentation, it must be done in an automated and standardized way. Documentation help should therefore refer to existing knowledge and to context-sensitive selection criteria. It does not seem practical to force the user to always give a full-text description in the obligatory final documentation of activities. Rather, the processing method of a measure should be documented automatically, in so far as possible, and it should primarily consist of statistically calculated, yet customizable proposals in the end user documentation.

In addition, thanks to the creation of standardized documentation, there is a constantly growing knowledge base, which supports not only the analysis phase, but the functional activities of employees as well.

6.4 Granular Key Performance Indicators

Based on the fact that real-time business monitoring is predominantly based on Business Process Intelligence and thus on key figures from business processes, we shall show you an example of how to extract granular KPIs from the business process for complete sales order processing (see Figure 6.4).

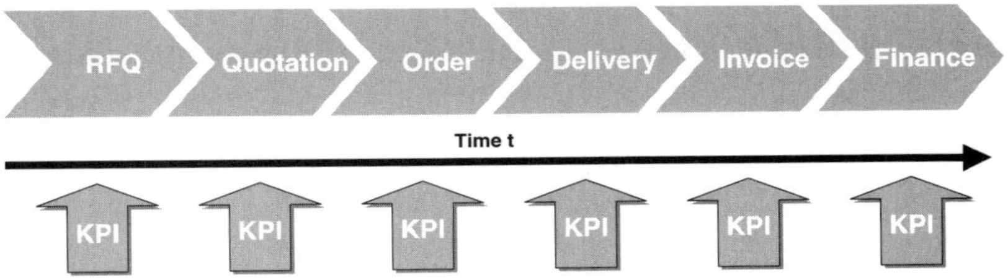

Figure 6.4 Example: The Sales Order Processing Business Process

The RBM key figures should yield conclusions for both the efficiency—relationship between input and output—and the effectiveness—what impact is obtained with the output. The strength of the system lies in the fact that performance values need to be compiled and checked very quickly and the focus is on monitoring the measures. The short-term nature of this aspect highlights the need to observe operational key figures for day-to-day activities.

Because input for a business process often builds on the output of a saved business process, statements on efficiency must be based on the interior dimension of the organization. Therefore, they must be relative percentage values, which can be seen, for example, in the business process for sales order processing.

Inquiry

In many enterprises, the process of sales order processing begins with the processing of customer inquiries. When answering inquiries, the problem frequently arises that, initially, customer requirements are not presented completely, or they're conflicting and need to be resolved before an offer can be made. Also, simultaneously, the customer must be answered as soon as possible. For such cases, RBM can monitor customer inquiries for which a processing deadline due to additional clarification must be monitored and that must be answered within a predefined reaction time. RBM can also be set to measure how long it takes before the agent responsible for an A-classified (= very important) customer starts to process an incoming inquiry. In this way, you can achieve a predefined service level for such customers.

Quotation The next step in the sales order processing procedure is usually to draw up the quotation. The relationship of the number of inquiries to quotation is of course a very interesting key figure, but it is of no direct significance for the short-term functional area that is what is most relevant to us here. Note that an important monitoring value is the delivery of quotations within the specified time and, with it, deadline monitoring. Other key figures that are relevant for monitoring are offers with certain products, for example, during a product introduction phase, or offers for certain customers who need particular attention from a team of responsible sales and service employees.

Sales Order If there is an order, this gives rise to a range of key figures that can be monitored. Naturally, sales management is interested in the current incoming orders to ensure that it can react quickly to exceptional situations. The observance of sales order conditions can be monitored by a set of rules. In addition to order receipt, another focus in the key figures is the monitoring of service performance. The availability of bottleneck resources for service performance can serve as a basis for a key figure set. Blocked or delayed goods entry for material that is specifically acquired for sales orders will require a quick response and should therefore be included in the key figures.

Delivery Key figures from the area of delivery are among the most short run and, as such, are the most important figures for real-time monitoring. Date and completeness check are prerequisites that influence customer satisfaction most. The relevant key figures are thus called "On time" or "Quota of overdue orders."

Billing Document The billing document should be issued as quickly as possible to keep the order-to-cash cycle short. Monitoring this cycle forms part of the area of operational key figures and the exception situations call for immediate attention. Therefore, the "Quota of orders with billing blocks" is a trigger for short-term action.

The key figures for the last part in the sales order process are "cash receipt" and "dunning level." If the agreed-on terms of payment are exceeded, and there is any additionally arranged tolerance deadline, Sales must determine the reasons for the delayed payment.

Finance

6.5 Summary

In this chapter, you have learned about the importance of real-time business monitoring and how it can be used as a functional enhancement for business intelligence. We have also examined—by following the course of an existing process chain—how key figures are derived. The following overview of the most important differences between traditional methods of BI compared to those of the RBM will round off the chapter.

Traditional Model	Real-Time Business Monitoring
Employees spend one to two hours/day struggling through reports.	Employees work efficiently with automatic messaging when an anomaly or problem arises.
Employees lose over a day between the time when the problem arises and the time when they resolve the problem.	Employees can immediately and directly start to eliminate the problem.
Employees may be made aware of the problem by customers or the boss.	Employees eliminate the error before the customers complain.
Employees are unsure of which method of resolution they should use; they depend on solutions from a third party.	Employees find the solution thanks to defined workflows and the use of solution databases.
Employees have to call to see if the problem has been resolved.	Employees are continuously supported by the system so they can follow the incident to its solution and have access to all previous problems and their solutions.
... and then the problem occurs again (back to start).	Root-cause analysis—problems are presented graphically and clearly; it is possible to permanently eliminate the error.

Table 6.1 Comparison of Traditional and Real-Time Business Monitoring

Enhanced scope for action—real-time determination of key figures and the possibility to react to forecast values—creates extra time to identify irregularities in time and introduce corrective measures. In this way, you can access development actively before it is too late to influence the result.

Efficient risk management—the coupling of monitoring and issue management control loops—helps to ensure that when an exceptional situation arises, the correct measures can automatically be implemented. Adherence to defined deadlines is actively monitored and, if necessary, escalated. In this way, the system actively supports you in the operational error-elimination process.

In addition, you get the gap-free documentation of all measures and their reasons by detecting the error because of its omission, that is, via its elimination.

When combined with the possibility to forecast, you have a tool to help you run efficient, proactive risk management.

7 Summary

With many enterprises having made high investments in building up complex system landscapes over the past years, the focus has shifted to the consolidation of their investments.

The economic environment dictates the development of IT investments and projects. During the 1990s, a lot of money was sunk into building integrated information systems. Then, the Y2K problem had to be addressed, and for many countries in Europe, there was also the conversion to the Euro. Internet euphoria also ate up a lot of money; however, this was not always to the investors' advantage. Today's economically strained environment places more emphasis on optimizing and consolidating investments already established. Very complex system landscapes have evolved over just a few years. Business processes run beyond components and platforms, resulting in increased demands on an already optimized system operation. So, what can enterprises do to protect and optimize their investments in an SAP solution landscape?

Optimization Strategies

Enterprises can decide to optimize the use of the existing solution landscape or, they can opt to change the landscape in some way—they can intervene in the structures of the solution landscape. Such restructuring would, of course, require follow-on investments. Now, let's look at the different strategies individually.

Increase Productivity

The goal of our first strategy is to improve the productivity of the usage of existing IT systems. Here, we must differentiate between the system side and the user side.

System Side

On the system side, everything must be done to maintain or to elevate the performance and availability of the solution to the defined service level. The service level is defined in accordance with the necessary and economically acceptable support by the information systems. Not every solution has to be available with optimal performance 24/7. Business processing, and, in particular, critical functions, which, if they fail or are obstructed, can lead to serious problems with business processing, must be identified and their required availability and throughput must be stipulated. The improvement of system performance and the optimal usage of hardware resources are integral to all SAP installations. System performance depends on many factors: *Expensive* SQL statements, non-optimally self-programmed ABAP code, system parameters of SAP Basis, the configuration of memory sub-systems, and system settings made when customizing the SAP systems can all be optimized. Data archiving is another measure that unquestionably should be considered.

User Side On the user side, the improvement of know-how—in relation to process development with the SAP systems—is an important area for optimization. Refresher courses and testing knowledge levels can help to clarify what action is needed.

Service & Support The productivity of IT usage is, not least of all, positively influenced by an optimized Service & Support infrastructure and organization. The support processes must be analyzed and checked for suitability. In the SAP Solution Manager, SAP provides a tool for improving the productivity of both implementation projects and the maintenance of existing solutions. Before optimization measures can be taken, the problem must be identified. The SAP Solution Manager provides you with tools to help you track down problems. It also provides you with a view of the system landscape and business processes, which can run across several systems and software components.

Adjusting Structures Another approach is based on adjusting the given IT structures. Whereas before, the trend was on having several decentralized SAP systems that were often independent of each other, today, the pendulum is swinging in the other direction. Many enterprises are centralizing their service infrastructure to just a few locations. The possibilities offered by improved networks and hardware resources contribute to the implementation of such options. The result is that several SAP systems have to be consolidated. There is, of course, the option of concentrating all SAP systems in one location and then using a single support infrastructure, however, frequently, enterprises choose a different, more advanced path. There is great potential benefit in merging different systems, however, in order for this to work, you must align processes and data. Not only does this open the way for a comprehensive and shared use of business processes, for example, centralized purchasing for all enterprises in a division on the same system, but, it also paves the way for future joint projects, for example, mySAP CRM. SAP refers to this type of project as System Landscape Optimization (SLO). In most cases, aligning data and processes leads to the need to change data directly on the database (for example, number ranges). It is very important that you check data consistency after this data conversion. If you are considering structural measures, you should also consider whether to outsource the IT infrastructure and organization.

Adjusting Business Processes

Optimizing system usage can also be determined by whether or not the business processes are optimally supported by the SAP components. To answer this question, you must understand how processes are handled—from both a business and a technical perspective—as these two levels must be in accord. For example, you need to check whether the business processes are consistently supported by the SAP system, or, if a special type of system support is used for individual tasks in a business process against media breaks, for example, an export price list in MS Excel and the manual transfer of the calculated prices into the SAP R/3 system. In a case like this, you should consider seeking a solution for this task within the range of SAP functions. The question of reengineering can also frequently arise from the perspective of changed business development. The ability to react to changes in the business environment, in the long- and short-term, is a clear competitive advantage because no solution is designed to last forever.

SAP Reverse Business Engineer

The *SAP Reverse Business Engineer* (RBE) is a general procedure to analyze the SAP functions used. The RBE loads a data extract from one or more production systems in a single offline database and enables far-reaching analysis of customizing and of master and transaction data, and, in this way, allows you to draw conclusions on system usage. The question of restructuring a specific business process can also frequently arise. SAP provides both sector-specific and cross-sector reference processes in the form of Business Maps. You can use these reference processes as templates to restructure business processes.

Workflow/ WebFlow

The automation of business processes with Business Workflow/WebFlow offers additional potential for optimization. Surprisingly, although this tried-and-tested technology has been available for years, it's still underestimated. A workflow can react to system events and can, for example, send information to the people responsible in an email or an SMS, or trigger a transaction. In this way, you can respond to critical situations immediately and detect any irregularity in the business process early on. Workflows can even communicate with the outside world via a browser or with another workflow and receive data from there. The technical prerequisites for real-time business and the related possibilities become available for enterprises. Identifying situations that are relevant to decision-making is one side; acting, that is, taking measures, is the other. The *Real-Time Business Monitor* (RBM) links these two fundamental control loops.

The world does not stop turning, however, and the promises of the *e-age*, namely, the universal and global networking of business processes, are becoming a reality, albeit a bit more slowly than expected during the initial euphoria. The cross-system and cross-company networking of business processes requires an infrastructure to control the flow of data to and from the enterprise. The *SAP Exchange Infrastructure* (SAP XI) fulfills all requirements for providing this service.

SAP Solution Management Optimization

With *Solution Management Optimization*, SAP offers a portfolio of services to help ensure the optimal operation of a mySAP solution landscape. SAP can provide these services on site, remotely, or as self-service. The services are suitable for eliminating existing problems and for the proactive identification and removal of potential problems. Solution Management Optimization services support the following areas: Performance, application integration, data volumes, and system administration. To determine the benefits of Solution Management Optimization, SAP recommends that you execute a Safeguarding Check. Based on this check, SAP can put together a customized list of optimization measures.

8 Management Summary

If, during the 1990s, the motto for matters of IT investment was "The main thing is to be there," in today's difficult economic environment, the focus is now on the following two criteria: *Return on Investment* (ROI) and *Total Cost of Ownership* (TCO). When calculating the TCO, the cost of the entire lifecycle of IT investments is examined; in ROI calculations, the business benefits are evaluated.

The optimal cooperation among the three pillars of *strategic planning, IT infrastructure,* and *system management* is what determines success.

We recommend that you use this book as a guide for aligning these three pillars, and for discovering and realizing optimization potential. The optimization of SAP systems is arranged on different levels:

System-Side Optimization: The performance and availability of the systems is examined and efficiency strategies can be determined by optimizing system parameters, with customer-defined developments, and by optimizing the database.

System Landscape Optimization: Whereas before SAP systems were implemented locally, today, efforts are underway to reverse this procedure and consolidate systems both technically and logically. This can lead to the alignment of processes and data and to the consolidation of the IT infrastructure, which has great potential benefits.

Optimization of Service and Support: The productivity of IT usage depends largely on the effectiveness of the service and support organization. Here, we have highlighted the support processes and how these same processes are supported via software solutions. The primary means of optimization is the SAP Solution Manager, which increases productivity for the implementation and operation of projects.

Optimizing Business Processes: The question arises as to whether the business processes are optimally supported by the SAP systems. We have examined the processes for inefficiencies such as media breaks, inconsistently distributed information, and overloading users with complex transactions. Another possibility for optimizing business processes is automation, which, technically, is mapped by Workflow. The potential savings via the use of automation techniques is still, in our experience, underestimated.

Real-Time Business Monitoring: An information process level, which serves to keep management informed, is, in principle, always layered on top of the business process level. This is usually reflected in reports and data warehouses. The problem with this method is that obtaining information usually creates a high manual workload, in particular, the reading and interpreting of reports. If a problem is detected, the resulting tasks are also, in turn, distributed manually. We have suggested another method of procedure—completely integrated Key Performance Indicator (KPI) monitoring with integrated forecast calculation and, in a second control loop, a completely automated distribution of to-dos with integrated control and escalation mechanisms. Not only does this procedure open up great potential operational benefits, it also supports management in the fulfillment of legal requirements such as the *Sarbanes-Oxley Act*.

The points listed here are addressed in more detail in the individual chapters and suggested solutions are presented as directly workable consultant knowledge. We have also taken care to ensure that the individual chapters can be read independently of each other.

A Sources and Further Reading

Sources

Brand, Hartwig: *SAP R/3 Implementation With ASAP. The Official SAP Guide.* Sybex 1999.

CIO Insight™ Magazine: *Spending Survey*. June 2002 edition.

CIO.com Research Reports: *Measuring IT Value*. February 2001.

Fritz, Stefan: *IT-Systeme intelligent betreiben*. notes magazin 5/2003.

Hammer, Michael; Champy, James: *Reengineering the Corporation: A Manifesto for Business Revolution.* Harper Business 1993.

IT Infrastructure Library (ITIL)/CCTA—The Government Centre for Information Systems: *An Introduction to Business Continuity Management*. The Stationery Office 1995.

IT Infrastructure Library (ITIL)/CCTA—The Government Centre for Information Systems: *Service Support*. The Stationery Office 2000.

IT Infrastructure Library (ITIL)/CCTA—The Government Centre for Information Systems: *Service Delivery*. The Stationery Office 2001.

IT Infrastructure Library (ITIL)/OGC: *Planning to Implement Service Management*. The Stationery Office 2002.

IT Infrastructure Library (ITIL)/CCTA—The Government Centre for Information Systems: *IT Services Organization*. The Stationery Office 1993.

Rademann, Cay; SAP AG: *Introduction into mySAP.com Landscapes.* SAP Service Marketplace 2002.

SAP AG: *White Papers for mySAP Technology*. SAP Service Marketplace 2002.

SAP AG: *White Papers SAP Solution Management*. SAP Service Marketplace 2002.

Schneider, Thomas: *SAP Performance Optimization Guide.* Third Edition, SAP PRESS 2003.

Links

http://www.itil.co.uk	Official ITIL Web site
http://www.itil.itsm-world.com	ITIL and ITSM directory

http://www.itsmf.com	IT Service Management Forum Germany
http://service.sap.com	SAP Service Marketplace
http://www.sap.com	SAP Web Site
http://www.sapinfo.info/en	SAP Information Glossary

Further Reading

Buck-Emden, Rüdiger (Ed.): *mySAP CRM. Solution for Success.* SAP PRESS 2002.

Egger, Norbert: *SAP BW Professional. Tips and tricks for dealing with SAP Business Information Warehouse.* SAP PRESS 2004.

Färber, Günther; Kirchner, Julia: *mySAP Technology Roadmap.* Galileo Press 2003.

Hagemann, Sigrid; Will, Liane: *SAP R/3 System Administration. The Official SAP Guide.* Second Edition, SAP PRESS 2003.

Heinemann, Frédéric; Rau, Christian: *Web Programming with the SAP Web Application Server.* SAP PRESS 2003.

IBM Business Consulting Services: *SAP Authorization System. Design and Implementation of Authorization Concepts for SAP R/3 and SAP Enterprise Portal.* SAP PRESS 2003.

Kagermann, Henning; Keller, Gerhard (Ed.): *mySAP.com Industry Solutions: New Strategies for Success with SAP's Industry Business Units.* Addison-Wesley 2001.

Missbach, Michael; Hoffmann, Uwe M.: *SAP Hardware Solutions.* Prentice Hall 2000.

Missbach, Michael; Wilhelm, Mathias; Stelzel, Josef; Sosnitzka, Ralf: *SAP System Operations.* SAP PRESS 2004.

Oswald, Gerhard (Ed.): *SAP Service and Support. An A-to-Z guide to optimizing ROI and TCO.* SAP PRESS 2003.

SAP Labs: *System Administration Made Easy, 4.6C/D.* Johnson Printing Service 2002.

Stefani, Helmut: *Archiving your SAP Data. A comprehensive guide to plan and execute archiving projects.* SAP PRESS 2002.

Will, Liane: *SAP APO System Administration. Principles for effective APO System Management.* SAP PRESS 2003.

B About the Authors

Daniel Baumann is Managing Director at SNP AG (Schweiz), Dübendorf.

A physics graduate, he has worked in the SAP environment since 1995. He joined the SNP group in 2003, having previously worked as a consultant, project leader, and IT manager in the consultancy field. His expertise lies with linking business and technical matters, particularly in the area of system consolidation.

Dr. Björn Gelhausen is Technical Manager and Banking Sector Manager at SNP Schneider-Neureither & Partner AG, Heidelberg.

After obtaining his doctorate in chemistry in 1998, he began work as an SAP technology consultant at SNP AG. Since then, he has held different positions within the company. SAP Basis consulting, SAP banking solutions, and the SAP Enterprise Portal are his main areas of expertise. His skill set also includes system management solutions.

Johannes Hurst is head of the Service & Support business unit at SNP Schneider-Neureither & Partner AG, Heidelberg. He has worked in IT consultancy since 1990.

After studying, he started his professional career in the field of system engineering for the mainframe and client/server environment. Having managed several large projects, for several years he was IT manager for an SAP implementation at a large multinational corporate group. Since 2000, Johannes Hurst has been Manager of the Services & Support area at SNP AG, specializing in the setup and optimization of SAP Customer Competence Centers (CCCs). Johannes Hurst is a Certified IT Service Manager.

Gerhard Krauss is a Technical Manager at SNP Schneider-Neureither & Partner AG, Heidelberg. He is responsible for the area of SAP Basis Consulting and for internal technical SAP infrastructure.

Having studied mechanical engineering, he became a Basis consultant for SNP AG in 1998. Since then, he has overseen several large projects as consultant and senior consultant. His main areas of expertise include systems operation, archiving, and central system monitoring.

Dr. Andreas Schneider-Neureither is the Chief Executive Officer of SNP Schneider-Neureither & Partner AG, Heidelberg. He is responsible for operational business and sales.

Having studied and obtained a doctorate in theoretical physics, he first worked as an IT consultant and developer on numerous large projects in well-known companies. In 1994, together with his wife Petra Neureither, he founded Schneider-Neureither & Partner GmbH. After the company became a stock corporation [AG] in 1998, he assumed the role of CEO of SNP Schneider-Neureither & Partner AG.

Achim Westermann is a member of the executive board at SNP Schneider-Neureither & Partner AG, Heidelberg. He is responsible for the area of SAP consultancy, specializing in technologies, application development, and workflow.

He has worked in IT consultancy since 1992. After studying IT at Karlsruhe TH, he worked as a technology consultant at SAP AG, Walldorf. During his time there, he was responsible for numerous customer projects in mid-sized companies and multinational corporations in various different sectors. He joined SNP AG in 2002.

SNP Schneider-Neureither & Partner AG is an SAP consultancy firm that supports customers in the implementation and optimization of their SAP solutions. The company was established in 1994 by Dr. Andreas Schneider-Neureither and his wife Petra Neureither as Schneider-Neureither & Partner GmbH. In 1998, it became a stock corporation and was launched on the stock exchange in 2000. SNP Schneider-Neureither & Partner AG currently employs 80 people. The head office is in Heidelberg, Germany. They also have offices in Stuttgart, Düsseldorf, Leuna, Vienna, Linz, and Zürich.

The strategy at SNP Schneider-Neureither & Partner AG is to concentrate on technology, process, and application consultancy for the SAP market. Consequently, competencies are constantly being developed in mySAP Technology consulting, Enterprise Application Integration, Optimization, Service & Support, System Landscape Optimization, SAP Workflow, Monitoring, and Process and Application Consulting. SNP Schneider-Neureither & Partner AG has developed the SNP Real-time Business Monitor to optimize company performance. This solution, which is based 100% on SAP technology, can be used to automate the control of business performance. This is done using real-time monitoring of critical key figures and business processes and the automatic implementation and tracking of error elimination. SNP AG also offers, among other things, services to optimize Service & Support organizations and solution management on the basis of the SAP Solution Manager or the SAP Support Desk.

Index

S

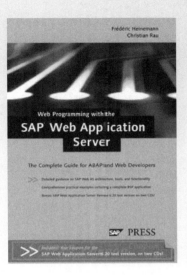

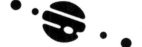

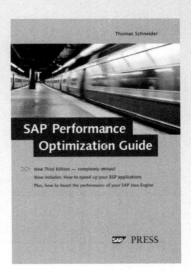

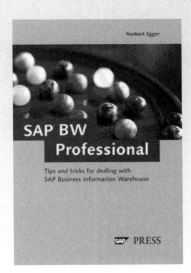

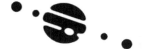